The Sephardic Kitchen

The
Sephardic
Kitchen

The Healthful Food
and Rich Culture of the
Mediterranean Jews

RABBI ROBERT STERNBERG

HarperCollins*Publishers*

HarperCollins books may be purchased for educational, business, or sales promotional use. For information please write: Special Markets Department, HarperCollins Publishers, Inc., 10 East 53rd Street, New York, NY 10022.

FIRST EDITION

Designed by BTD/Beth Tondreau

Library of Congress Cataloging-in-Publication Data

Sternberg, Robert.
    The Sephardic kitchen : the healthful food and rich culture of the Mediterranean Jews / Robert Sternberg. — 1st ed.
        p.   cm.
    Includes index.
    ISBN 0-06-017691-1
    1. Cookery, Jewish. 2. Cookery, Mediterranean. 3. Sephardim—Social life and customs. I. Title.
    TX724.S748
    641.5'676—dc20   96-5390

96 97 98 99 00 ❖/RRD 10 9 8 7 6 5 4 3 2 1

Contents

Preface

*a*shkenazic" and "Sephardic" are familiar terms that are used to describe the two main divisions of Jewish ethnic communities. "Ashkenazic," from the Hebrew word *Ashkenaz* (meaning "Germany"), refers to all Jews of European ancestry except those of Southern Europe. "Sephardic," from the Hebrew word *Sepharad* (meaning "Spain"), has been applied to all the others.

The purpose of this book is to introduce you to the fragrant foods and fascinating culinary traditions of the Sephardim and their descendants as well as those of other Jewish communities in the Mediterranean region.

Sephardic food is Mediterranean food. Parts of the cuisine were fully developed between the eighth and twelfth centuries when Spain was an Islamic country. Arabic influence on Sephardic cuisine was, at that time, very strong. The cuisine of the Sephardic Jews continued to develop under Christian rule in Spain until 1492 and in Portugal until 1496. In those years, Jews and Muslims in the two countries were forced to choose between converting to Christianity or being expelled. The majority chose exile and migrated to various Mediterranean countries or to Holland. Most of the Sephardic Jews who left Spain and Portugal went to Islamic countries.

In the Mediterranean, ancient history lives side by side with modernity. Mysticism, the supernatural, romance, and poetry appear in all facets of everyday life, including cooking. Many aspects of food preparation and presentation are infused with vivid imagination and artistic nuances. For example, the Sephardic Shevuot bread called *Los Siete Cielos* ("Bread of the Seven Heavens") was created as a culinary representation of the world beyond the earthly realm. *Pescado Ahilado con Abramela* ("Baked Fish in Sour Plum Sauce") is named for a story about Abraham, the patriarch of the Jewish religion.

On the other hand, some aspects of Mediterranean culture are marked by simplicity, understatement, and informality. In the cooking of Mediterranean Jews, the natural flavor and appearance of food are emphasized. Herbs are added to enrich and enhance the natural taste of the raw ingredients. Sauces are unpretentious and straightforward. Spice adds an element of surprise and mystery.

Jews and Muslims, especially in the countries of the Ottoman Empire, intermingled freely and, in the process, shared many culinary traditions and secrets. They had a great influence on each other, especially regarding food preparation and presentation. Turkey and Greece, for example, had indigenous Jewish communities prior to the exile of the Spanish and Portuguese Jews, but the Ladino-speaking Sephardic Jews eventually outnumbered all the others in these countries. Sephardic culture became the dominant culture and Sephardic cuisine became the dominant cuisine, contributing much to the local cuisines and, at the same time, borrowing from them. Morocco, on the other hand, had a large Jewish community prior to the exile of Jews from Spain and Portugal and the numbers of Jews of Spanish and Portuguese descent were never greater than that of the indigenous Jewish population. In Morocco, therefore, and in other parts of North Africa where Sephardic Jews settled, Moorish culture and cuisine were preeminent over Sephardic. Jews of Spanish and Portuguese descent in Morocco and Algeria retained a few individualistic habits, like a disdain of turmeric (which Moroccan cooks use as an inexpensive substitute for saffron), but for the most part their cuisine did not differ from that of other Jews in the region.

The recipes in this book are adapted from ancient Spanish and Portuguese sources and from the Sephardic kitchens of Italy, southeast France, Morocco, Algeria, Tunisia, and the countries and cities of the former Ottoman Empire (Turkey, Greece, Bulgaria, Bosnia, Serbia, Albania, parts of Romania, Egypt, Lebanon, Syria, and Jerusalem). There are also a few recipes from the Sephardic communities of Amsterdam, London, the southern United States, and Curaçao. In these non-Mediterranean, non-Islamic communities, Sephardic cooks assimilated foods and cooking techniques from Northern Europe and Latin America. The Iberian influences that were preserved in their cuisine are, therefore, easily discerned. All of these recipes have been preserved in Sephardic and other Mediterranean Jewish families as part of their ethnic and culinary heritage.

I encountered Sephardic and other forms of Mediterranean Jewish cooking for the first time in Israel, where I lived as a student from 1972 to 1974. I was fascinated with the types of foods produced in the kitchens of the families of some of my non-Ashkenazic Israeli friends and in the ethnic restaurants and kiosks of Jerusalem and Tel Aviv. The Mediterranean Jewish foods were very different from the Jewish food I had grown up with. I constantly asked the mothers of my Israeli friends about the dishes they cooked, what they put into them, and how they made them. I wrote down recipes and when I finally rented my own apartment, I tried to cook some of these foods myself. I loved to wander the neighborhoods of Jerusalem and Tel Aviv looking through the markets for interesting foods. I would go back often to some of my favorite places to learn more about the *borekas* or the *buleymas*, the *felafel*, or the Sephardic and Arabic breads. When possible I would ask about ingredients and write things down. I had no intention at that time of ever writing or publishing a book on Sephardic cooking. I simply wanted to know how to prepare these foods because I loved them so much.

One of the other interesting things I learned was that Sephardic Jews had their own language, Ladino. Because Ladino is a Jewish language, wherever possible I try to give Ladino as well as English names to the recipes in this book that are of Sephardic origin. Jews from other Mediterranean countries who were not of Sephardic origin spoke dialects of Arabic, French, or Italian, which are not specifically Jewish languages. I therefore give no foreign language names to these recipes.

I also learned that Sephardic and other Jews from Mediterranean countries had as rich a folklore as the Yiddish-speaking Jews of Central and Eastern Europe. When possible, I intersperse folktales of Sephardic or Arab/Jewish origin among the recipes.

In 1992, the Jewish community of Turkey celebrated its five-hundredth anniversary. The date was chosen to coincide with the invitation extended by Sultan Beyazit II in 1492 to the Jews of Spain and Portugal to make their homes in the Ottoman Empire. It was a celebration of five hundred years of peace, tolerance, and friendship between Jews and Muslims in Turkey, a relationship that has been marked, for the most part, by a spirit of openness, tolerance, and mutual respect. The Sultan was rumored to have said to King Ferdinand of Spain when he opened the doors of his empire to Jewish immigration that, ". . . By expelling the Jews you have made your country poor and my country rich." The Ladino-speaking Jews of Turkey called the five-hundredth anniversary a celebration of *Anyos Munchos y Buenos* ("good years and many more"). Through the centuries of living together, Jews and Muslims in Turkey learned an important lesson, which is summed up in a Ladino proverb: *Boca dulce abre puertos de hierro* ("Kind words open iron gates").

No kinder gesture of friendship can be made than the sharing of food with others. May the joy of working creatively with Mediterranean Jewish cooking give you "good years and many more," and may this book open gates for you to new experiences and new friendships.

B'Tayavon ("With a good appetite")

Acknowledgments

a book like *The Sephardic Kitchen* cannot be produced without the help of many people. Special thanks go to Miri and Yakov Varol, Rabbi Susan Talve, Rabbi James Stone Goodman, the Zargari family, and the Ben David family for their recipes, stories, and folklore. Thanks also to Charlotte Bright, Ellen and Elliot Wallach, Peter Wallach, John Wallach, Judith Cleavelin, and Tristan Cleavelin for emotional support, for inspiration, and for help in testing recipes. Special thanks to Diana Finch of the Ellen Levine Literary Agency for much professional assistance and support, and to Iris Salsman and her public relations staff for their special help and support over many years. A special word of appreciation to Susan Friedland at HarperCollins for a tremendous amount of editorial support, mentoring, and helpful suggestions and ideas, and an overall high level of professionalism in working with me on this endeavor. Thanks also to Jennifer Griffin and Sue Llewellyn of HarperCollins, to copy editor Estelle Laurence and designer Beth Tondreau, and to Merrilyn Lewis and David Nussbaum of Lisa Ekus Public Relations for the time and care they have taken in bringing this project to fruition and making it succeed. Thanks to my mother-in-law, Nelly Komras, who is my premier taster and tester of recipes and who spreads the word of what's cooking in my kitchen all over Montreal and the East Coast; and last but not least to my wife, Henrietta, editor in chief and partner in the entire *Sephardic Kitchen* endeavor.

A Short History of Sephardic Jewry

*U*ntil the first century of the Common Era, most of the world's Jews lived in or in proximity to Jerusalem. This was because the Hebrew Temple, built on top of the mountain on which the spirit of the Creator was believed to dwell, was located in Jerusalem. The Jews of this period worshiped only at this Temple. The Temple was both a gathering place and a house of worship. Business and trade were conducted there as well as prayer. The entire spiritual, social, economic, and cultural life of the Jewish people was centered strictly on the Temple, its daily rituals, and its seasonal festivals. Jerusalem was also the capital city of the Roman province of Judea.

The people of Judea suffered greatly under Roman rule. The Jewish leadership rejected the worship of pagan gods and goddesses in the Temple and, because of this, earned the enmity of the Roman governors. Many attempts were made to overthrow Roman rule in Judea. In the year 70 C.E., the Roman army laid siege to Jerusalem and in the summer of that year, on the ninth day of the Hebrew month of Av, Jerusalem was captured and the Temple destroyed. Throughout the Roman Empire thousands of Jews were murdered and thousands more sent into exile, some as slaves. The Sanhedrin, a body of seventy-one Rabbinic scholars appointed by Rabbi Yochanan ben Zakkai with permission from the Roman General Vespasian, became the leadership of the Jewish community after the destruction of the Temple. One of the steps taken by the Sanhedrin to ensure the survival of the Jewish community was the reorganization of Jewish life around studying, codifying the Hebrew Bible and oral tradition, and the creation of new houses of worship called synagogues. The synagogue, called in Hebrew *bet knesset* (which means "house of gathering") or *bet hamidrash* (which means "house of study"), came to serve a similar function to the Temple. Because of the foresight of the Sanhedrin, the Jews of Judea and other places, unlike their pagan neighbors, did not assimilate into the Roman world. The majority of them continued to live according to the laws of the Jewish religion and remained a part of cohesive, well-organized Jewish communities throughout the Roman Empire.

In 313 C.E. the Roman Emperor Constantine I adopted Christianity as his personal religion and embarked on a campaign to make Christianity the official religion of the Roman Empire. Most Christians by this time considered their religion to be separate from Judaism. Over the next several centuries, paganism would disappear from Europe and would be replaced by Christianity.

In the early part of the seventh century C.E., Muhammad of Arabia developed another monotheistic religion, Islam, based on what he had learned of the principles of Judaism and Christianity—belief in one God and a body of moral, ethical, and spiritual laws to create a just and good society. Islam became the religion favored over paganism in the Middle East and North Africa just as Christianity was favored in Europe. In time, only Judaism remained as a separate minority religion in the countries of the Mediterranean region.

During this period of history the largest Jewish populations in the world were in Babylonia, Persia, and the lands of the Middle East. Smaller numbers of Jews lived in North Africa and Iberia and even smaller numbers lived in France, Italy, Sicily, Germany, and Byzantium (today Greece, Bulgaria, and the Balkan republics).

It is believed that the first Jewish settlers came to Spain in the days of the First Hebrew Temple (953–586 B.C.E.). By the fourth century C.E. there were well-established Jewish communities all over Iberia. In 711 C.E., Tarik, the general of the Muslim Moors of North Africa, crossed the Strait of Gibraltar and within four years, all of Spain was under Muslim control.

Overall, Jewish life prospered under Muslim rule more than it did under Christian rule. The Muslim rulers of Spain were especially tolerant. Though the official language of Muslim Spain was Arabic, and Islam the official religion of the court, all people in Muslim Spain enjoyed equal opportunities regardless of ethnic background or religion. The Jews of Muslim Spain worked in many occupations. They were farmers, vintners, tailors, goldsmiths and silversmiths, businessmen, scientists, physicians, mathematicians, astronomers, poets, and philosophers. Many Jews served as diplomats and interpreters for the Spanish government. This "Golden Age" in Spain lasted almost five hundred years and produced some of the greatest thinkers, scholars, writers, and leaders in Jewish history. Among them were the physician/diplomat Hasdai Ibn Shaprut (915–970 C.E.), the poet/philosopher Solomon Ibn Gabirol (1021–1058 C.E.), the *Talmud* commentator Isaac Alfasi (1013–1103 C.E.), the philosopher/poet Yehuda Halevi (1075–1148 C.E.), and Maimonides (1135–1204 C.E.), philosopher, physician to the Spanish court, and codifier of Rabbinic law.

Jews in Christian Europe did not live as comfortably as those in Islamic countries. In some parts of Europe, the practice of Judaism was outlawed by the Church, or Jews were subject to special restrictions concerning where they could live or what work they could do. These restrictions were designed to make the Jews uncomfortable and ultimately encourage them to abandon their Jewish faith and become Christians.

The twelfth century was also the beginning of the end of the "Golden Age of Spanish Jewry." As Christian kings slowly gained control of the various provinces of Spain, efforts to convert Jews and Muslims increased. In 1391, a massive outbreak of persecutions led to wholesale conversions by Jews to Christianity. The conversions were made under duress and many Jewish converts practiced Judaism in secret and taught their children to do likewise. Much criticism was levied against these *conversos* for not behaving as "true proselytes." When Isabella of Castile and Ferdinand II of Aragon married, the two great Christian kingdoms of Spain became one. Queen Isabella set out on a campaign to make all of Spain a Christian land. She created an

Inquisition to deal with the "scandal" of "New Christians" relapsing into Judaism. The "work" of the Inquisition was hampered because it had no authority over the large numbers of Jews who never accepted conversion. The Spanish Inquisition became increasingly brutal, subjecting people under its control to unspeakable tortures and burning them at the stake for committing heresy against the Church.

On August 2, 1492, all the Jews of Spain were given the choice of converting to Christianity or going into exile. The Jews who chose exile had to abandon all their property and possessions, which were then confiscated by the King and Queen. The voyage of Christopher Columbus, which took place on August 3, 1492, one day after the exile of Spanish Jewry, was financed by the confiscated Jewish assets. It is estimated that as many as 250,000 Jews left Spain in 1492. Most Spanish Jews fled to Muslim countries in North Africa and the Ottoman Empire, where they were welcomed by leaders like Sultan Beyazit II of Turkey. Salonika (Thessaloniki, Greece) became a particularly important center of Sephardic Jewry. All of the Spanish towns that had large Jewish communities before the exile were represented in Salonika by their own congregations. Smaller numbers of exiled Spanish Jews went to Italy and the Netherlands. Not all of the Jewish exiles fared well. Many died in poverty or were robbed and killed by greedy ship captains before they ever arrived at their intended destinations.

Many of the Jews who accepted forced conversion to Christianity and remained in Spain were persecuted even more intensely by the Inquisition. Large numbers went to Portugal, where the Inquisition was less brutal and where many continued to practice Judaism in secret. Eventually, these Jews slipped out of Portugal, in smaller numbers than those who went openly in 1492 and in 1496 with the exiles. Some moved to the Spanish and Portuguese colonies of North, Central, and South America, where the terror of the Inquisition was not as oppressive. Holland, especially Amsterdam, became the largest center for Jewish emigrés from Portugal. This migration of "secret" Jews occurred over two centuries and many of the Jews who settled in reestablished

Sephardic Jewish communities in Western Europe and the Americas were not well educated about the Jewish religion.

The Edict of Expulsion remained officially in force until 1968, when it was formally rescinded by the Spanish government.

The descendants of Spanish and Portuguese Jews are called *Sephardim,* after *Sepharad,* the Hebrew word for Spain. Sephardic Jews still preserve the synagogue rituals and liturgies of Spain and Portugal. Many of the descendants of Spanish Jews still speak Ladino.

Ladino, also called Latino, Judezmo, and Judeo-Spanish, is composed of ancient Spanish dialects intermingled with Hebrew, Arabic, Turkish, Greek, and medieval French words. Until recent years, Ladino was written in Hebrew rather than in Roman characters. There is no sufficient historical evidence to confirm that Ladino originated as a Jewish language. More likely, it was a dialect or several dialects of medieval Spanish. However, after Jews were expelled from Spain, Ladino evolved as a specifically Jewish language because the exiled Spanish Jews were the only Spanish-speaking people in the world to preserve words in their Spanish, which had become archaic. Ladino was spoken in Greece, Turkey, Yugoslavia, Bulgaria, Romania, North Africa, southern France, Eretz Israel, and, to a lesser extent, the United States and Latin America.

The Jews who emigrated from Portugal between the sixteenth and seventeenth centuries spoke primarily Portuguese rather than Ladino and they wrote their language in Roman rather than Hebrew characters. They also used Spanish, mostly for business and as a semisacred language for Bible translation.

The nineteenth century marked the beginning of the end of Sephardic Jewry in Europe. After World War I, the Ottoman Empire was dissolved. Unstable governments in many countries led to massive immigration from Greece and Turkey to Western Europe, America, and especially Latin America. Before quotas were put on immigration in the United States, fifty to sixty thousand Sephardic Jews emigrated to the United States, especially after the Young Turk Rebellion in 1908.

The Holocaust decimated the remaining populations of Sephardic

Jews. In Holland, the Sephardim were the last to be deported by the Nazis to death camps but their number was reduced to one-tenth its original size. In the Balkans, victimization of Jews was carried out on a large scale, particularly in Yugoslavia. The Bulgarian government played a heroic role in saving almost its entire Jewish population, but it did nothing to protect the approximately eleven thousand Jews of Thrace and Macedonia, which were put under its jurisdiction by the Nazis. In Greece, most of the Jewish community was concentrated in Salonika. The small Jewish community in Athens was saved by its Greek Orthodox patriarch Damascenes, but Jews in other parts of Greece did not fare as well. Of the seventy-three thousand pre–World War II Jewish population of Greece, over sixty-five thousand were murdered by the Nazis and their collaborators. Only the Sephardic Jewish communities of North Africa, the Middle East, and Turkey were untouched by the Holocaust.

Today there are living Sephardic Jewish communities in Israel, France, Latin America, South Africa, and the United States. The largest community in the United States is in New York City with sizable populations in Los Angeles, Seattle, Portland, Miami, Chicago, Philadelphia, and Atlanta.

The Sephardic Jews pronounce the Hebrew language itself according to a specifically Sephardic dialect known as *Havarah Sephardit* (the Sephardic pronunciation).

The Jews of Central and Eastern Europe are called *Ashkenazim,* after the Hebrew word *Ashkenaz,* which means "Germany." Most, but not all, Ashkenazic Jews trace their ancestors back to Germany or to other parts of Central Europe. Ashkenazic Jews have their own synagogue rituals and liturgies and their own way of pronouncing the Hebrew language, called *Havarah Ashkenazis* (the Ashkenazic pronunciation). Many Asheknazic Jews also speak Yiddish, a mixture of medieval German and Hebrew with some Polish, Russian, and Ukrainian words mixed in.

Jews native to the countries of the Middle East, Central Asia, and North Africa are called in Hebrew *Edot Hamizrach* ("the Ethnic Communities of the East" or "the Ethnic Communities of the Orient").

Included in the *Edot Hamizrach* are the Jews of Iran, Iraq, Kurdistan, Armenia, Uzbekistan, Bukhara, Georgia, Azerbaijan, Yemen, Aden, Turkey, Syria, Lebanon, Egypt, Libya, Tunisia, Algeria, and Morocco. The *Edot Hamizrach*, or "Oriental" Jews, are very diverse. Synagogue rituals and liturgies are many and varied but the pronunciation of the Hebrew language among these communities resembles the Sephardic rather than the Ashkenazic.

The Israeli government appoints an official Chief Rabbinate to deal with matters of religious law in the State of Israel. Because large numbers of Sephardic Jews settled in Middle Eastern and North African countries, their religious practices, over time, have become somewhat blended with those of the Oriental Jews in the countries where they settled. The Israeli government designates two Chief Rabbis, one to serve the Jews of Ashkenazic descent and the other to serve the Sephardic and Oriental Jewish communities. These two rabbis are called by the Israelis the Ashkenazic and the Sephardic Chief Rabbis. The Chief Rabbi of the Sephardic and Oriental Jews is also called the *Rishon L'Tzion* ("First" or "Head" in Zion). For these reasons, Jews whose ancestors came from the *Edot Hamizrach* have often been mislabeled "Sephardic."

Because the government of Israel also chose the *Havarah Sephardit* over the Ashkenazic pronunciation of Hebrew as its official standard, confusion over who should properly be called Sephardic is further exacerbated.

Sephardic, Oriental, and Ashkenazic Jews have both similarities and differences where foods and food rituals are concerned. Generally speaking, the foods eaten by all Jews are dictated by the climates, the growing seasons, and the produce available where they live and are adapted to conform to the laws of *kashrut*. Some similarities are found in the bread (*challa*) baked for the Sabbath and festivals and in the preparation of the slow-cooked Sabbath stews called *hamin*. Differences lie mainly in what is put into the recipes. In the case of *hamin*, Sephardic and Oriental Jews use rice, chick-peas, and spices like saffron whereas Ashkenazic Jews use potatoes, barley, and sweet paprika.

The food rituals in each community relate much more to ethnic culture, folklore, folk beliefs, and lifestyles. The Sephardic world embraced the mystical teachings of Judaism and made them central to the practice of the Jewish religion. Therefore it is not surprising to find Kabbalistic customs like *Yehi Ratsones* on Rosh Hashono, "making *brochot*" at the Friday night Sabbath meal, and the Tu B'Shevat *Seder* ceremony called *Las Frutas* common practice among Sephardim. Ashkenazic Jewish life revolved primarily around *Talmudic* and Rabbinic scholarship, so the religious rituals of the Jewish mystics are less prevalent.

This poem was written when Yehuda Halevi left Spain due to the intense persecution of Jews and attempted to move to Eretz Israel. The poet journeyed to Egypt and is believed to have died there, never reaching the Holy Land.

In Remembrance of Home
　　I will not weep for the garden I have planted
　　　　and watered, so flowers may grow there . . .
　　I will almost forget the synagogue
　　　　where in the classroom I studied my scripture.
　　I will forget the joys of all the Sabbaths,
　　　　the pleasures of the holidays, the wonderful Passovers,
　　As for the tributes I would have paid to others,
　　　　I bequeath my own praises to those less fortunate than I.
I have exchanged my orchards and vineyards for the shadows of the briars.
　　And the strength of my trellises for the protection of the thorns.
My soul, filled with the aroma of the most delectable spices,
　　is now satisfied with the scent of thistles.
I now no longer walk on my hands and knees,
　　　　but have placed myself in the bosom of the sea,
　　until I find the footstool of my God. . . .
　　　　　　YEHUDA HALEVI (1075–1148 C.E.)

Homemaking and Hospitality Among the Mediterranean Jews

The days of cold are past
   And days of spring have buried winter's rain
We see the doves returning to our land
   They flock near to the newly sprouting leaves
So my friends, be true and keep your word
   Be careful and do not disappoint your friend
Come into my garden
   Roses are waiting, beautifully fragrant and ready to pluck
Come and drink with me, among the buds and birds
   Gathered there to sing the summer's praises
Wine, red as my tears for loss,
   Of friends, or red as the blush on lovers' cheeks.

SAMUEL THE NAGID (993–1055 C.E.)

This romantic poem, written by the Sephardic poet Samuel the Nagid, is an invitation to partake of the beauty of the season, the garden, and the bittersweet joys of love. Samuel the Nagid was also a Talmudic scholar, statesman, and a leader of the Jewish community in Spain during its Golden Age. The openhearted spirit of Mediterranean hospitality contained in this poetic invitation, despite its bittersweet lament at the end, gives a little insight into the importance of hospitality in Mediterranean cultures.

t he people of the Mediterranean countries, including the Jews, are famous for their hospitality. Hospitality is so important that there are specific codes of behavior that apply to it. A person is obligated to extend hospitality at every opportunity and all interaction among people, including business meetings and visits to shops, is considered a chance to do so. Shopkeepers love to play host to potential customers and often invite shoppers to sit down in their store for a casual cup of coffee and conversation before proceeding to conduct business. Only after getting acquainted does the process of bargaining begin in earnest. And bargain one must—it is a way of life! It is a match of wits, a setting and resetting of upper and lower limits. Nerves can get frazzled. Blood can boil. People become aggressive. But bargaining is lots of fun, too, and the ultimate outcome of striking a good bargain can be the beginning of a buyer-and-seller relationship that is based on mutual trust, honor, and sometimes genuine friendship.

When visiting the home of a Jew from a Mediterranean country, one is usually greeted with an apology by the host or hostess for the poor and limited quality of the food being served. The apology is generally followed by a lavish buffet with a dazzling array of mouthwatering appetizers and salads. A minimum of three to four appetizers must precede a meal and when company comes, more than this is preferred. Appetizers include dips made with legumes like chick-peas; mashed potatoes with garlic, yogurt, fresh herbs; pureed vegetable salads; chopped vegetable salads; marinated olives; cold fish dishes; and savory pastries like *borekas, buleymas,* or *boyos.* Only after everyone has eaten fully of the appetizers is the main entree brought out. Sometimes it is served with rice, bulgur, or *couscous.* Or it is served on its own with crusty Mediterranean-style bread to soak up the sauces.

Meat and fish are not the only kinds of foods eaten as main dishes. Many entrees are vegetarian or made of just eggs or cheese. Desserts are simple—usually plain fresh fruit or simple sweets made of dried fruits stuffed with marzipan or pistachio paste. Sweet pastries are eaten with coffee or tea as a repast separate from a regular meal.

In Mediterranean countries, there are strict rules governing invitations to partake of food. One never, ever, refuses an invitation to eat or drink. Refusing a gift of food is the greatest insult one can give to a person from a Mediterranean country. It is considered to be an affront—crude, ill-mannered, and vulgar. Another rule is that one should eat most but never all of the food on one's plate as this is a signal to the hostess that the guest is still hungry. The hostess will invariably whisk away a fully cleaned plate and ceremoniously appear with another containing a second serving of everything. Once this happens, it is considered a grievous insult not to eat heartily of the second portion.

The order of serving courses is different than in the United States. After the appetizers are served, all of the dishes except the sweets appear on the table at the same time and people help themselves to whatever they want. This relieves the hostess of having to bustle about from kitchen to dining room, allowing her to sit with her guests, relax, and entertain them with conversation as well as food. The atmosphere at such meals is comfortable, casual, and informal. Italy is an exception to this protocol, where the formality of serving separate courses (*antipasto, primo, secundo, insalata, dolci*) is a long-established tradition.

Sephardic Jews have some interesting and unusual social rituals connected with the serving of foods on Sabbaths and festivals. One of them is the custom of "making *brochot*" ("blessings"). Psalms 24:1 says "The earth is the Lord's and the fullness thereof," which means that everything in the earth is considered sacred and a gift from God and must be blessed before it is used. The subject of making blessings over food in Jewish tradition is very complex. There are different blessings prescribed for different kinds of foods. Foods made from plants that grow in the ground have one blessing, "*borei p'ri ha'adamah*" ("We thank you, Oh Lord, for the fruits of the earth"). Foods made from plants that grow on trees have another, "*borei p'ri ha'etz*" ("We thank you, Oh Lord, for the fruit of the trees"). Grains and all dishes made of grains except yeast-risen breads have a third blessing, "*borei minay m'zonot*" ("We thank you, Oh Lord, for the kinds of grains"). Breads made with yeast and wine each have separate blessings, "*hamotzi lechem min ha'aretz*" ("We thank you, Oh Lord, for bringing forth bread from the earth") and "*borei p'ri hagafen*" ("We thank you, Oh Lord, for the fruit of the vine"). Every kind of food that does not fit into the above categories is blessed with a generic blessing, "*shehakol ni'hieh bid'voro*" ("We thank you, Oh Lord, for every kind of sustenance, which was created by Your command").

To complicate things even more, Jewish tradition gives foods a "pecking order." Bread is considered the most important of all foods and before eating bread one has to wash the hands, recite a blessing over the hand washing, and then recite the blessing over the bread. If bread is eaten with a meal, foods in all the other categories are exempted from being blessed separately because the blessing for bread includes them. If bread is not eaten with the meal, each item requires a separate blessing. The "catchall" blessing of *"shehakol ni'hieh bid'voro"* is really intended for nonplant foods like meat, poultry, eggs, fish, dairy products, and beverages other than wine. But if a variety of foods are not eaten at a meal and this "catch-all" blessing is recited, it is considered sufficient and the other foods do not have to be blessed separately. However, the *shehakol* blessing is considered lowest in the "pecking order" of blessings. So one should not use this blessing to cover the foods that have their own specific blessing. *Shehakol* is considered a sufficient blessing only if it is recited by mistake before any of the other blessings are recited.

Sephardic Jews have developed a custom of reciting extra blessings over food on Sabbaths and festivals based on a Kabbalistic belief that reciting more blessings on the Sabbath brings you closer to God. Since the Sabbath is a day for praising God and developing a personal relationship with the Creator, extra blessings are recited. Before serving the Sabbath meal, extra blessings are recited on fruits, a "fruit" of the ground, and savory pastries.

I observed this custom of reciting extra blessings for the first time in Israel in the home of my Sephardic friend David Zargari. We came home from the synagogue on Friday night and sat down at a beautifully set, low, round table. At each place setting was a small dish containing seasonal fruits, a small pickling cucumber (unpeeled), and three *borekas*. We sang several songs, including the traditional *"Shalom Aleichem,"* which welcomes the Guardian Angels of the Sabbath to the table and then David's father made the *kiddush* blessing over some delicious sweet homemade wine. After we all drank some wine, the carafe was set on the table. Yitzchak, David's father, took a silver fish-shaped container, which held aromatic spices, and recited a blessing over the aroma of spices. The spice box was passed from person to person and everyone took a sniff. This was something new to me. As an Ashkenazic Jew I thought spices were used only at the conclusion of the Sabbath during the *Havdallah* ceremony. That evening I learned that Sephardic Jews like the Zargaris welcomed the Sabbath as well as said good-bye to it with a ceremony involving sniffing ritual spices. The Zargaris also had two different spice boxes, one for use during the Friday night dinner and the second, filled with different aromatics, for the conclusion of the Sabbath.

After blessing the spices, Yitzchak picked up an apricot that sat on the small dish in front of him, recited the blessing over "fruit of the trees," and then ate it. Everyone at the table answered "Amen" to the blessing. David then took a turn. Following his father's lead, he picked up his apricot, recited the blessing, and bit into it. Everyone at the table answered "Amen" to this blessing. We then went around the table, every person reciting this blessing out loud, and then eating his or her apricot. After the recitation of each blessing, everyone responded "Amen!" The ritual continued with a new round of blessings. When we came to eat the cucumber, the blessing over "fruits of the earth" was offered. Then we performed the same ritual with the *borekas,* which contained a delicious sweet pumpkin filling. The blessing over grains was offered this time, since the pastries were made of wheat flour. Every round of blessings was followed by a chorus of "Amens."

After the "making *brochot*" ceremony was concluded, we sang "*Yedid Nefesh,*" a beautiful Sabbath song about peace, the relationship between ourselves and God, and the healing spirit the celebration of the Sabbath brings to the Jewish soul. "*Yedid Nefesh*" was followed by the ritual hand washing and the blessing over the Sabbath bread. In typical Mediterranean fashion, we began with an assortment of salads and appetizers, followed by a wonderful *hamin.* We ate, we drank lots of wine, we sang lots of songs and told stories late into the night. This first of many Sabbaths with the Zargari family was one of my most memorable experiences in Israel.

I also observed the "making *brochot*" ceremony in another context. One Shabbat when I was with the Zargaris, a death had occurred in the home of their next-door neighbor. The family was in the middle of *shiva*, the seven-day mourning period. The laws of *shiva* are lifted on the Sabbath. I went with David, his father, and his brother to visit the neighbor and pay our respects to the bereaved and was surprised to be greeted with another "making *brochot*" ceremony. The family served wine, fruits, bananas (which are considered a "fruit of the earth"), Sephardic bagels, and pastries to the many visitors who were present. Before partaking of the foods, each guest recited aloud the appropriate blessing while everyone present smiled their approval and answered "Amen." It was understood that each visitor was expected to partake of each kind of food and recite the appropriate blessing. David explained to me that in this case, the blessings were offered on behalf of the deceased to help open the Gates of Paradise and ease the soul of the departed on its journey back to the Creator. In the Jewish tradition, visiting a house of mourning on the Sabbath when these special blessings were recited was considered to be one of the greatest acts of kindness.

For Mediterranean Jews, food is an intergral part of all special occasions. This includes life cycle events, especially weddings and circumcisions, which are occasions for great community celebration. This book contains some of the special Mediterranean Jewish folk customs connected with foods.

Menus are organized in two different ways—Mediterranean style and Western style. This will enable you to work with the cuisines in a variety of different ways.

A Ladino proverb says, "Whether you ate or did not eat is not what matters. What matters is that you sat down at the table." This illustrates the essence of what is considered the most important element of a Mediterranean Jewish meal—sharing in the experience of being with people, enjoying their hospitality, and savoring the joy and conviviality of human relationships. At a table where people celebrate the joy of being with one another, the art of eating is elevated to the art of dining.

A Garden of Fruits and Essences: The Raw Materials of the Jewish Mediterranean Kitchen

Your lips, my bride, drop honey—
    honey and milk are under your tongue . . .
Your shoots are a pack of pomegranates
    with precious fruits
    henna with spikenard plants
    spikenard and saffron
    calamus and cinnamon
with all trees of frankincense
myrrh and aloes, with all the chief spices. . . .

SONG OF SONGS 4:11, 13–14

king Solomon was one of the first to describe the abundance of fruits, herbs, and spices for which the Mediterranean region is famous. His evocative poetic language was also a harbinger of what would be written about Mediterranean gardens in later centuries by Greek, Roman, Arab, Jewish, Turkish, French, and Italian poets. These gardens were cultivated for their fragrances as well as for food and for aesthetic pleasure. Sweet herbs, fruit and flower essences, heady spices, and brilliant colors are all important elements in the composition of a Mediterranean meal.

A staggering variety of fruits, vegetables, herbs, and grains grow well in the Mediterranean climate. Some food materials are available year-round but most are seasonal. Spring brings artichokes, asparagus, spinach, early lettuces, young perennial herbs like chives, chervil, mint, marjoram, and dill, the first annual herb. Almonds, tomatoes, eggplants, olives, peppers, cucumbers, green beans, broad beans, leeks, melons, green and yellow squashes, celery, and all the lettuces are available from late spring through the summer and autumn harvests and well into the winter rainy season. Fruits like cherries, plums, apricots, grapes, peaches, and fresh figs are also abundant in this long growing season. The herbs are at their peak during the summer months. Autumn is the time for pumpkins, pomegranates, fennel bulbs, walnuts, quinces, apples, and pears. Lemons are available year-round, but oranges and other citrus fruits begin their season just after the autumn harvest and are in season all winter. Some herbs, like thyme, oregano, lemon verbena, mint, sage, and marjoram are dried for winter use. Although the ground rarely freezes in the Mediterranean region, the heavy winter rains and the lower amount of sunlight detract from the flavor of the herbs. Wheat is harvested in early summer and late autumn. In rice-growing regions, the harvest occurs in the same seasons as wheat.

Because of the vast array of plants, all Mediterranean cuisines, including those of the Mediterranean Jews, favor plant foods over animal foods. But none is exclusively vegetarian. Fish is eaten more often than meat, which is reserved for special occasions, like the Sabbath and the festivals.

For thousands of years, Mediterranean Jews have coexisted with their non-Jewish neighbors, a culturally and ethnically diverse population that includes Christians and Muslims, Turks, Greeks, Arabs, Berbers, Southern Europeans, and North Africans. Mediterranean people borrow aspects of culture from one another but do not blend together into one homogeneous community. Individual family, community, and tribal identities are strong, encouraging the groups to develop distinct regional styles and preferences.

Jewish cooks have made unique contributions to Mediterranean cuisine. The existence of kosher and Sabbath laws has promoted the techniques of lengthy braising and stewing, the separation of dairy and meat products, the exclusion of pork and shellfish, and the use of wine and spirits in cooking. Like Jews, Muslims exclude pork from their diets but they do not exclude shellfish. They also mix dairy with meat. Muslims forbid the use of alcohol, in cooking or for drinking. When you see wine or spirits used as an ingredient in a Middle Eastern recipe, the recipe is Jewish or Christian in origin.

Many plant foods like leeks, artichokes, and fennel were first used in Jewish cooking and later adopted by others. Jewish cooks in Italy, especially in Rome, are famous for their methods of preparing artichokes. Jews also adapted and modified recipes so that they would conform to the kosher laws. The Jewish recipe for moussaka, for example, is made without the béchamel custard in the classic Greek recipe because it contains milk and cheese, which according to Jewish tradition, cannot be mixed with meat.

There are strong regional preferences in the Mediterranean for various herb and spice combinations. In Greece, parsley and oregano are combined with garlic to flavor food, whereas in Turkey, garlic is combined with dill, mint, and parsley. North African cooks like to use a combination of garlic, parsley, cilantro, and hot paprika or cayenne pepper, sometimes adding mint for a cooling balance.

Sephardic Jews from Spain brought olive oil, almonds, citrus, saffron, and a love for sweets made with eggs and egg yolks with them into Ottoman and North African cities. They also substituted olive oil for the butter or fat from fat-tailed sheep that was used by Arab, Turkish, and Berber cooks. (Fat-tailed sheep are a North African breed with thick, fatty tails, from which cooking fat is rendered.) Spices and flower essences like rosewater and orange flower water were brought from Persia into Arab and North African countries and were eventually absorbed into all the Jewish cuisines of the Mediterranean. Spices, especially cumin seeds, are always roasted before grinding to bring out their flavors.

Grains and nuts are also subject to regional preferences. Jews of Sephardic descent love rice, the favored grain of Andalusia and Valencia, their ancestral home. North African cooks prefer wheat in the form of *couscous*. Turkish and Arabic cooks like wheat in the form of *trahanas*, which is similar to bulgur. But they use rice just as frequently. Turks and

Macedonians use walnuts in their pastries. In North African and Arab countries almonds and pine nuts are used more often than walnuts.

Jewish kitchens in the Mediterranean countries were much more prosperous than those of Eastern Europe. The poor Eastern European Jew's lament is expressed in a Yiddish folk song:

Sunday, potatoes,
Monday, potatoes,
Tuesday and Wednesday, potatoes.
Thursday, potatoes,
Friday, potatoes,
And on Shabbat a *cholent* with—potatoes!

The outcry of the beggar from southern France seems far less pathetic by comparison:

Lettuce on Sunday,
Crumbs and water Monday,
Leeks Tuesday,
Leftover leeks Wednesday,
Dry lentils Thursday,
Leftover lentils Friday,
While on Shabbat it seems wise not to dine
    on too much meat or too much wine!

A JEWISH PAUPER'S LAMENT
Medieval Hebrew poem from French Provence

The ingredients needed to produce authentic Mediterranean Jewish dishes are available in most American supermarkets. It is a good idea to keep some items, like olive oil, fresh lemons, yogurt, rice, and a variety of fresh and dried herbs and spices on hand in your kitchen.

A Word About Kashrut

*k*ashrut, the Jewish dietary laws, are laid out in the biblical books of Leviticus and Deuteronomy and in the *Talmud* and various Codes of Rabbinic Law. Some rules of *kashrut* are determined by customs and traditions, that varied from Jewish community to community. Most of the differences between Ashkenazic and Sephardic practices of *kashrut* lie in local custom or tradition.

GENERAL RULES OF *KASHRUT*

Vegetarianism

The laws of *kashrut* apply only to the consumption of animal products. All plant foods are kosher—fruits, vegetables, nuts, herbs, spices, grains—everything that grows in the ground or on trees. If a person is a strict vegetarian and does not eat any animal products, including dairy products, that person is keeping strictly kosher. Vegetarianism is considered to be an ideal lifestyle according to Jewish tradition but it is not a requirement of Jewish law. There is a principle in Jewish tradition called *n'zirut,* which means the "taking on of extra customs which are helpful to evolving a higher spiritual relationship with the Creator." Extra fast days, refraining from drinking alcohol, vegetarianism, and not cutting the hair are all practices of *n'zirut.* Many Jewish holy men and women throughout the centuries have taken voluntary vows of *n'zirut,* which has included vegetarianism. During the Depression and during the Nazi occupation of Europe, my grandmother, Miriam Brizman, an immigrant to America from Lithuania, fasted from sunup to sundown every Monday and Thursday, the weekdays when the *Torah* is read in the synagogue. She also refused to eat meat except on Sabbaths and Jewish holidays during this time. She did these things as a way of asking God to restore the world to wholeness and alleviate hunger and starvation. They were acts of *n'zirut.*

On Shabbat and Yom Tov the *Talmud* says "*Ain Simcha Eloh B'Yayin*" and "*Ain Simcha Eloh B'Bassar,*" which mean "There is no joyous occasion without wine" and "There is no joyous occasion without meat." For this reason, most Jews do not follow a strict vegetarian lifestyle. Mediterranean Jews, like other Mediterranean people, ate more vegetables and fruits than they did meat and ate meat only on special occasions.

There is one period during the Jewish calendar year when it is customary not to eat meat. This is the three weeks during the summer which precede the Fast of Tisha B'Av, which commemorates the destruction of the First and Second Hebrew Temples in Jerusalem. For Mediterranean Jews, Tisha B'Av also marks the occasion of the Exile of the Jewish community of Spain, which occurred in 1492. The nine days before Tisha B'Av are particularly solemn. At this time of year observant Jews around the world practice vegetarianism.

The Eating of Meat

There are a few strict rules concerning the eating of meat:

1. The animal must have split hooves and chew its cud. This explains the Jewish prohibition on pork. Pigs have split hooves but do not chew their cud.
2. It must be domesticated—hunting is strictly forbidden according to Jewish law. The law of domestication applies to poultry as well as meat.
3. It must be killed according to a strictly prescribed ritual by a ritual slaughterer called a *shochet.*

4. After the animal is killed, its meat must be soaked in cold water for 30 minutes and salted with coarse or kosher salt for 1 hour in order to remove all blood. Jewish law forbids the consumption of blood.

The Eating of Fish

There are a few laws that apply to the eating of fish:

1. Fish must have fins and scales in order to be considered kosher. This explains the prohibition on shellfish and on fish that do not have scales like eels and catfish.
2. Fish do not have to be killed by a *shochet*, nor do they have to be soaked and salted to remove the blood.
3. There is a tradition not to mix fish and meat in the same dish but they are often eaten in the same meal as separate courses.
4. Fish eggs must come only from kosher fish (those that have fins and scales).

The Eating of Dairy Products

1. Dairy products must come from kosher animals.
2. Dairy foods may not be cooked or eaten with meat. Jewish homes have separate sets of dishes, pots and pans, and cutlery for meat meals and dairy meals.
3. There is also a waiting period between eating meat and eating dairy. The amount of time varies with local tradition and can be as long as five hours or as short as one hour. This tradition only applies to the eating of dairy after meat. If dairy is eaten first, there is no waiting period.

The Eating of *Pareve* Foods

Fish and eggs are considered *pareve* products, neither meat nor dairy, and, therefore, may be cooked or eaten with dairy foods. Eggs must come from kosher poultry and not from birds of prey or from reptiles (like turtles). Eggs must also be checked for blood spots. If a blood spot is found on an egg, it must be discarded.

If a person is vegetarian but also eats fish and eggs, there is no need to have two sets of dishes, pots and pans, and cutlery because these foods are *pareve*.

Passover

On Passover there is an additional dietary restriction—no bread or baked goods leavened with yeast, baking powder, or baking soda. Observant Jews have additional sets of cooking and eating utensils for Passover. Glass is considered a nonabsorbent material and therefore a kosher home does not need more than one set of glassware. But glass must be specially prepared for Passover use by soaking it in water for twenty-four hours.

Mediterranean Jews have different Passover customs from the Jews of Northern, Central, and Eastern Europe. The Ashkenazic Jews do not eat rice, corn, or legumes on Passover because in ancient times, unleavened breads were made of these foods. Mediterranean Jews do not consider breads made of rice flour, corn flour, or legumes *hametz* (leavened) because the flat dough cannot rise even with leavening. Therefore they eat them on Passover. There is even a tradition in some Mediterranean Jewish communities to eat rice during the Passover *seder*. Special Passover delicacies are made of rice and fava beans, which are just coming into season, for the Mediterranean Jewish Passover.

Let me emphasize that one does not have to maintain a kosher kitchen to prepare the dishes in this cookbook. But preparing them with kosher ingredients adds to the creativity and spirit of the cuisines. After all, they evolved in kosher homes! Experiment yourself and see if using kosher ingredients makes a difference for you.

Appetizers

Ajada (ROASTED GARLIC SPREAD)

Ajada de Aves (TURKISH-STYLE BEAN DIP)

Humus (ARABIC-STYLE CHICK-PEA DIP)

Salata de Haminados (TURKISH EGG AND POTATO SALAD)

Olivos Marinados (GREEN AND BLACK OLIVES IN HERB MARINADE)

    Black Olives in Savory Herb Marinade

    Green Olives in Sweet Fennel Marinade

Olivada

    Olivada with Black Olives

    Olivada with Green Olives

Canton de Sardellas (PORTUGUESE-STYLE ANCHOVY SALAD)

Salata de Atun y Sardellas (SEPHARDIC-STYLE SALAD NIÇOISE)

Marinated Fried Fish

    Marinated Fried Fish, British Style

    Marinated Fried Fish, Dutch Style

Yaprakes de Oja (STUFFED VINE LEAVES)

Ajada

ROASTED GARLIC SPREAD

 Ajada is made of smoky roasted garlic, mashed potatoes, eggs, tangy lemon juice, and herbs. Similar to Greek *skordalia*, it is a dip for vegetables or a spread for bread or crackers. The primary ingredient in this spread is *ajo* ("garlic"), from which the dish gets its name. In Sephardic cooking, *ajada* is served as an appetizer with many different kinds of vegetable salads.

ROASTING TIME (GARLIC): **1 hour**
PREPARATION TIME: **1$^1/_2$ hours**
SERVINGS: **8–10**

    1   medium head garlic (10–12 cloves)
    1   tablespoon plus $^1/_4$ cup olive oil
    4   medium red-skinned potatoes
$^1/_4$ teaspoon salt (optional) plus 1 teaspoon
$^1/_4$ cup cold water (optional)
    2   large eggs
$^1/_3$ cup plus 1 tablespoon freshly squeezed lemon juice
    1   teaspoon Hungarian hot paprika, plus additional for garnish (optional)
$^1/_4$ cup finely chopped fresh parsley, plus additional for garnish (optional)
$^1/_4$ cup finely chopped fresh chervil or 1 teaspoon dried chervil
        Celery sticks, carrot sticks, red and green pepper strips, blanched cauliflower florets, blanched broccoli florets, zucchini sticks, scallions, blanched green beans, mushrooms, and radishes

1. Preheat the oven to 350 degrees.
2. Cut off the top of the head of garlic and place the head in a small clay garlic roaster or on a small baking pan. Spoon 1 tablespoon olive oil over it. Cover with the lid of the garlic roaster or with foil and bake 1 hour. The garlic will be lightly browned and the cloves very soft. Remove the garlic from the oven and cool to room temperature.

(continued)

3. Peel the potatoes and cut into chunks. Bring a large pot of salted water to a boil and cook the potatoes until soft (about 15–18 minutes). The potatoes may also be cooked in a microwave oven in a 2-quart microwave-safe casserole. Cut the potatoes into cubes and combine in the casserole with $^1/_4$ teaspoon salt and $^1/_4$ cup cold water. Cover the casserole and microwave on high for 9–10 minutes. Stir once during cooking after $4^1/_2$ minutes. Remove the potatoes with a slotted spoon.

4. Place the eggs gently into the boiling water, remove from the heat, and leave for $1^1/_2$ minutes. If the potatoes have been cooked in the microwave, bring a small pot of water to boil on top of the stove, remove from the heat, and place the eggs in the water for $1^1/_2$ minutes. Remove the eggs from the pot with a slotted spoon.

5. While waiting for the eggs to heat, mash the potatoes in a mixing bowl with a potato masher or a fork.

6. Break the eggs into the potatoes, add the lemon juice, and mix gently but thoroughly.

7. Remove the roasted garlic pulp from the paper-thin shells that hold it in place and mash it in a bowl. Add this to the potatoes and mix gently.

8. Add the paprika, salt, parsley, chervil, and remaining oil to the potatoes and mix in thoroughly but lightly. The *ajada* should have the texture of thick mayonnaise. *Ajada* may be served immediately or chilled until ready to serve.

9. To serve *ajada,* spread the paste across a platter and sprinkle it, if you wish, with more hot paprika or chopped parsley. Serve it with fresh vegetables as a dip.

SERVING SUGGESTIONS:

Ajada is traditionally served together with a variety of salads and other appetizers as a first course in a Mediterranean meal but it may also be served Western style as a course all on its own. Served this way it makes a delicious cocktail appetizer or light vegetarian entree on a hot summer day. If serving *ajada* as a main dish, accompany it with good, crusty bread, crisp flat bread, and one or two kinds of cheeses. Serve with an array of fresh vegetables for dipping. Serve a white wine with the meal.

Ajada de Aves

TURKISH-STYLE BEAN DIP

Ajada de aves can be made with either chick-peas or white kidney beans. Herbal accents vary with the seasons. In spring, dill and parsley are used. In late summer and autumn, savory and sage leaves replace the dill. Paprika and lemon juice are a constant in every season. This dish can be easily made with canned chick-peas or beans without compromising the flavor or texture of the dish. If using canned beans or chick-peas, rinse them with cold water before using to rid them of the "canned" taste.

SOAKING TIME (BEANS): **12 hours or overnight**
COOKING TIME (BEANS): **$1^1/_2$–2 hours**
PREPARATION TIME: **20 minutes**
SERVINGS: **8–10**

$^1/_2$ pound dried chick-peas or white kidney beans or two 16-ounce cans chick-peas or white kidney beans

4 fresh whole sage leaves and 2 sprigs savory or $^1/_3$ cup finely chopped fresh dill leaves

$^1/_3$ cup plus 2 tablespoons olive oil

2 medium onions, peeled and finely chopped

2 large garlic cloves, peeled and finely chopped (1 scant tablespoon)

$^1/_3$ cup plus 1 tablespoon freshly squeezed lemon juice

1 teaspoon salt

$^1/_4$ cup finely chopped fresh parsley
Freshly ground black pepper

1 teaspoon Hungarian hot paprika

1. If using dried chick-peas or beans, soak 12 hours or overnight in cold water to cover by 1 inch. Drain and rinse. Bring 3 quarts of unsalted water to a boil in a stockpot and drop in the chick-peas or beans. If using sage and savory, add to the boiling water. Reduce the heat to a simmer, partly cover the pot, and cook $1^1/_2$–2 hours or until tender. Drain. The savory and sage can now be discarded as they have ren-

dered their flavor. Do not use savory or sage with canned chick-peas or beans. If using canned chick-peas or beans, simply drain them, rinse under cold water, and use as directed.

2. Heat $1/3$ cup oil in a skillet over medium heat. Sauté the onions until soft and translucent (5–7 minutes). Add the garlic and cook 2 minutes longer. Remove from the heat and set aside to cool.

3. Put all remaining ingredients except the paprika and 2 tablespoons oil into a food processor or blender. Pulse/chop and then blend until smooth. Bean dip can either be served at this point or chilled until ready to serve. For full flavor, bring to room temperature before serving.

4. To serve *ajada de aves,* spread the paste onto a platter. Mix the hot paprika with the remaining oil and sprinkle over the paste. This makes an attractive as well as tasty paprika-oil garnish for the *ajada de aves.*

SERVING SUGGESTIONS:

Serve *ajada de aves* with crusty Mediterranean bread, crisp flat bread, or pita bread. It is traditionally served with a variety of other salads and appetizers. *Ajada de aves* makes an excellent vegetarian entree as well as an appetizer. When serving it this way, accompany the *ajada* with fresh vegetables for dipping as well as breads. Serve a light-bodied red wine with this entree.

Humus

ARABIC-STYLE CHICK-PEA DIP

Humus is not a dish of Jewish origin but it is very popular among Jews from Middle Eastern countries and Turkey. It is one of those dishes that entered the Jewish repertoire via Arab neighbors. Garlic, lemon, and *tehina* (sesame paste) are the essence of *humus* and, in combination, bring out the full nutty flavor of the chick-peas. Turkish Jews sprinkle paprika oil over their *humus* as a decoration and for additional flavor before serving it. It is pungent and tangy in flavor. This dish can be easily made with canned chick-peas that are already cooked with no loss to its flavor. Simply drain the canned chick-peas and rinse with cold water before using.

SOAKING TIME (CHICK-PEAS): **12 hours or overnight**
COOKING TIME (CHICK-PEAS): **$1^1/_2$–2 hours**
PREPARATION TIME: **20 minutes**
SERVINGS: **8–10**

> 4 cups cooked chick-peas ($^1/_2$ pound dried)
> 5 large cloves garlic, peeled and chopped ($2^1/_2$ tablespoons)
> $^3/_4$ cup *tehina* paste
> $^3/_4$ cup freshly squeezed lemon juice
> $^1/_3$–$^1/_2$ cup cold water
> 1 heaping teaspoon salt
> 2 tablespoons olive oil
> 1 teaspoon Hungarian hot paprika

1. Place everything but the olive oil and paprika in a food processor or blender. Pulse/chop until you have a smooth puree. *Humus* can be used immediately or chilled until ready to use. Bring to room temperature before serving in order to get the full flavor. *Humus* tastes best if made a day in advance and then served. The flavors strengthen as they meld together.

2. To serve *humus,* spread it onto a large platter. Mix the olive oil and paprika until paprika is dissolved into the oil. Dribble it over the *humus.*

(continued)

Humus is traditionally served with pita bread, sliced tomatoes and cucumbers, and olives. It is equally delicious with other kinds of breads and a variety of vegetables for dipping.

Salata de Haminados

TURKISH EGG AND POTATO SALAD

This Turkish salad reminds me of the Ashkenazic favorite chopped eggs and onions. It is traditionally made with leftover *huevos haminados*, creamy hard-boiled eggs made by Sephardic Jews for the *desayuno,* a special Sabbath brunch served after synagogue services. The addition of boiled mashed potato gives the salad a creamy texture and less eggs are used than in the Ashkenazic recipe, a boon for the cholesterol-conscious! Herbs add a light, springlike freshness to an otherwise full-bodied dish.

PREPARATION TIME: **45 minutes, including boiling the eggs and potato**
SERVINGS: **6–8 as an appetizer, 4 as a vegetarian entree**

> 3 large eggs or *Huevos Haminados* (page 231)
> Cold water plus $1/4$ cup (optional)
> 1 very large red boiling potato
> 3 tablespoons olive oil
> $1/4$ cup finely chopped fresh parsley
> $1/3$ cup finely chopped fresh dill leaves
> $1/3$ cup thinly sliced scallions
> Salt and black pepper

1. Place the eggs in a small saucepan that will hold them comfortably and cover with cold water. Bring this to a boil over medium heat.

Then remove the pot from the heat source, cover, and let stand 20 minutes. Drain and cover the eggs with cold water.

2. To boil the potato, cook it in a large pot unpeeled in boiling salted water to cover, for 25 minutes. The potato may also be cooked in the microwave in a 2-quart microwave-safe casserole. Prick the unpeeled potato twice with a fork. Add $^1/_4$ cup water and cover the casserole. Microwave on high for 15–16 minutes. Potato will be soft and cooked through at the end of cooking. Plunge the cooked potato into cold water when done and peel when cool enough to handle.

3. Peel and chop the eggs. Mash the potato. Mix together with the remaining ingredients. Serve at room temperature. You may chill the dish but be sure to bring it back to room temperature before serving.

SERVING SUGGESTIONS:
Serve *salata de haminados* with a variety of vegetable salads, appetizers, and savory pastries as part of a vegetarian buffet.

Olivos Marinados

GREEN AND BLACK OLIVES IN HERB MARINADE

 Olives are a staple of the Mediterranean Jewish kitchen. Plain olives are soaked in a salt brine solution and eaten just as they are. Sephardic Jews have developed some splendid herb and garlic marinades for serving olives on special occasions. Lemon juice, garlic, and seasonal fresh herbs give these marinated olives a fragrant bouquet and a variety of savory taste sensations. Good quality black olives have a generally mellow, smoky flavor because they have ripened on the tree longer than those that are picked while still green. The taste of green olives is more crisp and sharp than that of black. Different kinds of marinades complement each of the different kinds of olives.

The following recipes are made with ready-to-eat olives that can be bought in the market. It is important to get the best quality olives for these dishes. The tastiest marinade will do very little to improve the flavor of insipid canned olives whose briny flavors have been leached out in a water bath before canning.

Black Olives in Savory Herb Marinade

PREPARATION TIME: **10 minutes**
MARINATING TIME: **24 hours**
SERVINGS: **8–10**

This is a savory herb marinade that black olives take to. The flavors of the herbs marry well with the smooth, fermented natural taste of black olives. This marinade can also be used for green olives with an entirely different effect.

    4 cups good quality black olives (Niçoise, Kalamata, Sicilian, Moroccan)
    2 bay leaves
    3 large cloves garlic, peeled and cut in half lengthwise
    6 sprigs fresh thyme or lemon thyme
    1 cup extra virgin olive oil
  $2/_3$ cup freshly squeezed lemon juice
    1 heaping teaspoon dried oregano
  $1/_2$ teaspoon freshly ground black pepper

1. Place the olives in a mixing bowl or in a large glass jar with a tight-fitting lid.
2. Place the bay leaves, garlic cloves, and thyme sprigs among the olives.
3. Whisk together the oil, lemon juice, oregano, and black pepper. Pour over the olives. Cover tightly and marinate for 24 hours at room temperature in a cool, dark place before serving. The olives can be chilled in the refrigerator after the first 24 hours of marinating. They keep well for several weeks.

Green Olives in Sweet Fennel Marinade

PREPARATION TIME: **10 minutes**
MARINATING TIME: **24 hours**
SERVINGS: **8–10**

This marinade for green olives adds sweetness to balance the sharpness and crispness of the olives. The orange zest and juice and the fennel seeds contribute a sweetly fragrant herbal essence. I do not recommend this marinade for black olives except for Greek Kalamata olives, which are not entirely black and carry a little of the raw freshness of ordinary green olives.

   4 **cups good quality green olives (California or Sicilian)**
   1 **tablespoon freshly grated orange zest**
   1 **tablespoon freshly grated lemon zest**
   2 **tablespoons fennel seeds**
   2 **bay leaves**
   4 **large garlic cloves, peeled and cut in half**
   $^1/_2$ **cup freshly squeezed orange juice**
   $^1/_2$ **cup freshly squeezed lemon juice**
   1 **cup olive oil**

1. Place the olives in a mixing bowl or in a large glass jar with a tight-fitting lid.
2. Sprinkle the orange zest, lemon zest, and fennel seeds over the olives and mix.
3. Place the bay leaves and garlic cloves among the olives.
4. Whisk together the orange juice, lemon juice, and oil; pour over the olives. Cover tightly and marinate at room temperature in a cool, dark place for 24 hours before serving. The olives can be chilled in the refrigerator after the first 24 hours of marinating. They keep well for several weeks.

Olivada

 Olivada is a mellow-tasting, herb-scented olive spread or dip that is popular throughout the Mediterranean. It can be made with either black or green olives. It is spread on crisp flat breads, pita, or crusty Mediterranean white bread or used as a dip for fresh vegetables.

Olivada with Black Olives

PREPARATION TIME: **20 minutes**
YIELD: **1$^1/_2$ cups dip**

- 1 cup pitted good quality black olives
- 2 large cloves garlic, peeled and chopped (1 tablespoon)
- 1 tablespoon capers, drained and rinsed
- $^1/_3$ cup extra virgin olive oil
- $^1/_4$ cup chopped fresh parsley

Place everything in a blender or food processor and puree until smooth. *Olivada* will have the consistency of a thick paste. Transfer to a glass jar with a tight-fitting lid and chill until ready to use. *Olivada* will keep 4–5 days refrigerated.

SERVING SUGGESTIONS:
Follow the serving suggestions for *Olivada* with Green Olives (below).

Olivada with Green Olives

PREPARATION TIME: **20 minutes**
YIELD: **1$^1/_2$ cups dip**

- 1 cup pitted good quality green olives
- 2 large cloves garlic, peeled and chopped (1 tablespoon)
- 1 teaspoon Hungarian hot paprika
- 1 teaspoon freshly grated lemon zest
- 1 tablespoon freshly squeezed lemon juice
- $^1/_3$ cup chopped fresh parsley

Place everything in a blender or food processor and puree until smooth. *Olivada* will have the consistency of a thick paste. Transfer to a glass jar with a tight-fitting lid and chill until ready to serve. *Olivada* will keep 4–5 days refrigerated.

SERVING SUGGESTIONS:
Serve *olivada* with crisp flat breads, pita bread, or crusty Mediterranean white bread and fresh raw vegetables as a dip.

Canton de Sardellas
PORTUGUESE-STYLE ANCHOVY SALAD

Sardellas is the Portuguese name for salt-cured anchovies, a favorite Sephardic appetizer. They can be purchased at any Italian or Middle Eastern grocery. *Sardellas* are also considered a gourmet item in Provence and Sicily, where they are used in many ways. To prepare *sardellas* for eating, just soak them for 1 hour in cold water to cover and then rinse them thoroughly to rid them of the excess salt in which they were cured. They are much, much tastier than tinned anchovies and also much larger. Portuguese Jews eat them all by themselves with fresh lemon slices and chopped parsley. *Canton de sardellas* is a delicious anchovy salad featuring these salty fish. The orange juice provides a sweet and unusual counterpoint to the saltiness of the fish.

SOAKING AND RINSING TIME (ANCHOVIES): **$1^1/_4$ hours**
PREPARATION TIME: **15 minutes**
SERVINGS: **4**

8 Italian salt-packed anchovies, rinsed and drained, or one 8-ounce can
   flat anchovies packed in oil (imported are best)
   Cold water (for salt-packed anchovies)
1 medium red onion, peeled and very thinly sliced
$^1/_3$ cup good quality green olives
1 large tomato, cut into thin wedges
$^1/_3$ cup extra virgin olive oil
$^1/_3$ cup freshly squeezed orange juice
$^1/_4$ cup freshly squeezed lemon juice
   Freshly ground black pepper
$^1/_4$ cup finely chopped fresh parsley

1. If using Italian salt-packed anchovies, place the fish in a bowl and cover with cold water. Soak for 1 hour, then rinse well and dry with paper towels. If using imported oil-packed anchovies, this step is unnecessary.

2. Place the anchovies, onions, olives, and tomato in a medium bowl. Mix the oil and fruit juices in a glass jar with a tight-fitting lid. Shake well and pour over the anchovy mixture. Toss gently and carefully.

3. Divide the salad among four plates. Sprinkle some of the black pepper and some of the parsley over each portion. Serve immediately.

SERVING SUGGESTIONS:

Canton de sardellas should be served with plenty of good crusty Mediterranean bread.

Salata de Atun y Sardellas

SEPHARDIC-STYLE SALAD NIÇOISE

 This marvelous salad is similar to the Provençal salad Niçoise, though the vegetables are different. Balsamic vinegar, while not traditional in Sephardic cooking, adds its own special qualities to the vinaigrette, so I have suggested it as an alternative to the traditional wine vinegar. This recipe is probably Spanish in origin.

PREPARATION TIME: 45–50 minutes
SERVINGS: 6 as an appetizer, 2 as an entree

- 8 ounces 1-inch-thick fresh tuna steak
  Olive oil for brushing
- 2 large yellow bell peppers
- 4 large, meaty tomatoes
- 1 medium red onion
- 2 large cloves garlic, peeled and chopped (1 tablespoon)
- $1/_2$ teaspoon salt
- $1/_2$ teaspoon Hungarian hot paprika
- $1/_3$ cup plus 1 tablespoon freshly squeezed lemon juice
- $1^1/_2$ tablespoons balsamic or red wine vinegar
- $2/_3$ cup extra virgin olive oil
- 3 hard-boiled eggs, peeled and quartered
- 2 tablespoons capers, drained and rinsed
- 6–8 imported flat anchovy fillets packed in olive oil, drained
  Freshly ground black pepper
- $1/_3$ cup finely chopped fresh parsley

1. Preheat the outdoor grill or oven broiler. Brush the tuna steak with olive oil. Grill 7 minutes on one side. Turn the fish over and brush again with olive oil. Cook another 7 minutes. The tuna will be dark around the edges and cooked through. Set aside to cool. When cool, cut the steak into $1/_2$-inch cubes.

2. Roast the peppers over the same grill, turning until each side is blackened. Wrap in dish towels or place in a plastic bag and cool. Peel, seed, and cut the peppers into thin strips.

(continued)

3. To peel and seed the tomatoes, bring some water to boil in a 2-quart saucepan on top of the stove and plunge each tomato into the boiling water for $1^1/_2$ minutes. Remove with a slotted spoon and cool. The peels will slip right off. Cut each tomato widthwise so the seeds show through in their compartments. Using the scooping end of a vegetable peeler or a spoon, remove and discard the seeds. Chop the tomatoes into chunks.

4. Peel and slice the onion into very thin rounds. Separate into rings.

5. Put the tuna cubes and vegetables into a large mixing bowl.

6. Place the garlic and salt into a mortar and pound to a paste. Put into a glass jar together with the paprika, lemon juice, balsamic vinegar, and olive oil. Shake this vinaigrette well and pour over the fish and vegetables. Mix together thoroughly.

7. Divide the salad among four plates. Garnish with the hard-boiled egg quarters, capers, and anchovies. Add some of the black pepper and some of the parsley to each portion before serving.

SERVING SUGGESTIONS:

This wonderful salad makes a fine appetizer or entree. Serve plenty of crusty Mediterranean bread with it and a glass of chilled white wine.

 Marinated Fried Fish

This appetizer was brought to the Netherlands by Spanish and Portuguese Jews, introduced into Dutch cuisine, and later into British, when the descendants of Spanish and Portuguese Jews settled there in the seventeenth century. From Great Britain it spread to the various British colonies where Jews settled. It is still very popular among British, South African, and Australian Jews.

The Jewish method of frying fish was so loved by the British that they adopted it as their own but changed the batter to one containing beer. Spanish and Portuguese Jews make their fish with a much lighter batter and serve it hot for dinner with egg/lemon or garlic and herb sauce. A large quantity of the fish is fried so that some of it can be marinated and eaten cold on the Sabbath as an appetizer.

British fish and chips, served with malt vinegar, is an adaptation of this original Sephardic recipe. It is as popular in England as hot dogs and hamburgers are in America.

This recipe includes two variations on the marinade, the first popular among British Jews and the second a Dutch recipe used by Jews in Holland, Curaçao, and Surinam.

Marinated Fried Fish, British Style

PREPARATION TIME: **30 minutes**
MARINATING TIME: **12 hours or overnight**
SERVINGS: **6–8**

  1 **recipe Sephardic-Style Fried Fish (page 105)**
$^1/_2$ **cup peanut oil in which the fish was fried**
  2 **bay leaves**
  1 **tablespoon fresh rosemary leaves**
  2 **tablespoons flour**
  4 **tablespoons malt vinegar**
$1^1/_2$ **cups cold water**
    Salt and freshly ground black pepper

1. Place the freshly fried fish in a glass or enamel container in one layer.
2. Place the hot oil in a $1^1/_2$-quart saucepan together with the bay leaves and rosemary and let it steep while you prepare the remaining ingredients for the marinade.
3. Place the flour and vinegar in a food processor or blender and blend until smooth. Add the cold water, salt, and pepper; blend thoroughly.
4. Heat the oil and add the ingredients from the processor. Stir constantly as the mixture cooks. When sufficiently thickened (sauce will be thin), pour over the fish and marinate, covered, in the refrigerator for 24 hours before serving. The fish will keep at least a week and improves with standing. Serve chilled.

(continued)

Marinated fried fish is served all by itself as an appetizer with bread, usually *challa* for the Sabbath.

Marinated Fried Fish, Dutch Style

PREPARATION TIME: **30 minutes**
MARINATING TIME: **12 hours or overnight**
SERVINGS: **6–8**

1 recipe Sephardic-Style Fried Fish (page 105)
1 small lemon, thinly sliced
$^1/_4$ cup peanut oil in which the fish was fried
1 cup malt or cider vinegar
2 bay leaves
1 teaspoon whole black peppercorns
1 large clove garlic, peeled and finely chopped ($^1/_2$ tablespoon)
1 dried hot red cayenne pepper or other red pepper
6 whole cloves
5 whole allspice

1. Place the freshly fried fish in a glass or enamel container in one layer. Cover with the lemon slices.
2. In a $1^1/_2$-quart saucepan, heat the oil over medium heat. Add the remaining ingredients and bring to a boil. Boil for 5 minutes. Remove from the heat and cool. Pour over the fish and marinate in the refrigerator for at least 24 hours before serving. Serve chilled. The fish will keep at least 1 week in the refrigerator.

SERVING SUGGESTIONS:
Follow the serving suggestions for Marinated Fried Fish, British Style (page 17).

Yaprakes de Oja

STUFFED VINE LEAVES

There are many different versions of this dish throughout the Mediterranean. The recipe is not Jewish in origin, but this particular seasoning mixture is pure Sephardic Jewish. Sephardic Jews, like Greeks, make two different kinds of stuffed vine leaves. One is a cold appetizer. The Jewish version of the appetizer is vegetarian. The other is a hot entree made with lamb or ground beef and served with an egg/lemon sauce (*Agristada*, page 305). This Sephardic-style stuffed vine leaf appetizer is full of spicy and herbal accents that titillate the palate with a variety of taste sensations.

ASSEMBLY TIME: **45 minutes**
PREPARATION TIME: **$2^1/_4$–$2^1/_2$ hours, plus 20 minutes for soaking**
CHILLING TIME: **3 hours**
YIELD: **makes about 24 stuffed vine leaves**

$^1/_2$ pound preserved vine leaves
    Cold water
  2 cups uncooked long grain white rice
  3 medium tomatoes, peeled, seeded, and finely chopped
$^1/_2$ cup finely chopped scallions
$^1/_3$ cup pine nuts
  4 large cloves garlic, peeled and chopped ($1^1/_2$–2 tablespoons)
$^1/_4$ cup finely chopped fresh parsley
$^1/_4$ cup finely chopped fresh mint leaves
$^1/_4$ teaspoon ground allspice
$^1/_4$ teaspoon ground cloves
    Salt and freshly ground black pepper
$^1/_2$ cup olive oil
$^3/_4$ cup cold water plus more, if needed
$1^1/_2$ teaspoons sugar
$^1/_3$ cup plus 1 tablespoon freshly squeezed lemon juice

1. Vine leaves are generally preserved in a salt brine. To prepare preserved vine leaves for cooking, the excess salt needs to be removed.

(continued)

To do this, place the leaves into a large bowl and pour boiling water over them to cover. Soak for 20 minutes and drain.

2. Return the leaves to the bowl and pour cold water over them. Taste the water for salt and, if necessary, drain and soak them in cold water an additional 20 minutes. If you have access to fresh vine leaves and are using them in the recipe, skip steps 1 and 2. Just plunge the leaves into boiling water and drain. This softens them enough to be rolled.

3. Mix the rice with the tomatoes, scallions, pine nuts, garlic, herbs, and spices in a large bowl.

4. Take one vine leaf and spread it out across a plate. Take 1 heaping tablespoon filling and spread it along one side of the vine leaf lengthwise, as illustrated in figure 1.

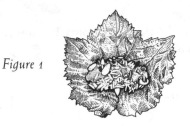

Figure 1

5. Fold the end of the leaf over the filling, as shown in figure 2.

Figure 2

6. Fold the two end pieces of vine leaf over this, as shown in figure 3.

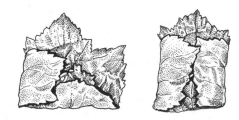

Figure 3

7. Roll the stuffed vine leaf up like a thin tube, as shown in figure 4. Set into a 4-quart stockpot or casserole.

Figure 4

8. Repeat steps 4 through 7 with the remaining vine leaves and filling until all the whole leaves are used up. You will probably have some torn or damaged vine leaves left which are unsuitable for stuffing. Lay them across the stuffed vine leaves in the pot. They will help protect the stuffed leaves from popping up and unfolding as they cook.

9. Mix the remaining ingredients together and pour over the vine leaves in the pot or casserole. Put several plates on top of the leaves to weight them down and keep them pressed into the pot while they cook. The liquid in the pot should cover the vegetables. Cover the pot tightly and bring to a boil slowly. Simmer the stuffed vine leaves for 2 hours. Check the pot from time to time and add cold water, if needed. After 2 hours of cooking, take the pot off the heat and cool to room temperature.

10. After the vine leaves have cooled, remove the plates and the leaves that cover the stuffed vine leaves. Place them gently onto a serving platter. *Yaprakes de oja* are generally served chilled. Chill at least 3 hours before serving. This dish is best prepared a day ahead of time, which allows the flavors to meld and strengthen.

SERVING SUGGESTIONS:
Yaprakes de oja are very versatile and make an attractive appetizer when served with a legume puree like *Humus* (page 7) or *Ajada de Aves* (page 5), marinated black and green olives (page 9), and *Toureto* (page 31) or Cucumber Salad with Kasseri Cheese (page 32). They are also a good buffet dish, served together with other appetizers and salads.

The Cooking of My Deceased Wife
A LADINO FOLK TALE

Once there was a man who was married to a woman he loved very much. The woman died young, and after many years of grieving and living alone, he decided to marry for the second time. His second wife knew how to cook very well. She would make him excellent dish after excellent dish but could never please him. Each time he tasted her cooking, he would complain, saying, "This is not like the cooking of my *deskansada* ['deceased wife']!"

One day the young woman was so frustrated she put something on the stove and forgot to watch it. It cooked so long that it burned. When she saw she had no time to prepare anything else, she was heartbroken but she had to serve what she had prepared. When her husband tasted it, he was ecstatic. "Ah!" he sighed. "This! This is like the cooking of my *deskansada!*"

Salads

Anjinara (HERB-MARINATED ARTICHOKES)

  Anjinara, Greek Romaniot Style

  Anjinara, Italian Style

Toureto (HERBED CUCUMBER PUREE)

Cucumber Salad with Kasseri Cheese

Salata Sepharadi (SEPHARDIC SUMMER SALAD)

Salata de Verdura (ROMAINE LETTUCE AND ARUGULA SALAD, ANDALUSIAN STYLE)

Salata de Maror (PASSOVER BITTER HERB SALAD)

Salata de Naranja y Verdura (FENNEL AND ORANGE SALAD)

Salata de Spinaca (SEPHARDIC-STYLE SPINACH AND YOGURT SALAD)

Salata de Panjar (BAKED BEET SALAD)

  Salata de Panjar y Carnabeet (BEET AND CAULIFLOWER SALAD)

Moroccan Carrot Salads

  Sweet Carrot Salad

  Hot and Savory Carrot Salad

Roasted Pepper Salads

  Simple Lemon Vinaigrette

  Paprika Vinaigrette

  Olivada Vinaigrette

  Bulgarian-Style Walnut Vinaigrette

Eggplant Salads

  Grilled Eggplant Salad, Balkan Style

  Roasted Eggplant Salad, Arabic Style

  Sautéed Eggplant Salad with Walnut Sauce

Anjinara

HERB-MARINATED ARTICHOKES

Artichokes are loved and appreciated throughout the Mediterranean and they are prepared in many interesting ways. Italian cooks have the greatest known variety of artichoke recipes and Italian Jews have created a number of those dishes. The recipe below has Italian, Greek Romaniot, and Sephardic variations. The Greek Romaniots, called in Ladino *Romaniotes,* are those Jews whose ancestors lived in Greece prior to 1492. When the Sephardic exiles from Spain and Portugal settled in Greece, which was a part of the Ottoman Empire, they called the Jews who were there by the name *Romaniotes* because they had been settled there since Roman times.

The herbs that dominate this dish vary from country to country and community to community but the technique of preparing the vegetable is basically the same. The artichokes are trimmed of all their inedible parts, braised in a lemon, herb, and garlic sauce, and then left to marinate in the liquid in which they were braised. The chilled marinade serves as a sauce for the finished dish.

The preparation of artichokes for cooking is a little lengthy but not complicated. And *anjinara* is so delicious, it is worth the time and effort it takes to make it.

ASSEMBLY TIME: **45 minutes (includes trimming of artichokes)**
PREPARATION TIME: **$1^1/_2$ hours**
CHILLING TIME: **24 hours**
SERVINGS: **6–8 or more**

  2 large lemons
     Cold water plus 1 cup cold water
6–8 whole artichokes with stems
 $1/_2$ cup olive oil
  1 teaspoon salt
 $1/_2$ cup chopped fresh parsley
 $1/_3$ cup chopped fresh dill leaves

$^1/_3$ cup chopped fresh mint leaves

3 medium cloves garlic, peeled and chopped ($1^1/_2$ teaspoons)

1. Squeeze the juice of $1^1/_2$ lemons into a large bowl of cold water to acidulate it. Throw in the lemon shells. The acid from the lemon juice prevents the artichokes from discoloring while you trim off the inedible parts of each artichoke.

2. Remove and discard all the outer leaves of one of the artichokes. These leaves are pure cellulose and cannot be digested. Then dunk the artichoke into the acidulated water.

3. Examine the leaves of the artichoke carefully. You will be able to feel, with careful attention and a little practice, how much of the top of each leaf you will need to cut off. Like the outer leaves, the top of most of the artichoke leaves is also pure cellulose. The edible parts of the artichoke are the heart, bottom, stem, and the parts of the leaves closest to the heart and stem. With a pair of scissors, cut the tops off the leaves, leaf by leaf. As you work your way into the artichoke, you will be cutting off less and less from each leaf. When you reach the innermost leaves, which are completely tender and, therefore, completely edible, you will know that you have cut off enough. Dunk the artichoke into the acidulated water again. Rub the cut surfaces with one of the squeezed-out lemon halves.

4. Gently pry open the center of the artichoke. Here, you will see purple-colored, hairy fibers, which are also made of tough, inedible cellulose. This part of the artichoke is called the choke and, if you make the mistake of eating it, you will discover how it got its name. It tastes like cotton. Pull this material out with your fingers and discard it. Brush out the inside of the artichoke with a pastry brush to eliminate all excess fibers. Dunk the artichoke into the acidulated water again.

5. With a vegetable peeler, peel the stem of the artichoke to get rid of the tough, fibrous outer layer. Put the artichoke back in the bowl of acidulated water. The artichoke is now ready to be stuffed and cooked.

6. Repeat steps 1 through 5 with the remaining artichokes.

(continued)

7. The artichokes will be poached just like pears. Make sure you have a stockpot wide enough and deep enough to hold them all in one layer, bottom facing upward.

8. Put the olive oil, salt, juice of the remaining $1/2$ lemon, and 1 cup cold water into the stockpot.

9. Combine the herbs and the garlic in a small bowl and divide this mixture among the artichokes, stuffing a portion into the cavity of each artichoke. Put the stuffed artichokes, stems up and leaves downward, into the stockpot. If there is any herb mixture remaining, scatter it all over the artichokes.

10. Cover the stockpot with foil and then put on the lid of the pot; this provides a tight seal. Bring the pot to a boil over medium-high heat and reduce the heat to simmer. Simmer for 1 hour. Artichokes should be cooked through and soft but not mushy.

11. Check the quantity of liquid in the pot. There should be no more than $3/4$ cup. If necessary, remove the artichokes, set them head down onto a platter, and boil down the liquid until it is sufficiently reduced.

12. Remove the pot from the heat and cool to room temperature, partially uncovered. When the artichokes have cooled, cover the pot again and chill for 24 hours before serving.

13. To serve *anjinara,* place the artichokes on a flat platter or on individual serving plates, head down and stem up. Spoon some of the sauce from the pot over and around the artichoke. For diners with smaller appetites, serve a half rather than a whole artichoke.

SERVING SUGGESTIONS:
This is an elegant appetizer that should be served on its own with good, crusty Mediterranean bread and a light white wine.

VARIATIONS:
Anjinara, Greek Romaniot Style
The herbs in the above recipe are the Sephardic formula. For a Greek Romaniot version, substitute 2 tablespoons fresh thyme leaves and 1

tablespoon dried oregano for the dill and mint. Proceed as directed, using all the other ingredients for *anjinara* in the preceding recipe.

Anjinara, Italian Style

For an Italian recipe, use 2 tablespoons fresh thyme leaves, $1/4$ cup chopped fresh basil leaves, 2 tablespoons fresh marjoram leaves, and the mint. Do not use dill. Proceed as directed, using all the other ingredients for *anjinara* in the preceding recipe.

Toureto

HERBED CUCUMBER PUREE

Toureto is a specialty of the Sephardic Jews of Turkey. The mint and cucumber have a cooling, soothing effect on the palate that contrasts vividly with the hot paprika oil which is dribbled over the finished puree. Hot paprika oil is a favorite topping on vegetable puree dishes in Turkey and other parts of the Middle East.

PREPARATION TIME: **25 minutes**
CHILLING TIME: **2–3 hours**
SERVINGS: **6–8**

> 4 cups cut-up stale French or sourdough white bread (cut into chunks)
> Cold water
> 1 very large or 2 medium cucumbers
> 2 large cloves garlic, peeled and chopped (1 tablespoon)
> $1/3$ cup olive oil
> $1/3$ cup plus 1 tablespoon freshly squeezed lemon juice
> $1/3$ cup chopped fresh mint leaves
> 1 teaspoon salt
> $1/8$ teaspoon ground white pepper
> $1/4$ cup olive oil mixed with $1/4$ teaspoon Hungarian hot paprika

1. Soak the chunks of bread in cold water to cover until softened. Drain and squeeze dry.
2. Peel the cucumber(s). If using English cucumbers, proceed to the next step. If using American cucumbers, cut in half lengthwise and remove the seeds and discard.
3. Place all the remaining ingredients except the hot paprika oil in a food processor or blender and process into a smooth puree.
4. Pour the puree into a bowl or spread it onto a flat platter. Chill in the refrigerator, covered, for 2–3 hours before serving. When ready to serve, dribble the oil and paprika mixture decoratively over the cucumber puree. Serve immediately.

SERVING SUGGESTIONS:
Toureto makes an excellent appetizer served alongside other salads, appetizers, and savory pastries. It is also an excellent addition to a vegetarian buffet.

Cucumber Salad with Kasseri Cheese

 This is a favorite Sephardic *desayuno* dish. *Desayuno* is a warm-weather meal, eaten on Saturday in the late morning or early afternoon after coming home from the synagogue. Rich with tangy homemade yogurt and salty, soft, white kasseri cheese and fragrant with the cooling taste of mint, it is enjoyed throughout the Mediterranean world.

PREPARATION TIME: **1 hour and 10 minutes**
CHILLING TIME: **several hours or overnight**
SERVINGS: **6–8**

2 medium cucumbers, peeled and seeded
Coarse salt

1 1/2 cups plain yogurt
  3 large cloves garlic, peeled and chopped (1 1/2 tablespoons)
1/4 teaspoon salt
1/3 cup finely chopped fresh mint leaves
  1 tablespoon freshly squeezed lemon juice
     Freshly ground white pepper
1/2 pound soft, white kasseri cheese (or brynza, chèvre, or soft, white
     farmer's cheese)

1. Slice the cucumbers very thinly and place in a colander in the sink. Sprinkle with coarse salt to cover all the cucumber slices and cover with plastic wrap. Place several plates on top of the plastic to weight the cucumbers down and let them stand for 1 hour. The excess moisture will be drained out of the cucumbers.

2. Place a fine wire mesh colander over a mixing bowl and line it with two layers of cheesecloth. Put the yogurt into the cheesecloth-lined colander and allow it to drain for 45 minutes. The excess water will be drained out of the yogurt, creating a thicker, cheeselike yogurt.

3. Crush the garlic and salt together in a mortar and put into a medium mixing bowl. Add the mint leaves, lemon juice, and white pepper and mix.

4. Crumble the cheese and add it to the garlic mixture. When the yogurt has drained for 45 minutes, combine it with the cheese.

5. Remove the plates and plastic wrap from the cucumbers. Rinse and dry the cucumbers carefully and squeeze out the moisture before adding them to the mixing bowl.

6. Mix everything together well and chill several hours or overnight before serving.

SERVING SUGGESTIONS:
Serve this salad with *Huevos Haminados* (page 231), sliced fresh tomatoes, marinated olives, and savory pastries for a delicious *desayuno*. This salad is also a welcome addition to an array of appetizers and salads served before a fish entree.

Salata Sepharadi

SEPHARDIC SUMMER SALAD

This salad is a summer delight! It is made of the freshest seasonal summer vegetables. *Salata sepharadi* is not a "catch-all" minced vegetable salad. Each element in the composition of this salad is chosen for its visual appearance and distinctive flavor. The overall composition is defeated by adding vegetables just because you think they happen to look good that day in the market or because they are in the refrigerator and need to be used up.

PREPARATION TIME: **30 minutes**
SERVINGS: **6–8**

    1   small sweet red onion, peeled and very finely diced
    1   large long, narrow cucumber, peeled, or 1 large English hothouse
        cucumber, unpeeled
    1   large yellow bell pepper, cored and seeded
    1   large green bell pepper, cored and seeded
    3   large, meaty, best quality ripe local tomatoes
    8   large red radishes
  $1/2$ medium head romaine lettuce
    2   scallions
  $1/2$ cup finely chopped fresh parsley leaves
  $1/3$ cup finely chopped fresh dill leaves
  $1/3$ cup finely chopped fresh mint leaves
    1   very large or 2 medium cloves garlic, peeled
    1   teaspoon salt
        Juice of 1 large lemon
  $2/3$ cup extra virgin olive oil
        Freshly ground black pepper

1. The most important thing about making this salad is chopping the vegetables into fine dice. Begin by finely dicing the onion and placing it in a large mixing bowl.
2. Finely dice the cucumber, peppers, tomatoes, and radishes and add them to the onion.

3. Using a large chef's knife, chop the leaves of romaine lettuce into fine dice and the scallions into very fine slices. Add them to the vegetables in the bowl.

4. Add the fresh herbs to the salad.

5. Chop the garlic and place it in a mortar. Grind it together with the salt to make a paste and place in a glass jar with a tight-fitting lid.

6. Add the lemon juice and olive oil to the jar, shake vigorously, and pour over the salad. Toss well to combine the vegetables with the dressing.

7. Add black pepper to taste and toss again. Serve immediately. Salad can be tossed $1^{1}/_{2}$–2 hours ahead of time and chilled until it is served. If doing this, do not mix the lettuce into the salad. Just before serving, toss it in. Bring salad to room temperature by removing it from the refrigerator 30 minutes before serving.

SERVING SUGGESTIONS:
Salata sepharadi can accompany any grilled meats or fish. It is equally delicious as part of an array of appetizers and salads or as part of a vegetarian buffet.

Salata de Verdura

ROMAINE LETTUCE AND ARUGULA SALAD, ANDALUSIAN STYLE

This subtly sweet treatment for slightly bitter romaine lettuce may have been part of the Sephardim's Andalusian cuisine. The delicate, sweet flavor of the orange juice, honey, and dill marry well with the peppery arugula leaves and the subtly bitter romaine. The taste of orange is highlighted by the grated orange zest in the vinaigrette.

PREPARATION TIME: **20 minutes**
SERVINGS: **6–8**

- 1 large head romaine lettuce, washed, dried, and torn into small pieces (approximately $8^1/_2$–9 cups)
- 1 small bunch arugula or watercress, washed, dried, and torn into small pieces ($1^1/_2$–2 cups, tightly packed)
- $1/_4$ cup snipped fresh chives
- $1/_3$ cup chopped fresh dill leaves
- 1 teaspoon freshly grated orange zest
- 1 tablespoon honey (preferably citrus flower honey)
- $1/_3$ cup freshly squeezed orange juice
- $1/_3$ cup freshly squeezed lemon juice
- $2/_3$ cup extra virgin olive oil
  Salt and freshly ground black pepper

1. Put $8^1/_2$ cups torn lettuce into a large mixing bowl. (If there is any lettuce left, save it for another salad.)
2. Add the arugula to the lettuce.
3. Add the chives and dill to the greens in the bowl.
4. Place the orange zest and honey in a glass jar with a tight-fitting lid. Add the orange juice and lemon juice. Stir well until the honey is dissolved.
5. Add the olive oil and salt to taste to the jar, cover tightly, and shake well to combine. Pour the dressing over the salad and toss.
6. Add black pepper to taste and toss again. Serve immediately.

This delicate and unusually flavored salad goes especially well with grilled fish or grilled chicken breasts. It is also excellent as part of a meal featuring *Pescado Ahilado con Abramela* (page 111) or *Pescado Sofrito à la Judia* (page 105).

Salata de Maror

PASSOVER BITTER HERB SALAD

In biblical Israel, Passover was one of the three "Pilgrim Festivals" during which Jews from all around Israel would travel to Jerusalem to worship at the Temple. All three Pilgrim Festivals, Sukkot and Shevuot as well as Passover, are agricultural as well as spiritual. Passover marks the coming of spring in the Jewish calendar, and foods that are eaten on Passover reflect this aspect of Jewish life.

Spring is remembered in a formal ritual at the Passover *seder* with the eating of the *karpas,* a spring vegetable or herb. Parsley, celery, chives, and dill are all used for the *karpas* ritual. Ashkenazic Jews of Northern and Northeastern Europe have a tradition of using potato for the *karpas* because spring usually does not arrive in the colder climates until after Passover and green herbs are often unavailable in March or April.

There is also another green plant used in a *seder* ritual—the *maror* or "bitter herb." The eating of the *maror* symbolizes the bitterness of slavery experienced by the Hebrews in Egypt. There are several plants that grow in the Mediterranean region that qualify as "bitter herbs" for the *maror* ritual in the *seder.* Three of them are lettuces—romaine, chicory, and endive. Sephardic Jews have a tradition of serving a salad made with these lettuces as part of the *seder* meal. This salad is cool and refreshing—a real culinary celebration of the spring season.

PREPARATION TIME: **20 minutes**
SERVINGS: 6–8

  1 leek, white part only
  5 cups torn romaine lettuce leaves
$2^1/_2$ cups torn chicory leaves
$2^1/_2$ cups torn endive lettuce leaves
$1^1/_2$ cups torn arugula or watercress
  2 scallions
$^1/_3$ cup chopped fresh parsley leaves
$^1/_4$ cup chopped fresh dill leaves
  1 tablespoon chopped fresh mint leaves
  1 large clove garlic, peeled and chopped ($^1/_2$ tablespoon)
  1 teaspoon salt
$^1/_3$ cup plus 1 tablespoon freshly squeezed lemon juice
  1 egg yolk
$^2/_3$ cup extra virgin olive oil
    Freshly ground black pepper

1. Carefully wash and dry the leek to remove all bits of sand. Cut it into very fine slices and place it in a large mixing bowl.
2. Add the romaine, chicory, endive, and arugula to the bowl. Wash and dry the scallions and slice them finely. Add them to the salad.
3. Sprinkle the chopped herbs over the salad.
4. Put the garlic into a mortar with the salt and grind into a paste. Put the paste into a glass jar with a tight-fitting lid. Add the lemon juice, egg yolk, and olive oil to the jar. Shake well to combine and pour over the salad. Toss well together.
5. Add black pepper to taste and toss again. Serve immediately.

SERVING SUGGESTIONS:

Serve this salad as a course all by itself. It is an excellent palate cleanser between courses. A Passover *seder* menu that includes this salad is found on page 326.

Salata de Naranja y Verdura

FENNEL AND ORANGE SALAD

The fennel plant, native to the Mediterranean and well known to the ancient Greeks, is a favorite herb in the cuisine of Mediterranean Jews. Fennel was actually not popular in Spain except as an herb to cook with fish, so the original Spanish recipe for this Sephardic salad may or may not have included fennel bulb. The Moroccan variation of the recipe omits fennel altogether. The flavors in this salad are a perfect balance of sweet, tart, and bitter. Romaine lettuce provides a slightly bitter counterpart to the sweetness of the orange sections while the fennel adds an herbal freshness.

PREPARATION TIME: **20 minutes**
SERVINGS: **6–8**

1 medium head romaine lettuce, washed, dried, and torn into small pieces ($6^1/_2$–7 cups)
2 fennel bulbs
1 tablespoon finely grated orange zest
1 large or 2 medium seedless navel oranges
1 leek, white part only
1 tablespoon honey (preferably citrus flower honey)
$^1/_3$ cup plus 1 tablespoon freshly squeezed lemon juice
$^2/_3$ cup extra virgin olive oil
Salt
Freshly ground black pepper

1. Place the lettuce in a salad bowl.
2. Remove the stalks and leaves from the fennel bulbs. Set aside a few feathery sprigs of the fennel leaves for the salad. Wash the fennel leaves and set on paper towels to dry.
3. Wash and dry the fennel bulbs and shred them thinly. Add to the lettuce leaves.
4. Place the orange zest in a glass bowl or jar. Peel the orange(s) and carefully remove the white membrane. Cut the orange into wedge-

shaped sections. If the orange is very large, cut the sections in half. Set aside.

5. Carefully wash and dry the white of the leek, getting in between each layer to make sure no sand or grit adheres. Finely shred the leek and add it to the lettuce and fennel.

6. Add the honey to the orange zest. Add the lemon juice and stir well to dissolve the honey completely.

7. Add salt to taste. Then add the oil and mix or shake the dressing.

8. Pour the dressing over the salad and toss. Add the oranges and any juice that has accumulated with them to the salad and toss again. Add black pepper to taste and toss one more time. Serve immediately.

SERVING SUGGESTIONS:
This salad goes well before a fish entree or with simple roasted or grilled chicken. *Salata de naranja y verdura* does not taste good when served with dishes cooked in tomato-based sauces or with dishes featuring eggplant.

Salata de Spinaca

SEPHARDIC-STYLE SPINACH
AND YOGURT SALAD

Spinach, yogurt, and dill have a remarkable affinity for one another. Turkish Jews serve this salad in the spring, when spinach and dill are in season. The gentle, sweet herbal fragrance of the dill is a welcome complement to the spinach.

PREPARATION TIME: **1 hour 25 minutes**
CHILLING TIME: **several hours**
SERVINGS: **6–8**

$1^1/_2$ cups plain yogurt, preferably homemade
  2 pounds spinach
   Cold water
  2 medium cloves garlic, peeled and chopped (1 heaping teaspoon)
  1 teaspoon salt
$^1/_3$ cup chopped fresh dill leaves
  1 tablespoon freshly squeezed lemon juice
   Freshly ground white pepper

1. Place a fine wire mesh colander over a large mixing bowl. Line it with two layers of cheesecloth. Pour the yogurt into the colander and allow it to drain for 45 minutes.
2. Carefully wash the spinach leaves but do not dry them. Place the spinach in a large saucepan and bring to a simmer, covered, over medium heat. Cook until the spinach leaves are wilted but still bright green. Be careful not to overcook.
3. To stop the spinach from cooking, pour it into another colander and run cold water over it until it feels cool to the touch. Allow spinach to drain as it cools.
4. Place the drained yogurt in a medium mixing bowl. It will have given off all its excess moisture.
5. In a mortar with a pestle, grind the garlic and salt to a paste. Add it to the yogurt, stirring well to combine.
6. Add the dill, lemon juice, and white pepper. Mix well to combine.
7. Squeeze the spinach gently to remove as much moisture as you can and dry with a paper towel. Place the spinach on a cutting board and chop it finely. Add to the yogurt mixture and mix well to combine. Chill several hours before serving.

SERVING SUGGESTIONS:
Serve *salata de spinaca* with *Huevos Haminados* (page 231), sliced fresh tomatoes, marinated olives, and a variety of savory pastries. The salad may also be served as part of an array of salads and appetizers or a vegetarian buffet.

Salata de Panjar

BAKED BEET SALAD

Beets are often thought of as a Jewish vegetable because Ashkenazic Jews make so many dishes with them. In Northern Europe, root vegetables are commonly grown, so the use of beets and other root vegetables by Ashkenazic Jews is not surprising. Beets are less popular in Sephardic cuisine because they are not cultivated widely in Mediterranean countries. However, in Serbia, Bulgaria, and Romania, where beets are abundant, Sephardic Jews prepare many dishes with them. In this recipe, the garlic and onions lend a savory balance to the natural sweetness of the beets. The beets are baked rather than boiled, which helps preserve most of the nutrients as well as the full flavor and rich red color.

BAKING TIME (BEETS): **1 hour**
PREPARATION TIME: **25 minutes**
SERVINGS: **8–10**

- 3 pounds beets
- 4 tablespoons plus $^1/_3$ cup sunflower oil
- 1 large onion, peeled and thinly sliced
- 2 large cloves garlic, peeled and finely chopped (1 tablespoon)
- 4 scallions, thinly sliced
- 1 tablespoon sugar
- $^1/_4$ cup freshly squeezed lemon juice
- Salt and freshly ground black pepper
- $^1/_4$ cup chopped fresh parsley

1. Preheat the oven to 350 degrees.
2. Wash and dry the beets. Wrap each beet individually in foil and place on a flat baking sheet. Bake for 1 hour or until beets are soft and cooked through. Remove from the oven and cool to room temperature.
3. Heat 4 tablespoons sunflower oil in a skillet over medium heat and sauté the onion until soft and translucent (5–7 minutes). Reduce the

heat slightly, add the garlic, and cook 2–3 minutes more until soft and translucent. Remove from heat.

4. Mix the remaining oil, sugar, lemon juice, salt, and pepper in a large mixing bowl.

5. Peel and dice the beets. Add them to the vinaigrette, mixing well.

6. Add the onion and garlic mixture with its cooking oil from the skillet. Add the scallions and mix the beets well again.

7. The salad may be served right away or it may be refrigerated until ready to serve. Just before serving, add the parsley and toss together. The salad keeps well covered in the refrigerator for several days.

SERVING SUGGESTIONS:

Salata de panjar is traditionally served as part of an array of appetizers and salads. It is also wonderful as part of a vegetarian buffet.

VARIATION:

Salata de Panjar y Carnabeet (Beet and Cauliflower Salad)

Add the parboiled florets of 1 small head of cauliflower to the beet salad before refrigerating. To parboil cauliflower, cook florets in a 2-quart saucepan in salted water to cover for 15 minutes. Or place the florets in a microwave-safe dish with $1/4$ cup water and cook for 8–10 minutes in the microwave on high. Drain and dry the cauliflower before adding it to the beet salad. Serve as you would *salata de panjar.*

Moroccan Carrot Salads

 Moroccan Jews prepare two types of carrot salads, one sweet and scented with orange flower water, and the other hot and savory with just a hint of sweetness. Here is a recipe for each.

Sweet Carrot Salad

PREPARATION TIME: **20 minutes**
CHILLING TIME: **2–3 hours**
SERVINGS: **6–8**

- 7 large carrots, peeled
- Salt
- $1/4$ cup honey (preferably citrus flower honey)
- $1/3$ cup freshly squeezed lemon juice
- 1 tablespoon orange flower water

1. Grate the carrots using the julienne blade of a food processor or by hand with the julienne blade of a mandolin or hand grater. Place in a medium mixing bowl and sprinkle with salt.
2. Stir the honey into the lemon juice until it dissolves. Pour over the carrots and mix well.
3. Pour the orange flower water over the carrots, toss again, and chill 2 or more hours before serving.

SERVING SUGGESTIONS:
Follow the serving suggestions for Hot and Savory Carrot Salad (page 45).

Hot and Savory Carrot Salad

PREPARATION TIME: **30 minutes**
CHILLING TIME: **2–3 hours**
SERVINGS: **8–10**

  7 large carrots, peeled and cut into thin rounds
    Cold water
$1/_2$ teaspoon sugar
$1/_3$ cup plus 1 tablespoon freshly squeezed lemon juice
$1/_2$ teaspoon ground cumin
$1/_2$ teaspoon cayenne pepper
    Salt and freshly ground black pepper
$1/_3$ cup olive oil
$1/_4$ cup finely chopped fresh cilantro

1. In a 2-quart saucepan, parboil the carrots in boiling salted water to cover for 10 minutes or until tender. Or microwave on high power in a microwave-safe dish with $1/_4$ cup water for 5–7 minutes. Drain and pour cold water over the carrots to stop them from further cooking. Cool to room temperature and place in a large mixing bowl.
2. In a glass jar, mix together the remaining ingredients except for the cilantro. Shake vigorously and pour over the carrots. Add cilantro and toss again. Chill salad before serving.

SERVING SUGGESTIONS:
Moroccan carrot salads are always served with an array of salads and appetizers at the beginning of a meal.

Roasted Pepper Salads

Mediterranean Jews prepare many different kinds of roasted pepper salads. Only eggplant is as ubiquitous or as versatile. All colors of bell peppers are roasted and can be used interchangeably. A mixture of colors (i.e., red, yellow, purple, and green) gives roasted pepper salads visual interest but they can be made with whatever peppers are available or look good in the market. Red bell peppers are the sweetest in flavor and green bell peppers are the sharpest. Nothing brings out the taste of peppers better than roasting. It mellows out their sharpness and, in sweet red peppers, brings out their sweetness. Roasted peppers also have a deliciously smoky quality. There are several kinds of vinaigrettes that blend well with the flavor of roasted bell peppers and each makes a different kind of pepper salad. The basic technique is the same for each salad.

ROASTING AND COOLING TIME (PEPPERS): **35–40 minutes**
PREPARATION TIME: **30 minutes**
SERVINGS: **8–10**

8 large bell peppers (green, red, yellow, or purple)
1 recipe vinaigrette (see below)

1. Wash and dry the peppers and place them either on a preheated outdoor grill or under the preheated broiler in your oven.
2. Grill or broil the peppers, turning them over to expose every side to the heat source. Turn the pepper whenever the side facing the heat begins to blacken and char. This usually takes about 5 minutes.
3. After all sides of the peppers are blackened, wrap them in a dish towel or put them in a plastic bag and let them cool to room temperature.
4. When cool, peel the peppers with your hands.
5. Slit them open and remove the seeds and cores. Slice them into thin strips and place in a medium mixing bowl and toss with one of the vinaigrettes below. Serve roasted bell pepper salads at room temperature for full flavor.

Simple Lemon Vinaigrette

YIELD: 1 cup vinaigrette

$1/_3$ cup freshly squeezed lemon juice
$1/_2$ cup extra virgin olive oil
   Salt and freshly ground black pepper
$1/_4$ cup chopped fresh parsley

Mix all the ingredients together and use as directed in the recipe.

Paprika Vinaigrette

YIELD: 1 cup vinaigrette

1 very large clove garlic, peeled and chopped (1 heaping tablespoon)
1 teaspoon salt
$1/_2$ teaspoon Dijon mustard
$1/_3$ cup freshly squeezed lemon juice
$1/_2$ cup olive oil
1 heaping teaspoon Hungarian hot paprika
$1/_4$ teaspoon sugar
1 teaspoon caraway seeds
   Freshly ground black pepper

1. In a mortar with a pestle, grind the garlic and salt to a paste. Place it in a glass jar with a tight-fitting lid.
2. Add the remaining ingredients to the glass jar. Shake vigorously to combine. Use as directed in the recipe.

Olivada Vinaigrette

YIELD: 1 cup vinaigrette

1 cup *Olivada* (page 12)

Shake *Olivada* well before using as directed in the recipe.

Bulgarian-Style Walnut Vinaigrette

YIELD: 1 cup vinaigrette

$^1/_2$ cup walnut oil or sunflower oil
1 medium onion, peeled and finely chopped
1 large clove garlic, peeled and finely chopped ($^1/_2$ tablespoon)
$^1/_3$ cup chopped walnuts
4 tablespoons red wine vinegar
Salt and freshly ground black pepper

1. Heat the oil in a large skillet over medium heat and sauté the onions until soft and translucent (5–7 minutes). Reduce the heat to low, add the garlic, and sauté 2 minutes more. Remove from the heat.
2. Stir the remaining ingredients into the onion mixture and mix well. Use as directed in the recipe.

Eggplant Salads

Eggplant is the most popular vegetable in the Mediterranean. There are so many different eggplant salads in the Jewish culinary repertoire alone that they could fill an entire book. I offer three examples of eggplant salads that come from different regions and represent three different methods of working creatively with this vegetable. In the first recipe, the eggplant is grilled and then sautéed in olive oil together with a variety of other vegetables and herbs. In the second, the eggplant takes the place of chick-peas in a lemony *tehina*-based sauce. The third recipe, from Macedonia, combines sautéed eggplant slices with tangy pomegranate juice, crushed walnuts, garlic, and cool mint.

Grilled Eggplant Salad, Balkan Style

Variations on this type of eggplant salad appear from as far west as the Adriatic coast, east into southern Russia and the Caucasus, and as far south as Turkey. The only region that does not prepare eggplant salad this way is that of Antakya (Antioch) in southern Turkey near the Syrian border. These Jews are culturally linked to the Arab-Jewish communities of Syria, Lebanon, and Iraq in the area of cooking as well as in synagogue liturgies and folk customs. Antakya Jews would be more likely to prepare the Arabic-style eggplant salad found on page 51.

The technique for preparing the salad is virtually the same throughout these regions. The eggplant is first grilled until it is blackened. Then it is peeled and sautéed together with a variety of other vegetables and seasonings. The grilling brings out the strong, natural flavor of the eggplant and gives it a smoky, sweet quality. The seasonings are kept to a minimum in order to emphasize the flavor of the eggplant itself. The herb seasonings also vary regionally, with oregano preferred in Greece, marjoram in the Balkans. Parsley is a constant everywhere. This is a versatile salad and cooks can be creative with it, trying out an endless variety of new herb and vegetable combinations.

PREPARATION TIME: $1^1/_4$ hours (includes 30–35 minutes grilling time for eggplants and peppers)
SERVINGS: 8–10 or more

- 2 large eggplants ($1^1/_2$ pounds each)
- 1 medium head garlic, cloves peeled and cut in half
- 1 large green bell pepper
- 1 red bell pepper
- $^1/_2$ cup plus 3 tablespoons olive oil
- 2 large onions peeled and finely chopped
- 1 medium carrot, peeled and cut into small dice
- $1^1/_2$ teaspoons dried oregano or marjoram
- 2 large tomatoes, peeled and seeded
- $^1/_3$ cup red wine vinegar
- $1^1/_2$ teaspoons salt
- Freshly ground black pepper
- $^1/_3$ cup finely chopped fresh parsley

1. Preheat the outdoor grill or your oven broiler. Cut small slits in the eggplants at intervals and insert $^1/_2$ clove garlic into each slit.
2. Grill the eggplants on all sides until they blacken (20–25 minutes); set aside to cool to room temperature. When cool, peel and cut into very small pieces. The peel should be discarded but the garlic does not have to be.
3. Grill the green and red peppers until they blacken on all sides (10–12 minutes). Wrap in a cloth towel or place in plastic bags. Cool to room temperature. When cool, peel, seed, core, and cut into small dice.
4. Heat $^1/_2$ cup oil in a deep, wide sauté pan over medium-high heat. Sauté the onions until soft and translucent (5–7 minutes). Add the carrot and continue cooking 4–5 minutes longer. Add the oregano or marjoram and mix in well.
5. Add all of the eggplant and continue cooking until the eggplant turns into a nice puree.
6. Add the peppers and cook 5 minutes more, stirring constantly. Remove from the heat.
7. Add the tomatoes, vinegar, remaining olive oil, salt, pepper, and parsley. Mix everything together well and put into a large serving bowl.

Salad may be served after it comes to room temperature or it may be chilled before serving.

SERVING SUGGESTIONS:

This delicious salad is traditionally served as an appetizer, either all on its own with dark bread or crisp flat breads, or as part of an array of salads and appetizers. It makes a wonderful addition to any vegetarian buffet.

Roasted Eggplant Salad, Arabic Style

This dish, called *baba ghanoush,* was popular in Turkey and in all the Arab countries. It is of Arabic origin and bears some resemblance to *Humus* (page 7). The eggplant is roasted in the oven rather than grilled. The flavor of oven-roasted eggplant is not quite as smoky as that of grilled eggplant. The *tehina* sauce, made with sesame paste, lots of garlic, and lemon juice is tangy and zesty, a beautiful complement to the roasted eggplant. Take care to roast the eggplant until it is completely done—it gets no additional cooking.

ROASTING TIME (EGGPLANTS): **1 hour**
PREPARATION TIME: **20 minutes**
CHILLING TIME: **3–4 hours minimum**
SERVINGS: **8–10**

2 **large eggplants (about $1^1/_2$ pounds each)**
5 **large cloves garlic, peeled**
$1^1/_2$–2 **teaspoons salt**
$^3/_4$ **cup *tehina* paste**
$^3/_4$ **cup freshly squeezed lemon juice**
$^1/_3$ **cup chopped fresh parsley**

1 Preheat the oven to 400 degrees.
2. Prick the eggplants all over with a fork. Lay them on a cookie sheet and roast for 1 hour, turning every 12–15 minutes. The eggplants will brown and then blacken. Some of their bitter liquid will leak onto the cookie sheet. When the eggplants are done, they will be very soft and

their skins will have sunken into their flesh in places. Cool the eggplants to room temperature and peel.

3. Place the eggplants, garlic, 1¹/₂ teaspoons salt, *tehina* paste, lemon juice, and parsley in a food processor or a blender in batches and process until a smooth puree is achieved. Transfer the eggplant salad to a bowl and taste for seasoning. If necessary, add salt. Chill 3–4 hours before serving.

SERVING SUGGESTIONS:

This salad is always served with a variety of other salads and appetizers before an entree. It is also excellent as part of a vegetarian buffet.

Sautéed Eggplant Salad with Walnut Sauce

This is a very elegant autumn dish with an unusual sauce. Tart pomegranate juice, cool mint, and musky walnuts combine well with the eggplant. This dish is often served for the second day of Rosh Hashono by Sephardic Jews because the pomegranate is rumored to have 613 seeds, one for each of the 613 *mitzvot* (commandments) in the Jewish religion.

SALTING TIME (EGGPLANT): **1¹/₂ hours**
PREPARATION TIME: **45–50 minutes**
SERVINGS: **8–10**

2	large eggplants (about 1¹/₂ pounds each)
	Coarse salt
¹/₂–³/₄	cup olive oil
3	thick pieces stale French or sourdough bread
¹/₂	cup Vegetable Stock (page 299)
¹/₂	cup pomegranate juice made from fresh pomegranate seeds or ¹/₃ cup bottled pomegranate juice (available in specialty food stores)
¹/₂	pound walnuts (approximately 4 cups)
	Salt and freshly ground black pepper
¹/₄	teaspoon ground cinnamon
¹/₈	teaspoon ground cloves
¹/₃	cup fresh mint leaves
	Fresh mint sprigs for garnish

1. Cut off the green top of the eggplants. Then slice them lengthwise into long, oval-shaped slices $1/4$ inch thick. Layer them in a colander in the sink, sprinkling each layer with coarse salt.

2. After sprinkling the last layer, cover the eggplant slices with plastic wrap and weight them down with several plates and cans of food. Allow them to rest $1^1/_2$ hours. This removes the bitter juices of the eggplant before cooking.

3. After the eggplants have drained, remove the plates, cans, and plastic wrap. Rinse the eggplant slices and gently squeeze out the juices into the sink. Dry the eggplant slices on paper towels.

4. In a large skillet, heat $1/4$ inch of the olive oil over medium-high heat. Sauté the eggplant slices two or three at a time until brown on both sides. Add oil as needed and regulate the temperature so that the oil doesn't burn. The eggplant slices will sauté quickly and not absorb too much oil. This is a little tricky. Eggplant is like a sponge: the oil must be hot but not so hot that it burns. Practice will teach you how to do this correctly. Drain the eggplant slices on paper towels as they brown.

5. After sautéeing the eggplants, soak the bread in the stock until soft. To make $1/_2$ cup freshly squeezed pomegranate juice, separate the seeds and fruit from two pomegranates and tie them into a double layer of cheesecloth. Squeeze by hand into a medium mixing bowl. Pomegranate juice cannot be made in a blender or juicer because the crushed seeds impart a bitter flavor to the juice. Put everything except the eggplant and the mint sprigs in a food processor or blender and process until smooth. This will make a thick puree.

6. To assemble the salad, spread 1 tablespoon pureed walnut mixture, which is the walnut sauce, on a slice of eggplant. Roll it up like a cigarette and place it on a platter. Repeat until all the eggplant slices are filled and rolled. There will be some leftover walnut sauce. The dish can be prepared several hours in advance up to this point and the salad and leftover sauce refrigerated until ready to serve.

7. Forty-five minutes before proceeding with step 8, remove the filled eggplant slices and the leftover walnut sauce from the refrigerator and bring them to room temperature.

(continued)

8. Spread the remaining walnut sauce over the tops of the stuffed eggplant, not too thickly. Serve immediately, garnished with sprigs of mint.

SERVING SUGGESTIONS:
Serve this elegant salad as an appetizer course all by itself as part of a special holiday dinner. Serve a light white wine with this dish.

Yuha Brings Eggplants from the Market
A SEPHARDIC FOLK TALE

Yuha, the proverbial fool of the Sephardic world, was always mixing things up. Once his mother wanted to send him to the market to buy some eggplants. Yuha told her he had never seen an eggplant. "Never seen an eggplant?" she queried in dismay. "But we eat eggplant at least twice a week."

"Mama, I know we eat it all the time. But I don't know what it looks like unless it is cooked. Please explain what I should look for in the market."

"An eggplant has a purple coat and it wears a green hat, just like this." With that, Yuha's mother put on a purple caftan and wrapped a green scarf around her hair. "See? This is what an eggplant looks like. Now go to the market and get me some."

With this clear, simple explanation in mind, Yuha ran off to the market. After a long time passed, he returned, all hot and tired. "I finally found the eggplant but he didn't want to come. I forced him here by tying his hands with a rope and dragging him through the street."

"What? You tied an eggplant with a rope and dragged it through the street?" cried Yuha's mother as she ran to the front door, only to see that her son had brought home an angry Turkish dervish with a purple satin robe over his shoulders and a green turban on his head!

Savory
Pastries
and Pies

Borekas

    Gomo de Queso Blanco (WHITE CHEESE FILLING)

    Gomo de Carne (SAVORY MEAT FILLING)

    Gomo de Spinaca (SPINACH AND HERB FILLING)

    Gomo de Spinaca y Queso (SPINACH AND CHEESE FILLING)

    Chandrajo (EGGPLANT FILLING)

Boyos

    Gomo de Spinaca y Queso (SPINACH AND CHEESE FILLING)

    Gomo de Berenjenna (EGGPLANT AND CHEESE FILLING)

    Gomo de Patata y Queso (POTATO AND CHEESE FILLING)

Buleymas or *Ojaldres*

Impanadas

Rodanchas

Pittas

    Pitta de Spinaca (SPINACH PIE)

    Pitta de Queso (CHEESE PIE)

    Pitta de Pescado (FISH PIE)

Pastilla

Minas (PASSOVER PIES)

    Mina de Pollo (CHICKEN AND SPRING HERB FILLING)

    Mina de Cordero (LAMB AND SPRING HERB FILLING)

Boyos de Pan (CHEESE/BREAD PASTRIES)

S avory pastries are an ancient culinary tradition in the Sephardic world. In medieval Spain and Portugal, savory meat pastries were regularly served on the Sabbath following the fish course. The placing of meat between two layers of dough was meant to represent the double portion of manna given to the Hebrews when they wandered in the Sinai desert. The Spanish Jews called these pastries *empanadas*. The custom of eating savory meat pastries on the Sabbath actually predates Spanish Jewry. The Babylonian *Talmud* mentions a Sabbath dish called *pashtida,* which is described as a kind of meat pie made with a raised yeast dough pastry. The term *pashtida* also appears in Rabbinic manuscripts from Spain, indicating clearly that this dish was part of their culinary repertoire.

The art of preparing many kinds of savory pastries and pies has been developed over the centuries by Sephardic cooks. The pastries are made with various kinds of doughs and many different fillings. A few kinds of savory pastries, like *Rodanchas* (page 74), are made only for special holiday meals or on special occasions. Some are small, individual samplings. Others are large pies or tarts which are sliced before serving. A complete index of Sephardic savory pastries and pies is almost impossible to create because the names of the dishes are interchanged by the cooks. Small pastries can be interchangeably called *Borekas* (page 61), *Boyos* (page 66), or *Buleymas* or *Ojaldres* (page 71). Large pies are generally called by the name *pitta* (page 77) if prepared from dough and *mina* (page 83) if prepared with *matzoh*. I have tried to simplify this complex subject by giving names to my savory pastry recipes based on the type of dough used to prepare them and maintaining the traditional names for the larger pies, which is easy to do.

Borekas

Borekas are the simplest and most popular Sephardic savory pastry. They are a Turkish dish that was absorbed into Sephardic cuisine by Jewish immigrants after the Spanish exile in 1492. In modern Israel, *borekas* are eaten as snacks or light meals, the way Americans would eat pizza or hot dogs. *Borekas,* or one of the other savory pastries, are also a part of nearly every festive meal in a Sephardic home. The fillings for *borekas* are varied and include seasonal herb and spice mixtures with meat, spinach, eggplant, potatoes, or cheese as the main ingredient. While fillings vary, the recipe for *boreka* dough is the same virtually everywhere. It is a simple mixture of flour, oil, water, and salt. The liquids are first heated together with the salt and then the flour is mixed into the hot liquid. The result is a soft, pliable dough that doesn't break easily and has good keeping qualities. It is an ancient recipe and might even predate the use of yeast in bread making. If flattened and grilled or baked on tiles, *boreka* dough makes a delicious flat bread similar to Indian *parathas* or *chapatis*. It is also an extremely easy dough to work with.

PREPARATION TIME (DOUGH): **15 minutes**
PREPARATION TIME (BOREKAS): **1 hour 45 minutes**
(not including preparation of filling)
YIELD: **makes 30 *borekas***

$^3/_4$ cup peanut or corn oil
$1^1/_4$ cups cold water
$^1/_2$ teaspoon salt
4–5 cups all-purpose flour
 1 recipe filling (see below)
 1 egg beaten with 1 tablespoon cold water (egg wash)
 Sesame seeds for sprinkling (optional)

1. Mix the oil, water, and salt in a saucepan and bring to a boil over high heat. Remove immediately from the heat and pour into a deep mixing bowl.

(continued)

2. Add the flour and mix together. The addition of the flour will cool the mixture so you can handle it. Mix the dough well and knead it with your hands until it is smooth and elastic. Add more flour, if necessary, to achieve the correct consistency. Cover the dough with a damp cloth and let it rest a minimum of 30 minutes or until you are ready to make the *borekas*. The dough will keep a couple of hours.

3. Prepare two well-oiled cookie sheets.

4. Have your filling(s) ready at your side while you work. Also have a small bowl of cold water. To make the *borekas,* take one walnut-sized lump of dough and roll it into a ball. Set it on a platter or a board. Repeat with the remaining dough. You will have approximately thirty balls of dough. Cover these with a damp towel.

5. Roll one of the balls into a flat oval about 3×4 inches and $1/4$ inch thick. Fill with 1 heaping teaspoon of the filling.

6. Fold in half across the 4-inch length to form an elongated half-moon shape. Brush the edge of the *boreka* with a little cold water. This will help hold the seal as the pastry bakes. Pinch gently or press with the tines of a fork to seal.

7. Using a spatula, transfer the *boreka* to one of the cookie sheets. Repeat until all the dough has been used up.

8. Preheat the oven to 400 degrees.

9. While oven is preheating, brush the *borekas* lightly with the egg wash and sprinkle with the sesame seeds, if you wish. Bake in the oven for 25–30 minutes or until the *borekas* are golden brown. They may be served warm or at room temperature. *Borekas* will keep for a few hours without refrigeration and several days refrigerated.

SERVING SUGGESTIONS:

Serve *borekas* with a variety of appetizers and salads either before a main entree or as a light meal. The dairy versions of *borekas* are traditionally part of the *desayuno* meal served on Shabbat.

Gomo de Queso Blanco
(White Cheese Filling)

PREPARATION TIME: **10 minutes**
YIELD: **2^1/$_2$–3 cups filling**

- 1 pound brynza, soft, white kasseri, or feta cheese
- 2 large eggs, beaten
- 2 tablespoons finely chopped fresh parsley
- 1 tablespoon finely chopped fresh mint leaves
- 1 tablespoon finely chopped fresh dill leaves
  Salt and freshly ground white pepper

Combine all the ingredients to form a paste and use as directed in the recipe.

Gomo de Carne
(Savory Meat Filling)

PREPARATION TIME: **20 minutes**
YIELD: **2^1/$_2$–3 cups filling**

- 3 tablespoons olive oil
- 1 medium onion, peeled and finely chopped
- 1 medium clove garlic, peeled and chopped (^{1}/$_2$ heaping teaspoon)
- 1 pound lean ground beef
- ^{1}/$_4$ cup cold cooked rice or mashed potatoes
- ^{1}/$_2$ teaspoon ground cinnamon
- ^{1}/$_4$ teaspoon ground cloves
  Salt and freshly ground black pepper

1. Heat the oil in a skillet over medium-high heat and sauté the onion until soft and translucent (about 5–7 minutes). Reduce the heat slightly, add the garlic, and cook 1 minute longer.
2. Add the meat and continue to cook until no trace of pink is left.
3. Remove from the heat and add the remaining ingredients. Mix together well, cool to room temperature, and use as directed in the recipe.

Gomo de Spinaca
(Spinach and Herb Filling)

> PREPARATION TIME: 30 minutes,
> including time to cook and chop spinach
> YIELD: 2 1/2–3 cups filling

- 3 tablespoons olive oil
- 1 medium onion, peeled and finely chopped
- 2 leeks, white part only, very finely sliced
- 1 medium clove garlic, peeled and finely chopped (1/2 heaping teaspoon)
- 2 pounds fresh spinach, cooked, drained, and chopped
- 1/4 cup finely chopped fresh parsley
- 1 tablespoon finely chopped fresh dill leaves
- 2 eggs, beaten
- Salt and freshly ground black pepper

1. Heat the oil in a skillet over medium-high heat. Sauté the onion until soft and translucent (about 5–7 minutes). Reduce the heat slightly and add the leeks and garlic. Cook, stirring constantly, until the leeks are soft. Remove from the heat.
2. Put the contents of the skillet into a mixing bowl and add the remaining ingredients. Mix well to combine and use as directed in recipe.

Gomo de Spinaca y Queso
(Spinach and Cheese Filling)

> PREPARATION TIME: 30 minutes,
> including time to cook and chop spinach
> YIELD: 2 1/2–3 cups filling

Substitute 1 cup crumbled feta cheese for the leeks in the previous recipe and use as directed.

Chandrajo
(Eggplant Filling)

PREPARATION TIME: **1 hour 40 minutes**
YIELD: **$2^1/_2$–3 cups filling**

1 large eggplant ($1^1/_2$ pounds)
Coarse salt
$^1/_3$–$^1/_2$ cup olive oil
1 large onion, peeled and finely chopped
1 large clove garlic, peeled and chopped ($^1/_2$ tablespoon)
4 large fresh tomatoes, peeled and chopped
$^1/_4$ teaspoon ground allspice
Freshly ground black pepper
Salt (optional)

1. Cut the unpeeled eggplant into small cubes and layer in a colander in the sink, sprinkling each layer with coarse salt. Cover the top layer with plastic wrap and place several dishes and cans of food on top of the eggplant to weight it down. Leave for $1^1/_4$ hours.
2. Remove the weights and plastic wrap. Rinse and gently squeeze the eggplant slices to remove the bitter juices. Dry with paper towels.
3. Put $^1/_3$ cup olive oil into a deep, wide sauté pan and heat over medium-high heat. Add the onion and sauté until soft and translucent (5–7 minutes).
4. Add the garlic, reduce the heat slightly, and cook 1 minute longer. Add the eggplant cubes and sauté about 15–18 minutes until soft and cooked through, stirring constantly.
5. Add the tomatoes and allspice and cook until the tomatoes soften and begin to disintegrate. The *chandrajo* will be thick and rich. Season with black pepper to taste and, if necessary, salt. Remove from the heat, cool to room temperature, and use as directed in the recipe.

Boyos

Boyos are savory cheese-filled pastries made with yeast dough. The unusual treatment of the dough, achieved by allowing it to rise in oil and then sprinkling it with a layer of flour and grated cheese, results in a flaky texture not typical of ordinary yeast dough. *Boya* dough is a little like strudel dough but thicker and more textured.

Boyos are a more elaborate pastry than *Borekas* (page 61) and are therefore prepared only for special occasions. In European Sephardic communities and in the Sephardic kitchens of Safed and Jerusalem, *boyos* are prepared for the Sabbath brunch called *desayuno*. This is a dairy meal featuring salads, savory pastries, and *Huevos Haminados* (page 231), slow-cooked, brown-colored, creamy hard-boiled eggs.

PREPARATION TIME (DOUGH): **2 hours**
PREPARATION TIME (BOYOS): **$1^1/_4$–2 hours,
including preparation of fillings**
YIELD: **makes 24 *boyos***

$5^1/_2$–6 cups all-purpose flour
  3 tablespoons grated Parmesan or Pecorino Romano cheese
$^1/_2$ teaspoon coarse salt
  1 teaspoon sugar
$2^1/_2$ cups lukewarm water
  1 tablespoon active dry yeast
    Olive oil
  1 recipe filling (see below)
    Cold water (optional)
  1 extra large egg beaten with 1 tablespoon cold water (egg wash)
    Sesame seeds for sprinkling (optional)

1. Set aside $^1/_2$ cup flour and mix with the grated cheese. Place 5 cups flour in a mixing bowl with the salt. Mix well.
2. Dissolve the sugar in the lukewarm water. Mix in the yeast and set aside in a draft-free place to proof (approximately 10 minutes). When the yeast is proofed, it will bubble up.
3. Make a well in the center of the mound of flour and pour in the

proofed yeast mixture. Stir it well and then begin to knead. If the mixture needs more flour, add it as you knead. The dough should be a little more sticky than ordinary bread dough because you will be adding more flour when the cheese mixture is added. When finished with this preliminary kneading, place the dough in an oiled bowl and cover with a damp towel. Allow to rest 30 minutes. Dough will rise a little.

4. Divide the partially risen dough into four equal parts. Roll each into a ball. Place each ball of dough in a large bowl with $1/2$ inch olive oil in it. Turn the dough over and around so that every part of the surface is well oiled. This is important for the texture of the dough. Cover these bowls with damp towels or with wax paper and allow to rest another 30 minutes. It will rise again.

5. While the dough is resting and rising, prepare the filling for the *boyos*.

6. Prepare two well-oiled cookie sheets.

7. On a well-oiled bread board, roll out one ball of dough to a 15-inch square. The dough will be very thin. Set aside one quarter of the cheese-flour mixture. Sprinkle half of the cheese-flour mixture you have set aside over the dough. Fold the two ends of the sheet of dough over the filling in toward the center, as you fold a towel (see figure 1), and have them meet at the center.

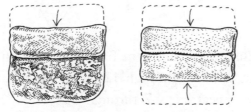

Figure 1

8. Sprinkle the remainder of the cheese-flour mixture you have set aside over this and then fold the sheet of dough in half (see figure 2).

Figure 2

(continued)

9. Cut the piece of dough into six equal square-shaped pieces (see figure 3).

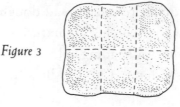

Figure 3

10. Roll one of the squares into a 5-inch square. Place 1 tablespoon filling in the center of the square (see figure 4).

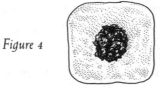

Figure 4

11. Fold each point of the square into the center of the pastry (see figure 5) and pinch the edges gently to seal. If you wish, you may brush lightly with cold water to secure the seal before pinching.

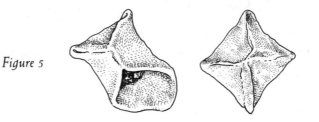

Figure 5

12. Using a spatula, gently place the finished pastry on a prepared cookie sheet. Repeat steps 10 through 12 with the remaining five pieces of dough. Then repeat steps 7 through 12 with the remaining dough and filling. You will have twenty-four *boyos*.
13. Preheat the oven to 400 degrees.
14. Brush the *boyos* with the egg wash and sprinkle lightly with the sesame seeds, if you wish. Bake until golden brown, about 20–25 minutes. Cool to room temperature before serving.

Gomo de Spinaca y Queso

(Spinach and Cheese Filling)

PREPARATION TIME: **20 minutes**
YIELD: **makes 5–6 cups filling**

- 3 pounds fresh spinach, cooked, drained, and chopped
- 1 cup freshly grated Parmesan or Pecorino Romano cheese
- 1 tablespoon bread crumbs or *matzoh* meal
- $3/_4$ cup soft, white farmer's cheese or brynza, feta, or soft, white kasseri cheese
- 2 large eggs, beaten
- $1/_3$ cup finely chopped fresh parsley
- $1/_3$ cup finely chopped fresh dill leaves
- Salt

Put all the ingredients into a mixing bowl and combine to form a thick paste. Use as directed in the recipe.

Gomo de Berenjenna

(Eggplant and Cheese Filling)

PREPARATION TIME: **1 hour 20 minutes**
YIELD: **makes 5–6 cups filling**

- 1 large eggplant (about $1^1/_2$ pounds)
- Coarse salt
- $1/_3$–$1/_2$ cup olive oil
- 1 medium onion, peeled and finely chopped
- 3 large tomatoes, peeled, seeded, and diced
- $1/_2$ cup freshly grated Parmesan or Pecorino Romano cheese
- $3/_4$ cup grated kashkaval cheese
- Freshly ground black pepper
- 2 large eggs, beaten
- Salt, if needed

1. Cut the eggplant into small cubes and place in a colander in the sink. Sprinkle coarse salt over the eggplant and mix with your hands to make sure all of it is covered with salt. Cover with plastic wrap and

place several plates and cans of food on top of the eggplant to weight it down. Allow it to rest $1^1/_4$ hours.

2. After the eggplant has rested, remove the weights and plastic wrap. Rinse the eggplant and gently squeeze to remove the bitter juices. Dry with paper towels.

3. In a wide, deep sauté pan, place $^1/_3$ cup olive oil and heat it over medium-high heat. Sauté the onion until soft and translucent (5–7 minutes). Add the eggplant cubes and, if necessary, a little more olive oil and cook until the eggplant begins to brown and soften.

4. Add the tomatoes and cook another 10–15 minutes, stirring constantly, until the eggplant is completely cooked and the tomatoes begin to disintegrate. The eggplant will be soft but not mushy. Remove from the heat and cool to room temperature.

5. When the eggplant mixture is cool, add the cheeses, black pepper, and eggs, and, if necessary, salt. Use as directed in the recipe.

Gomo de Patata y Queso
(Potato and Cheese Filling)

PREPARATION TIME: **30 minutes, including cooking of potatoes**
YIELD: **makes 5–6 cups filling**

  3 pounds red boiling potatoes, peeled and cut into chunks
$^1/_3$ cup water (optional)
$^1/_4$ teaspoon salt (optional)
  2 tablespoons olive oil
  1 medium onion, peeled and finely chopped
  1 cup soft, white farmer's cheese
  1 cup freshly grated Parmesan or Pecorino Romano cheese
  3 eggs, beaten
    Freshly ground black pepper

1. Cook the potatoes in boiling salted water to cover for 25 minutes until soft. Or for 18 minutes in the microwave on high in a covered 2-quart microwave-safe casserole with $^1/_3$ cup water and $^1/_4$ teaspoon salt. Drain and mash.

2. While the potatoes are cooking, heat the oil in a medium skillet over medium-high heat and sauté the onion until golden brown. Remove from the heat and put into a mixing bowl.

3. Add the mashed potatoes, farmer's cheese, Parmesan cheese, eggs, and salt and pepper to taste. Mix well and use as directed in the recipe.

Buleymas or Ojaldres

Buleymas, also called *ojaldres,* are savory pastries made with filo dough, a fine, paper-thin dough that is popular in Mediterranean and Middle Eastern cooking. *Buleymas* are the only kind of savory pastry prepared by Jewish cooks from North African countries except for Egypt. Other savory pastries are prepared by North African cooks, like *brik* or *cigares,* and all are made with filo dough. Filo dough is extremely difficult to make and most kitchens are not equipped to deal with it so I strongly recommend buying commercial filo. It can be stored almost indefinitely in the freezer but should be defrosted slowly so that the delicate sheets do not break apart. To prevent the sheets of filo from drying out and breaking, they must be kept covered with a damp cloth while resting. They must also be oiled quickly and thoroughly when being used for the same reason. Filo dough pastries are delicate and flaky.

PREPARATION TIME: **1 hour plus time for making fillings**
YIELD: **makes between 25–30 *buleymas***

> 1 pound filo dough
> 1 cup olive oil or melted unsalted butter (no butter with meat filling)
> 4$^1/_2$–5 cups filling (see Note)
> 1 large egg beaten with 1 tablespoon cold water (egg wash)
>   Sesame seeds for sprinkling (optional)

1. Preheat the oven to 350 degrees. Generously oil two cookie sheets.
2. Keep the filo dough covered with a damp cloth while working. Have oil or butter and a pastry brush at your side while you work. Place one sheet of the filo dough on a flat surface and brush it lightly with oil or butter.
3. Place a second sheet across it evenly and oil the second sheet.
4. Cut the sheets into three strips of equal width.
5. Place 1 scant tablespoon filling at the lower corner of each strip.
6. Fold the corner into a triangle and continue folding until the filling is completely wrapped. You will have a pretty triangle-shaped pastry. Place it on a prepared cookie sheet. Repeat steps 2 through 6 with the remaining dough and filling.
7. Brush each *buleyma* with egg wash and sprinkle, if you wish, with sesame seeds. Bake 20 minutes or until golden brown. Serve hot or cool to room temperature before serving.

NOTE:
You may use any of the fillings for *Borekas* (pages 63–65) or Boyos (page 69–71).

Impanadas

Impanadas are a Portuguese-Jewish savory pastry with a fish filling. The word *impanada* appears in a few old Rabbinic manuscripts and is used to designate a meat- or fish-filled pastry eaten on the Sabbath. *Impanadas* is probably the oldest name that Jews of Spanish and Portuguese descent give to this type of dish. The words *boreka* and *buleyma* are Turkish and Arabic in origin, whereas *impanada* is an archaic form of the Spanish *empanada,* which means "filled savory pastry."

Spanish and Portuguese Jews who settled in Holland, England, North and South America, and the Caribbean Islands continued to use the Spanish name for this dish. Spanish and Portuguese Jews settled in several parts of Latin America and the West Indies and played an active role in the manufacture and distribution of sugar, particularly in Brazil. A small number of Jews were important as sugar planters but their main role was in setting up sugar mills and as merchandisers of raw and refined sugar to European markets. Jewish entrepreneurs circumvented Portuguese trading restrictions by marketing in Amsterdam, which had sugar refineries owned by Jews.

This recipe for *impanadas* comes from Curaçao, a Dutch island colony in the West Indies that still has a Jewish community, mostly of Sephardic descent. The oldest synagogue in the New World still used as a house of worship is in Curaçao.

PREPARATION TIME (DOUGH): **15 minutes**
PREPARATION TIME (IMPANADAS): **2 hours,
including making the filling**
YIELD: **makes 30 *impanadas***

For the Filling
2   tablespoons olive oil
1   medium onion, peeled and finely chopped
1   large or 2 small stalks celery, finely chopped
1   large clove garlic, peeled and finely chopped ($^1/_2$ tablespoon)
Two $6^1/_2$-ounce cans good quality tuna packed in olive oil, drained
$^1/_3$ cup cold mashed potatoes or more as needed
$^1/_4$ cup finely chopped pimentos
    Salt and freshly ground black pepper
    Dash Tabasco or other hot pepper sauce

For the Dough
1   recipe *Boreka* dough (page 61)
1   egg beaten with 1 tablespoon cold water (egg wash)
    Sesame seeds for sprinkling (optional)

1. To prepare the filling, heat the olive oil in a skillet over medium-high heat and cook the onion until soft and translucent (5–7 minutes). Add the celery and garlic and cook 10 minutes longer, stirring constantly and regulating the heat so that the garlic doesn't burn while cooking. Remove from the heat and transfer to a mixing bowl.
2. Add the tuna, potatoes, pimentos, salt, pepper, and Tabasco to the mixing bowl and mix well.
3. Follow the instructions for *borekas*, steps 3 through 9. Cool the *impanadas* to room temperature before serving.

SERVING SUGGESTIONS:

Impanadas are a delicious alternative to *Borekas* (page 61) or *Buleymas* (page 71). They are especially good with an array of salads and appetizers that precede a fish entree.

Rodanchas

 Rodanchas are an autumn pastry made for the High Holy Days and Sukkot by Sephardic Jews. The autumn Jewish holidays are considered a time of spiritual renewal and many of the foods eaten at this time of year contain symbols of spirituality in them.

The filling for *rodanchas* is traditionally made from a kind of winter squash called *kalabasa,* which is not widely available in the United States. Fresh pumpkin and Hubbard squash are good substitutes. The seasoning in *rodanchas* is both spicy and sweet, typical of the Jewish dishes eaten at this time of year. The spiral shape of the pastry has folkloric significance. It symbolizes both the never-ending cycle of life and the ascent of the soul into the seven heavenly spheres.

Some Sephardic Jews eat *rodanchas* during the Rosh Hashono dinner as part of the *Yehi ratsones* ceremony, a recital of seven blessings over seven different foods. The seven blessings are made and seven different foods are eaten at the beginning of the meal. *Rodanchas* are used in this ceremony because of the pumpkin filling. The Aramaic word for pumpkin is *karah,* which, in spelling and pronunciation, is similar to the Hebrew words for "to recall" and "to be torn up." A special blessing asking the Creator to tear up stern judgments against us and to recall all our worth and good deeds on Rosh Hashono is recited before eating a piece of *rodancha.*

PREPARATION TIME: 2–2$^1/_2$ hours
YIELD: makes 30 *rodanchas*

  1 pound pumpkin or Hubbard squash, peeled and cut into small cubes
1$^1/_2$ cups sugar
  1 teaspoon ground cinnamon
$^1/_4$ teaspoon ground cloves
  1 cup ground walnuts plus finely chopped walnuts for sprinkling
  2 pounds filo dough (filo is generally sold in 1-pound packages)
  1 cup olive oil or melted unsalted butter
  1 large egg beaten with 1 tablespoon cold water (egg wash)

1. Put the pumpkin or squash into a pot of boiling water to cover and cook until soft and mashable (about 20 minutes). Alternately, steam the pumpkin or squash in a vegetable steamer until cooked through. When the vegetable has completely cooked, drain well and mash.

2. Return the mashed pumpkin to the saucepan and add the sugar and spices. Cook over low heat until the mixture is thick and pasty and most of the water has evaporated. This can take as little as 20 minutes or as long as 1 hour, depending on how much liquid the vegetable retains. Pumpkin takes longer to cook than Hubbard squash.

3. When the mixture is ready, remove from the heat and stir in the ground walnuts. Set aside to cool to room temperature.

4. When the filling has cooled sufficiently, you can start the pastries. Preheat the oven to 350 degrees. Prepare two well-oiled cookie sheets.

5. Place one sheet of filo dough on a flat surface. Cover the rest with a damp towel to prevent drying as you work. Have oil or melted butter

and a pastry brush at your side while you work. Brush the oil or butter over the sheet of filo. Place a second sheet over the first and repeat brushing.

6. Take 1 heaping teaspoon filling and lay it in a pencil-thin line across the longer part of one side of the filo sheets, as shown in figure 1.

Figure 1

7. Fold the two short ends of the sheets of filo over the filling to seal it in (see figure 2).

Figure 2

8. Roll the sheet up lengthwise like a thin tube and coil it as shown in figure 3.

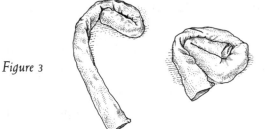

Figure 3

9. Using a spatula, carefully lay the *rodancha* on a prepared cookie sheet. Repeat steps 5 through 9 with the remaining filo dough and filling.

10. Brush the *rodanchas* with the egg wash and sprinkle lightly with the finely chopped walnuts. Bake for 20–25 minutes or until they are golden brown. Cool to room temperature before serving.

Pittas

 Pitta is the Greek word for pie. Sephardic Jews from Salonika and Romaniot Jews from other parts of Greece have many of their own recipes for large savory pies that are served as a main-dish meal. *Pittas* are large versions of *Buleymas* (page 71). Instead of making the dish into individual savory pastries, it is made into one big pie and cut into slices or wedges for serving. This way of preparing the dish is much less time consuming but considered to be more informal and, therefore, pitta is served as a weekday rather than as a Sabbath or holiday dish.

Nonetheless, traditional Sephardic cooks put a great deal of energy and creativity into preparing *pittas*. The Turkish grandmother of my friend and colleague Rabbi Susan Talve was so particular about her method of making *Pitta de Spinaca* that she insisted on listing the washing of the hands and the baking pans as part of her recipe. She also claimed that frozen spinach rather than fresh made the best, most authentic *Pitta de Spinaca*.

Here are recipes for *Pitta de Spinaca* and two other Sephardic *pittas*.

Pitta de Spinaca
(Spinach Pie)

PREPARATION TIME: **1 hour**
SERVINGS: **4–6**

10 sheets filo dough
$3/4$ cup melted sweet butter
4 cups Spinach and Cheese Filling for *borekas* (page 64)

1. Preheat the oven to 350 degrees. Butter a 9 × 13-inch rectangular baking dish.
2. Lay one sheet filo dough over the bottom of the prepared dish. Keep the others covered with a damp towel to prevent their drying out while you work. Brush this sheet with butter.

3. Fit five more sheets of filo dough over the first sheet, layering them one at a time and brushing each one with melted butter as it is laid down. Sheets of filo will slightly overhang the edges of the dish.
4. Spread the filling over the sheets of dough. The filling will fill the whole baking pan but there will be sheets of filo overhanging.
5. Cover the filling completely with the remaining four sheets of dough, placing them over the filling one at a time and brushing each one with butter.
6. Gently fold the overhanging sheets of filo dough from the bottom of the pie over the edge and roll them up to seal in the filling as the pie bakes. The rolled-up edges will make an attractive border around the pie.
7. Place the pie in the preheated oven and bake 45 minutes or until the pie is golden in color. Serve warm or at room temperature.

SERVING SUGGESTIONS:
Serve *pitta de spinaca* with *Olivos Marinados* (page 9) and a simple salad of cucumbers and tomatoes. This dish is also wonderful as part of a vegetarian buffet.

Pitta de Queso
(Cheese Pie)

> PREPARATION TIME: **1 hour**
> SERVINGS: **4–6**

Substitute the White Cheese Filling for *borekas* (page 63) for the spinach filling and prepare the *pitta* as directed above. Serve with *Salata de Verdura* (page 36), sliced fresh tomatoes, and olives for an elegant dinner.

Pitta de Pescado
(Fish Pie)

PREPARATION TIME: **1 hour**
SERVINGS: **4–6**

Use the filling for *Impanadas* (page 72) and prepare the *pitta* as directed above. Serve a *Salata de Naranja y Verdura* (page 39) and marinated green olives (page 11) with this delicious pie.

Pastilla

Pastilla is the Ladino name for the famous Moroccan pigeon pie called *b'stilla*. *Pastilla* is a Moorish dish that was brought to Morocco by Muslims of Andalusia, from whom the Spanish Jews borrowed the dish. The only Sephardic Jews that retained *pastilla* in their cuisine are the Jews of Morocco. The dish is made by Jews of both Moroccan and Sephardic origin in this country.

Pastilla is considered by Moroccan cooks to be a great delicacy and, because the preparations for it are quite elaborate, it is only made for special occasions, like weddings, or when entertaining very special guests. *Pastilla* contains three layers of fillings, each different. One is a spicy, aromatic meat mixture. The second a sugary almond mixture. The third a saffron-flavored egg custard. The Jewish version of *pastilla* is made with olive oil and the Muslim version is made with butter. Because pigeons are generally not available in American markets, I make my *pastilla* with chicken.

PREPARATION TIME: **$2^1/_2$–3 hours**
BAKING TIME (AFTER PIE IS ASSEMBLED): **30–35 minutes**
SERVINGS: **10–12 as an appetizer, 6–8 as an entree**

18 tablespoons olive oil

One 5-pound chicken, cut into eighths, including neck and gizzard

1 medium onion, peeled and chopped

Cold water

One 2-inch piece fresh gingerroot, peeled

5 black peppercorns

1 dried red hot pepper

1 tablespoon coarse salt

$1/8$ teaspoon saffron threads dissolved in $1/4$ cup boiling water

1 stick cinnamon

6 sprigs fresh cilantro

8 sprigs fresh parsley

6 large eggs plus 2 egg yolks

$1^1/_2$ cups sliced almonds

2 tablespoons sugar

$1/2$ teaspoon ground cinnamon

12 sheets filo dough

$1/2$ cup whole blanched almonds

2 tablespoons confectioners' sugar

Because *pastilla* is time consuming, it is good to divide the jobs over a 2-day period. Steps 1 through 6 may be done 1 day in advance.

1. Heat 4 tablespoons olive oil in a 4-quart stockpot over medium-high heat and brown the chicken pieces, a few at a time. Remove and set aside as they brown.

2. Add the onions and cook until soft and translucent (5–7 minutes).

3. Add cold water to cover and bring to a boil, stirring constantly. Reduce the heat to low, add the ginger, black peppercorns, red pepper, salt, saffron, cinnamon stick, cilantro, and parsley. Return chicken to pot and partially cover. Simmer 1 hour or until chicken is tender and cooked through.

4. Remove the chicken pieces with a slotted spoon and set aside on a plate. Pass the rest of the contents of the stockpot through a sieve, pressing down hard on the ingredients to extract all the flavor.

5. Separate $1^1/_2$ cups of the spicy stock and set aside. Put the rest into a

saucepan and reduce it by boiling it over high heat until all that remains is 4 tablespoons of glaze.

6. Separate the meat of the chicken from the bones. Discard the bones and chicken skin. Cut the meat into small pieces. If preparing the dish 1 day in advance, stop at this point and refrigerate the meat, stock, and glaze until ready to carry on.

7. Preheat the oven to 400 degrees. To assemble the *pastilla*, you will need a well-oiled, round, flat baking sheet. A pizza pan works well.

8. Beat the eggs and egg yolks in a mixing bowl until they are combined well but do not overbeat them.

9. Pour the $1\frac{1}{2}$ cups stock into a deep, wide sauté pan and turn the heat to medium. When the stock begins to heat up, pour 1 ladleful of stock into the beaten eggs. Whisk together well, reduce the heat under the pot to low, and pour the egg mixture into the stock. Cook, stirring constantly, until the mixture forms creamy curds. Remove from the heat and gently stir in the 4 tablespoons of glaze. This is the egg custard.

10. Heat 4 tablespoons olive oil in a skillet over medium heat. Add the sliced almonds and brown them in the oil, stirring constantly. When the almonds are browned, remove them from the heat. Cool slightly and stir in the sugar and cinnamon. Set aside. This is the almond filling.

11. Place filo dough sheets on a damp towel and cover them while you are working. Place one sheet on the surface of the prepared baking sheet. Brush it with some of the olive oil. Repeat this using five more sheets of dough. As you place each sheet of dough on the pan, slightly overlap them.

12. Place another sheet of the filo dough in the center of the baking sheet on top of the overlapping sheets. Oil it and fold it in half. Repeat with another sheet.

13. Spread the almond mixture over these two center sheets and cover with half the egg custard. Top this with strips and pieces of chicken meat. Cover the chicken with the remaining egg custard.

14. Lay the remaining four sheets of filo dough over the filling. Brush each sheet with oil after you lay it down.

15. Roll the overhanging edges of filo dough toward the center of the pie to make an attractive border and seal in the filling.

16. If the top looks too dry, brush the *pastilla* with more olive oil before putting it into the oven. Bake 30–35 minutes or until the *pastilla* is golden brown.

17. Remove the *pastilla* from the oven and cool to room temperature. Cut diagonal slashes into the pie in a crisscross pattern to make diamond shapes. Into each diamond shape, place a whole blanched almond. Sprinkle with the confectioners' sugar and serve. Present the whole pie for your guests to admire before cutting it.

SERVING SUGGESTIONS:

Pastilla is usually served as a course all by itself. It can be a first course in an elaborate Moroccan dinner or a main dish. If serving *pastilla* as a main dish, precede it with a *Salata de Naranja y Verdura* (page 39) and serve a light white wine with the meal.

Minas

PASSOVER PIES

Minas, also called *miginas* in Sephardic literature, are savory pies similar to lasagne. They are made with all kinds of vegetable and cheese or vegetable and meat fillings. The pastry dough for *minas* are Passover *matzot.* A variety of *minas* are always served during the Passover holiday, sometimes during the *seder* itself. *Minas* can be simple with only one filling or more elaborate with two or more fillings.

> PREPARATION TIME: **20 minutes plus time to make filling**
> BAKING TIME: **45–50 minutes**
> SERVINGS: **8–10 as part of a meal with other dishes**

> 6 *matzot*
> **Warm water or chicken stock for soaking (see Note page 84)**
> **Olive oil for brushing**
> 4$1/2$–5 **cups filling (see below and see Note page 84)**
> 3 **large eggs**

1. Preheat the oven to 350 degrees. Oil a rectangular 8 × 12-inch baking pan.
2. Soak the *matzot* in warm water or stock for 2 minutes. Remove each *matzoh* carefully and place it on a paper towel to drain.
3. Lay two *matzot* across the bottom of the baking pan in one layer. The *matzot* should cover all or most of the pan. Brush with olive oil.
4. Spread half the filling of your choice across the *matzot.*
5. Lay two more *matzot* over the filling. Brush with olive oil.
6. Spread the remaining filling over these two *matzot.* Top with the last two *matzot.* Brush the top with olive oil.
7. Beat the eggs and pour over the *mina* so that they cover everything completely. Bake 45–50 minutes or until *mina* is golden brown in color. Cut into squares and serve immediately.

NOTE:

You may use any of the fillings for *Borekas* (page 61), *Buleymas* (page 71), *Boyos* (page 66), *Impanadas* (page 72), or *Pittas* (page 77) or one of the two special Passover fillings below.

SERVING SUGGESTIONS:

Serve *minas* as part of a main dish during a Passover meal or any time of the year.

Mina de Pollo
(Chicken and Spring Herb Filling)

PREPARATION TIME (FILLING): **10 minutes**
YIELD: **4$\frac{1}{2}$–5 cups filling**

- 3 cups ground cooked chicken (ground in food processor or meat grinder)
- $\frac{1}{4}$ cup finely chopped fresh parsley
- $\frac{1}{4}$ cup finely chopped fresh dill leaves
- $\frac{1}{4}$ cup finely chopped fresh mint leaves
- 4 scallions, very thinly sliced
- $\frac{1}{2}$ cup cooked rice
- 2 tablespoons chicken stock
- 2 large eggs, beaten
  Salt and freshly ground black pepper

Combine all the ingredients in a mixing bowl and use as directed in the recipe.

NOTE:

When this filling is used for *minas,* use warm chicken stock instead of water to soak the *matzot.*

Mina de Cordero

(Lamb and Spring Herb Filling)

This filling is traditionally made for the second *seder* night with pieces of lamb leftover from the roast eaten the first night of Passover.

> PREPARATION TIME (FILLING): **with cooked lamb, 20 minutes; with uncooked lamb: 2 hours, 20 minutes**
> YIELD: **8 cups uncooked filling**

- 3 cups leftover pieces roasted lamb (cut into very small cubes) or 1 pound uncooked lamb cubes
- $2^1/_2$ cups chopped romaine lettuce
- 1 cup chopped arugula
- 1 cup chopped chicory
- 1 large clove garlic, peeled and chopped ($^1/_2$ tablespoon)
- 6 scallions, thinly sliced
- $^1/_3$ cup chopped fresh dill leaves
- $^1/_3$ cup chopped fresh parsley
- 2 large eggs
- Salt and freshly ground black pepper

1. If using uncooked lamb, place the cubes in a stockpot containing boiling salted water to cover. Cook at a simmer for 2 hours. If using leftover roast lamb (which is preferred), skip this step.
2. Combine everything in a bowl and mix together well. While the filling may seem a bit much for the six *matzot*, the lettuces cook down, like spinach, when they bake. Use as directed in the recipe.

Boyos de Pan

CHEESE/BREAD PASTRIES

 Boyos de pan are a delicious Sephardic snack food. They are an inventive and tasty way of using up stale bread. *Boyos de pan* made of leftover Sabbath *challa* are the best of all because the dough is enriched with egg, sugar, and oil. This delicious dish is also a wonderful light supper entree when served with a nice garden fresh salad like *Salata Sepharadi* (page 34). The traditional cheeses used in *boyos de pan* are kasseri and Pecorino Romano, but you may substitute other cheeses for other taste sensations.

PREPARATION TIME: **40 minutes**
YIELD: makes 35–40 *boyos*

- 1 loaf stale white bread or a mixture of stale bread pieces (1 loaf of bread will make 6 cups bread chunks)
  Cold water
- 5 large eggs
- $1/4$ cup sunflower or corn oil
- $1^1/_2$ cups freshly grated Pecorino Romano cheese
- 12 ounces soft, white kasseri, brynza, or soft, white farmer's cheese
- 2 cups all-purpose flour

1. Preheat the oven to 350 degrees. Grease two cookie sheets.
2. Break or cut the bread into chunks and soak in cold water to cover. Allow the bread to soften (about 3 minutes), then drain and squeeze dry.
3. Place the bread and everything else into a mixing bowl and mix together well. Have a bowl of cold water next to you as you work. Using wet hands, shape the bread mixture into 2-inch balls. Place the balls on prepared cookie sheets and flatten slightly with a spatula.
4. Bake *boyos* for 30 minutes or until they turn golden brown. Serve warm or at room temperature.

SERVING SUGGESTIONS:
Serve *boyos de pan* as a snack or a light dinner with a salad and a glass of white wine.

Two Jackasses at the Seder

A LADINO FOLK TALE

Once there was a well-educated woman who married an illiterate but very wealthy man. When Passover came, her husband, being illiterate, was unable to read the *Haggadah*. The woman was very sad about this. A year passed and the woman, concerned that the Passover *seder* would not be celebrated properly during her second year of marriage, asked her husband to bring home a guest from the synagogue to share their *seder*. The guest would then be able to lead in the recitation of the *Haggadah*. So the husband went to the synagogue and, after services were over, came home with a handsome young man who was in town on business and needed somewhere to celebrate Passover.

The husband and his wife and their guest sat down to a beautifully set table. The husband began by chanting the *kiddush* over the wine, which he knew by heart. Then he turned to his guest and said, *"B'kavod . . .* ['Please, honor us . . . ']," inviting his guest to begin the recitation of the *Haggadah*.

The guest responded, "Oh no. You are the *baal habayit* ['master of the house']. You should begin."

The husband looked sheepishly at his guest and said, "I wish I could but I cannot read or write."

"Neither can I," said the guest, looking just as sheepish.

"Very well," said the mistress of the house, with a disgusted look on her face. "I will recite the *Haggadah* for all of us." With this she began:

"Mah nishtanah halailah hazeh mikol haleylot?

Why is this night different from all other nights?

Sheb'chol haleylot yesh li hamor echad.

On all other nights I only have one jackass.

Halaila hazeh shney hamorim.

On this night, two jackasses!

"So much for the seder! We can now begin to eat! Let's enjoy our meal!"

Soups

Sopa con Huevos y Limon (EGG/LEMON SOUP)

Sopa de Ajo (GARLIC AND YOGURT SOUP)

Sopa de Trahanas (MACEDONIAN BULGUR SOUP)

Sopa de Aves (MEDITERRANEAN-STYLE WHITE BEAN SOUP)

Sopa de Spinaca y Lentijas (SPINACH AND LENTIL SOUP)

Sopa de Albondigas (MEATBALL SOUP)

Sopa con Huevos y Limon

EGG/LEMON SOUP

 This soup is traditionally served as two courses—first the soup, followed by the boiled chicken. It is an old, traditional Sephardic dish that also appears in Greek, Turkish, and Arabic cuisine. The Greek dish, *avgolemono* soup, is similar to *sopa con huevos y limon*. The origin of the dish is unclear. It is a mildly seasoned soup, ideally suited for the meal before the fast on Yom Kippur.

PREPARATION TIME: $1^3/_4$ hours
SERVINGS: **4–6**

One 5-pound chicken
1 medium onion, peeled and left whole
8 cups chicken stock
1 cup chopped celery leaves
1 cup white rice, rinsed
3 large eggs
$^1/_3$ cup plus 1 tablespoon freshly squeezed lemon juice
$^1/_4$ cup finely chopped fresh parsley
$^1/_4$ cup finely snipped fresh chives
Salt and freshly ground black pepper

1. Wash and dry the chicken. Stuff the onion inside the chicken and truss it.
2. Bring the stock to a rapid boil over high heat in a large stockpot. Lower the heat slightly and place the chicken in the pot. Skim off any scum as it rises to the surface of the pot.
3. After 10 minutes, reduce the heat to simmer, add the celery leaves and partially cover the pot. Simmer 1 hour.
4. Remove the chicken from the pot and cover with foil to keep warm. Add the rice to the stock and cook 20 minutes at the same simmer.
5. While the rice is cooking, beat the eggs with a wire whisk in a mixing bowl with the lemon juice. When the rice has finished cooking, pour 1 ladleful of soup stock slowly into the egg/lemon mixture and whisk together.

(continued)

6. Make sure that the soup is cooking at a low simmer. Slowly pour the egg/lemon mixture into the soup. Beat constantly and do not allow the soup to come to a boil or you will ruin the egg/lemon thickener by curdling the eggs.

7. When the soup has been nicely thickened by the egg/lemon mixture, remove from the heat and add the herbs, salt, and pepper. Serve immediately.

SERVING SUGGESTIONS:

Serve the soup as a first course. It is customarily followed by the chicken as an entree. Serve the chicken with *Salsa con Ajo* (page 307) and a side dish of potatoes with fennel or celery braised in tomato sauce (page 195). If you do not wish to serve the chicken as an entree, you can chill it and serve it cold at another meal or use it to make sandwiches, chicken salad, or *Mina de Pollo* (page 84).

Sopa de Ajo

GARLIC AND YOGURT SOUP

 This is a warm, nourishing winter soup from Salonika that is served with focaccia or some other kind of flat herb- or vegetable-topped bread on the side or with *Borekas* (page 61) or *Boyos* (page 66). The Swiss chard lends a savory herbal note to the sharpness of the yogurt and garlic. If Swiss chard is unavailable, kale or collard greens make a good substitute. Potato smooths out the flavor.

PREPARATION TIME: **45 minutes**
SERVINGS: **4–6**

$5^1/_2$ cups Vegetable Stock (page 299)
  2 tablespoons olive oil
  8 very large cloves garlic, peeled and sliced
  2 cups finely shredded Swiss chard
  1 very large or 2 medium red boiling potatoes (about 1 pound), peeled and cut into fine dice
  1 cup plain yogurt
  2 large eggs, beaten until frothy
$1/_4$ cup finely chopped fresh parsley
$1/_4$ cup finely snipped fresh chives
    Salt and freshly ground black pepper

1. Bring the stock and olive oil to a boil in a 4-quart stockpot over medium-high heat. Add the garlic, chard, and diced potato. Reduce the heat to the lowest simmer. Cook 15–18 minutes or until the potatoes are cooked through.
2. Beat the yogurt into the beaten eggs. Spoon 1 ladleful of broth into the yogurt mixture and whisk it in well. Slowly pour the yogurt mixture into the soup. Stir constantly and do not allow the soup to come to a boil or the yogurt will curdle. When heated through, remove the soup from the heat. Stir in the herbs, salt, and pepper. Serve immediately.

SERVING SUGGESTIONS:

This soup, like most Sephardic soups, is meant to be served as an entree after a variety of appetizers. *Borekas* (page 61) filled with cheese (page 63), or *Boyos* (page 66) filled with potato and cheese (page 70), marinated black olives (page 10), and *Salata de Panjar y Carnabeet* (page 43) are all good choices. This one is a vegetarian masterpiece. Enjoy it with plenty of good bread.

Sopa de Trahanas

MACEDONIAN BULGUR SOUP

 This is a hearty, body-and-soul-warming winter soup containing bulgur, cheese, and lots of garlic.

PREPARATION TIME: **35–40 minutes**
SERVINGS: **6**

$1/_4$ cup sunflower oil
  1 medium onion, peeled and chopped
  6 large cloves garlic, peeled and chopped (3 tablespoons)
  4 cups Vegetable Stock (page 299)
One 16-ounce can good quality tomatoes, chopped, with their liquid
  2 cups cooked bulgur
  4 large eggs, beaten
$1/_4$ cup finely chopped fresh parsley
$1/_4$ cup finely snipped fresh chives
   Salt and freshly ground black pepper
$1/_2$ cup freshly grated Pecorino Romano cheese

1. Heat the oil over medium-high heat in a stockpot and sauté the onion until soft and translucent (5–7 minutes). Reduce the heat, add the garlic, and cook 2 minutes longer, stirring constantly.
2. Add the stock and bring to a boil. Reduce the heat to a simmer, add the tomatoes, partially cover the pot, and simmer for 20 minutes.
3. Stir in the cooked bulgur and cook until heated through, about 10 minutes.
4. Remove from the heat and beat in the eggs. Add the herbs, salt, and pepper. Serve immediately, sprinkled with grated cheese.

SERVING SUGGESTIONS:
Sopa de trahanas is a main-dish soup that needs no accompaniment except good crusty bread. Precede the soup with a selection of appetizers

and salads for a delicious meal. *Borekas* (page 61) filled with spinach and cheese (page 64), *Boyos* (page 66) filled with spinach and cheese (page 69), marinated black olives (page 10), and *Ajada de Aves* (page 5) are all good choices.

Sopa de Aves

MEDITERRANEAN-STYLE WHITE BEAN SOUP

 This is a classic dish that is served throughout the Mediterranean countries with many variations. This Sephardic version uses fresh tomato sauce as well as aromatic vegetables like celery and carrots.

SOAKING TIME (BEANS): **8–12 hours**
PREPARATION TIME: **$2^1/_2$ hours**
SERVINGS: **6–8**

$^1/_2$ pound white kidney beans
    Cold water
  4 tablespoons olive oil
  1 large onion, peeled and chopped
  1 large clove garlic, peeled and chopped ($^1/_2$ tablespoon)
  2 stalks celery, thickly sliced
  2 large carrots, thickly sliced
$6^1/_2$ cups Vegetable Stock (page 299)
$1^1/_2$ cups Fresh Tomato Sauce (page 300)
  1 sprig fresh rosemary
  1 bay leaf
  5 sprigs fresh parsley
  1 tablespoon sugar
    Salt and freshly ground black pepper
$^1/_4$ cup finely chopped fresh parsley

1. Soak the beans overnight in cold water to cover by 1 inch. Drain and rinse.
2. Heat the oil in a stockpot over medium-high heat and sauté the onions until soft and translucent (5–7 minutes).
3. Add the garlic, celery, and carrots and sauté 5–7 minutes longer or until the vegetables start to soften. Stir constantly as you sauté.
4. Add the stock and tomato sauce and bring to a boil.
5. With kitchen string, tie together the rosemary, bay leaf, and parsley. Add the beans, herbs, and sugar, reduce the heat to simmer, partially cover the pot, and cook $2^1/_4$ hours.
6. Remove and discard bouquet garni. Add salt and pepper to taste and serve immediately, garnished with chopped parsley.

SERVING SUGGESTIONS:
Sopa de aves is a main-dish winter soup that is served with crusty Mediterranean bread. Precede the soup with an array of appetizers and salads for a delicious and nutritious meal. *Borekas* (page 61) filled with cheese (page 63), *Boyos* (page 66) filled with spinach and cheese (page 69), and *Olivada* (page 12) are all good choices.

Sopa de Spinaca y Lentijas

SPINACH AND LENTIL SOUP

 This spicy but delicate soup is common throughout the eastern Mediterranean with many variations. This particular recipe comes from the Jews of Macedonia.

PREPARATION TIME: **2 hours**
SERVINGS: **6–8**

　4　tablespoons sunflower oil
　1　medium onion, peeled and chopped
　1　large clove garlic, peeled and chopped ($^1/_2$ tablespoon)
$^1/_2$　teaspoon Hungarian hot paprika
　6　cups Vegetable Stock (page 299)
　2　large tomatoes, peeled, seeded, and chopped, or 8 ounces good quality
　　　canned tomatoes, chopped, with their liquid
$^1/_2$　pound brown lentils
　1　pound fresh spinach
　　　Salt and freshly ground black pepper

1. Heat the oil over medium-high heat in a stockpot. Sauté the onion until soft and translucent. (5–7 minutes).
2. Reduce the heat and add the garlic and paprika. Cook 2 minutes longer, stirring constantly and regulating the temperature so that the garlic and paprika don't burn.
3. Add the stock and tomatoes and raise the heat to medium-high. Bring to a boil and add the lentils. Reduce the heat to simmer, partially cover the pot, and cook 1 hour.
4. While the lentils are cooking, wash the spinach but do not dry. Add the spinach to the soup after the lentils have cooked 1 hour. Cook another 15 minutes and remove from the heat. The lentils should be well cooked and the spinach cooked but still nice and green. Season with salt and black pepper and serve immediately.

SERVING SUGGESTIONS:
Sopa de spinaca y lentijas is a main-dish soup that can be accompanied by crusty Mediterranean bread or *Boyos* (page 66) filled with potato and cheese (page 70). Precede it with a selection of appetizers and salads. *Canton de Sardellas* (page 13), marinated green and black olives (page 9), and cubes of feta cheese are good choices.

Sopa de Albondigas

MEATBALL SOUP

 This is a favorite Sephardic winter dish. The sweet flavor of cinnamon and allspice in the meatballs is sharpened by the tart egg/lemon sauce used as a thickener for the soup. Fresh parsley and chives lend an herbal note.

PREPARATION TIME: **2 hours**
SERVINGS: **6–8**

- 1 small onion
- 1 small clove garlic
- 1 pound lean ground beef or lamb
- $1/2$ teaspoon ground cinnamon
- $1/4$ teaspoon ground allspice
- Salt and freshly ground black pepper
- 3 large eggs
- $1/2$ cup bread crumbs
- 8 cups meat stock
- $1/3$ cup long grain white rice, rinsed
- Cold water
- Juice of 1 large lemon
- $1/3$ cup finely chopped fresh parsley
- $1/3$ cup finely snipped fresh chives

1. Place the onion and garlic in a food processor or blender and puree. Put the puree in a mixing bowl together with the meat, cinnamon, allspice, salt, pepper, 1 beaten egg, and bread crumbs. Mix together thoroughly by hand and set aside.

2. In a large pot, bring the stock to a boil. Add the rice and reduce the heat to a gentle boil.

3. Have a bowl of cold water next to you while you work. Wet your hands. Divide the meat mixture into six or eight parts and shape each

into a large meatball. Put these into the simmering liquid and partially cover the pot. Cook $1^1/_2$–$1^3/_4$ hours.

4. During the last 15 minutes of cooking, beat the lemon juice with the remaining eggs. Pour one ladleful of the stock into the egg/lemon mixture.

5. Reduce the heat under the soup to the lowest simmer and slowly add the egg/lemon mixture. Stirring constantly, allow the soup to thicken but do not let it come anywhere near a boil or the eggs will curdle, spoiling the sauce. When the soup is thickened, remove from the heat.

6. To serve, place one meatball per portion into a wide, deep soup bowl. Ladle the soup over this and sprinkle with the herbs. Serve immediately.

SERVING SUGGESTIONS:

Sopa de albondigas is an elegant one-dish entree. Serve with good crusty Mediterranean bread. Start the meal off with Marinated Fried Fish (page 16) followed by a selection of salads. Then serve the soup and complete the meal with assorted fresh fruits, some Sephardic cookies, and mint tea.

The Pomegranate Seed

A SEPHARDIC FOLK TALE

Once a poor young man stole a piece of food. Because of this, he was ordered by the Sultan to be hanged. On his way to the gallows, the man told the guard that he had a wonderful secret that he would like to reveal to the Sultan. If he could not tell his secret to the Sultan, it would die with him. The guard took the young man before the Sultan and told him to reveal his secret.

"Your Excellency," said the young man, "I know how to put a pomegranate seed into the ground and make it grow and bear fruit overnight. My father taught me how to do this and I thought it would be a shame if it died with me."

"All right," said the Sultan. "You have twenty-four hours to prove that you can do this. If you cannot, you will be hanged."

The next morning, the young man was taken out into the Sultan's garden. The Sultan and all his entourage were waiting there. The young man carefully dug a hole, and then he said, "This pomegranate seed can only be planted in the ground by a person who has never taken anything in his life that did not belong to him. Since I stole a piece of food, I am not able to plant it."

The Sultan pointed to one of his viziers. "You plant the seed," he said.

"I cannot, Your Excellency," said the vizier. "When I was a young man, I kept some money that belonged to my father and never gave it back to him."

Then the Sultan turned to his treasurer. "You plant the seed," he commanded.

"Your Excellency, I wish I could. But I have dealt with so many large sums of money that it is possible I might have entered too much or too little in the records. I cannot plant the seed."

Then they all turned to the Sultan and asked, "Why doesn't Your Excellency himself plant the seed?"

The Sultan turned red-faced and grumbled, "I am Sultan over so many lands. Who is to say I rightfully possess all of them?"

The young man looked at all of them, lowered his eyes, and said, "All of you are such great and powerful men. You are wealthy and not in want of anything. And yet none of you can plant this seed. I am just a little person who just stole a small piece of food for myself so I wouldn't starve. And I am going to be hanged right now while all of you are free to go on living."

The Sultan smiled at the young man, pleased with his trick. He gave the young man a pardon, and made him a member of his court. The young man was never hungry again.

Fish

Pescado Sofrito à la Judia (SEPHARDIC-STYLE FRIED FISH)

Pescado Ahilado (BAKED FISH WITH FRESH HERBS)

Pescado Ahilado con Tomate (BAKED FISH FILLETS WITH TOMATO SAUCE)

Pescado Ahilado con Abramela (BAKED FISH IN SOUR PLUM SAUCE)

Pescado Ahilado con Indivia (BAKED FISH WITH BITTER LETTUCES)

Pescado Ahilado con Legumbres or *Capama* (BAKED FISH WITH MEDITERRANEAN VEGETABLES)

Pescado con Tarator (TURKISH-STYLE FISH WITH WALNUT SAUCE)

Keftedes de Pescado (SAUTÉED FISH PATTIES)

    Albondigas de Pescado (POACHED FISH PATTIES)

    Keftedes or *Albondigas de Pescado, Turkish Style*

Pescado Sofrito à la Judia

SEPHARDIC-STYLE FRIED FISH

The word *sofrito* means "lightly fried." The technique has its origins in Andalusia, the ancestral homeland of many of the Jews of Spanish descent. Lightly fried foods, including fresh fish, are still prepared in this part of Spain and are justly famous. Another, more modern application of the word *sofrito* in Spanish cooking is for an aromatic vegetable mixture that is lightly fried in oil and used as a base for stews and braised meats.

Pescado sofrito à la Judia has had a strong impact on many cuisines but especially the British and the Dutch. It was brought to Holland and eventually to England by Spanish and Portuguese Jews and is quite probably the ancestor of British fish and chips. British Jews love *pescado sofrito* so much that they prepare it for Friday night instead of *gefilte* fish. They eat the fish cold, marinated in a spiced vinaigrette. Sephardic Jews also brought the dish to the United States. Thomas Jefferson, a famous gourmet of his time, added it to his personal collection of recipes and called it "Fried Fish in the Manner of the Jews." For an interesting article on Thomas Jefferson and two historical recipes for "Fried Fish, Jewish Fashion" that are presented in his name, see *The Jewish Holiday Kitchen* by Joan Nathan (Schocken Press, 1979), pages 222–23.

Before it is fried in a light batter, the fish is first soaked in salted water. This preliminary bath firms up the flesh of the fish and at the same time helps it retain moisture as it cooks. It also removes every trace of fishy odor and makes the fish taste as if it has just been taken out of the sea.

SOAKING TIME (FISH): **1 hour**
PREPARATION TIME: **25 minutes**
SERVINGS: **4–6**

$2^1/_2$ pounds fish fillets (halibut, cod, scrod, haddock, perch, and arctic char
 take well to this method)
 Coarse salt
 Cold water plus $^1/_3$ cup or more cold water
$^2/_3$ cup unbleached all-purpose flour
 2 large eggs, well beaten
$^1/_4$ teaspoon salt
 Peanut oil for frying

1. Wash and dry the fish fillets. Lay them in a deep, flat baking pan or casserole in one row. Sprinkle with the coarse salt. Pour cold water over the fish to barely cover. Refrigerate 1 hour.

2. Combine the flour, beaten eggs, $^1/_4$ teaspoon salt, and $^1/_3$ cup cold water. Beat well to make a smooth batter. If necessary, add more cold water by the tablespoon to achieve correct consistency. The batter will be smooth and not very thick.

3. Remove the fish from the salt water bath and dry it with paper towels. Heat the oil in a deep sauté pan to a depth of 1 inch, or in a wok to a depth of 2 inches, until just before it begins to smoke.

4. Dip one fish fillet in the batter. Let any excess batter drain back into the bowl. Drop the fish into the oil and fry until golden brown. If necessary, turn the fish over once while it is frying to make sure that it browns on all sides. The batter will puff up slightly. Do not fry too many fillets at one time. The fish must be completely submerged in the sizzling oil in order to fry well. Watch the heat and regulate, if necessary, to prevent burning. Drain fish fillets on paper towels before serving.

SERVING SUGGESTIONS:

Pescado sofrito is traditionally served with one or two sauces like *Caldo de Vinagre* (page 306), *Salsa con Ajo* (page 307), or *Agristada* (page 305). It may be served as well with fresh lemon wedges and salt. Vegetables and salads are served before, with, or after the fish. The following salads are recommended with the following sauces for the fish:

1. If serving fish with *caldo de vinagre,* serve *Salata de Maror* (page 37) or *Salata de Verdura* (page 36).
2. If serving fish with *agristada,* serve *Salata de Naranja y Verdura* (page 39) or a simple cucumber and tomato salad.
3. If serving fish with *salsa con ajo,* serve *Salata Sepharadi* (page 34) or a simple tomato and cucumber salad.

   Conclude the meal with assorted fresh fruit, cookies, and coffee.

Pescado Ahilado

BAKED FISH WITH FRESH HERBS

 This is a beautiful seasonal dish, simple and straightforward in both its ingredients and in its execution. In the spring and early summer, it is made with dill. In the late summer and autumn it is made with fennel. Delicate-textured fish like sole, red snapper, and flounder take especially well to this preparation.

PREPARATION TIME: **35 minutes**
SERVINGS: **4–6**

4–6 fish fillets ($2^1/_2$–3 pounds)
  1 large bunch dill or fennel leaves (about $3^1/_2$ cups tightly packed)
$^3/_4$ cup freshly squeezed lemon juice
  1 cup dry white wine
    Salt and freshly ground black pepper
  4 tablespoons unsalted butter

1. Preheat the oven to 375 degrees.
2. Wash and dry the fish fillets.
3. Lay all but six sprigs of the dill or fennel on the bottom of a 9 × 13-inch baking dish. Place the fish on top of this in one layer. Place one sprig of dill or fennel on top of each fish fillet.

(continued)

4. Combine the lemon juice and wine and pour over the fish. Sprinkle with salt and pepper.
5. Cut the butter into bits and scatter it over the top of the fish. Cover tightly with foil.
6. Bake the fish in the preheated oven for 25 minutes. Uncover and bake 10 to 15 minutes more. Remove from the oven.
7. To serve, place the fish on a serving platter or on individual plates. Pour a little of the sauce over the fish and serve the remaining sauce in a sauceboat.

SERVING SUGGESTIONS:

The fish may be served all by itself with just bread or it may be accompanied by rice pilav. *Pilafi con Piniones* (page 205) is a particularly good choice. Precede the fish with a selection of appetizers and salads. *Impanadas* (page 72) and *Salata de Spinaca* (page 40) or *Salata Sepharadi* (page 34) are all good choices. Conclude the meal with assorted fresh fruits, Sephardic cookies, and mint or lemon verbena tea.

VARIATION:

For a richer sauce, 4 tablespoons unsalted butter can be added. To do this, remove the cooked fish to a platter and strain the sauce from the baking pan into a small saucepan. Bring to a boil over medium heat and whisk in the butter 1 tablespoon at a time. Ladle a little sauce over each portion of fish and serve the rest in a sauceboat.

Pescado Ahilado con Tomate

BAKED FISH FILLETS WITH TOMATO SAUCE

 Special fish dishes are prepared by Jews for Friday night dinner. This tradition goes back many centuries and is rooted in the belief that fish are connected with the coming of the Messiah.

Rabbinic writings on the Book of Genesis state that all of the animals except the creatures of the sea were sinful during the time of Noah and therefore were not annihilated together with people in the Great Flood. Because the fish did not sin, it is believed that when the Messiah comes, a great feast will be held in his honor and fish will be the main course.

Jews also believe that the celebration of the Sabbath is a simulation of and a preparation for the coming of the Messianic Era. After the arrival of the Messiah, the rabbis say that time will be like one long Sabbath and people will be engaged in strictly spiritual pursuits like studying Scripture, singing hymns of praise to the Creator, and sharing in the peaceful and restful activities of Shabbat.

For these reasons, both Ashkenazic and Sephardic Jews traditionally welcome the Sabbath by eating fish on Friday night. Sephardic Jews have several special fish dishes that they serve on Friday night. *Pescado ahilado con tomate* is one of them.

This entree is delicious served hot or cold. The vegetables melt into a savory sauce for the fish. The recipe works particularly well with strong-flavored fish like fresh tuna, mackerel, or halibut. In Mediterranean countries, it is also prepared with salt cod, called *baccala*.

PREPARATION TIME: **45 minutes**
SERVINGS: **4–6 as an entree, 8–10 as an appetizer**

4–6 fresh tuna steaks or mackerel fillets ($2^{1}/_{2}$–3 pounds)
  4 tablespoons olive oil
  1 large onion, peeled and very finely chopped
  2 large cloves garlic, peeled and finely chopped (1 tablespoon)
  2 large green bell peppers, roasted, peeled, cored, seeded, and cut into thin strips (for technique, see page 46)
  6 anchovies packed in oil, drained and chopped
$^{1}/_{2}$ teaspoon Hungarian hot paprika
$^{1}/_{4}$ teaspoon ground allspice
  1 cup Fresh Tomato Sauce (page 300)
$^{1}/_{2}$ cup dry white wine
    Salt and freshly ground black pepper
$^{1}/_{4}$ cup finely chopped fresh parsley

1. Preheat the oven to 375 degrees.
2. Wash and dry the fish and place it in a 9 × 13-inch baking pan. Heat the oil in a skillet over medium-high heat and sauté the onion until soft and translucent (5 to 7 minutes).
3. Reduce the heat and add the garlic. Cook 1 minute more, stirring constantly. Add the peppers, anchovies, spices, tomato sauce, wine, salt, and pepper to the skillet. Stir together well and cook 5 minutes. Pour over the fish.
4. Cover the baking dish tightly and bake 25–30 minutes. Uncover and bake 10 minutes longer. When cooked through, the fish should flake when tested with a fork. The fish may be served immediately or cooled, chilled, and served cold. Before serving, sprinkle with the chopped parsley.

SERVING SUGGESTIONS:
This delicious baked fish should be served all by itself with crusty bread. Sephardic Jews will sometimes serve this fish as a cold appetizer in smaller portions. If serving as an entree, precede with a selection of appetizers and salads. Roasted Pepper Salad (page 46) with Simple Lemon Vinaigrette (page 47), *Borekas* (page 61) filled with spinach and herbs (page 64) or spinach and cheese (page 64), and marinated black olives (page 10) are all good choices. Conclude the meal with assorted fresh fruits, Sephardic cookies, and coffee.

VARIATION:
Pescado ahilado con tomate can also be made with salt cod. Soak $2^1/_2$ pounds salt cod in cold water to cover in the refrigerator for 24 hours. Change the water once during the soaking. Procede with the recipe as directed above.

Pescado Ahilado con Abramela

BAKED FISH IN SOUR PLUM SAUCE

Pescado ahilado con Abramela literally means "fish cooked with Abraham's fruit." In Sephardic folklore it is believed that Abraham sat under a sour plum tree after he was circumcised, so the Sephardim named the sour plum Abraham's fruit.

Male circumcision is the oldest commandment given to the Jewish people. By getting circumcised, Jewish men symbolically enter into a special covenant or relationship with God and become members of the Jewish community. The circumcision ceremony, which takes place on the eighth day after a boy is born, is a formal and joyous celebration for Sephardic Jews. A godmother and godfather are chosen. The godmother's job is to carry the infant through the streets on a special pillow to the synagogue accompanied by a crowd of people singing and dancing and playing guitars or mandolins. In the synagogue, the godfather sits in a special chair, called the *kisay shel Eliyahu* ("Elijah's chair") and receives the baby from the godmother. The entire synagogue is lit up by candles. Either the boy's father or a special ritual circumciser, called a *mohel*, performs the actual circumcision, proclaiming "The Holy One, Blessed be He, said to our father Abraham, 'Walk Before Me and Be Perfect in Form.'" After the ceremony, the child is given a name, usually after a living relative (Ashkenazim name their children after deceased relatives). Unlike Ashkenazim, who usually celebrate a *brit milah* by offering their guests an informal buffet, Sephardim consider the circumcision an occasion for an elaborate feast. Special dishes like stuffed *yaprakes* made out of vine leaves, peppers, tomatoes, eggplants, and zucchini; many kinds of savory pastries; and a large *mesa allegre* ("sweet table") containing sweets like *Travados* (page 268), a marzipan-stuffed, wine-scented pastry, and *nougada*, a confection made out of walnuts and a honey syrup are served by the family of the child after the conclusion of the circumcision ceremony. Lots of wine is served and drunk at a circumcision meal and there is generally also lots of singing and dancing.

The kind of sour plum traditionally used for this dish is not commercially available in the United States. Greengage or Santa Rosa plums make an acceptable substitute. Any fish can be prepared this way. Sea bass is traditional but the recipe is excellent with cod, haddock, scrod, or halibut. The dish can be made dairy or *pareve*. (See page xxix, chapter on *kashrut*)

MARINATING TIME (FISH): **at least 1 hour**
PREPARATION TIME: **$1^1/_4$ hours**
SERVINGS: **4–6 as a main dish, 8–10 as an appetizer or as part of a buffet**

$2^1/_2$–3   pounds fish fillets or steaks
  1   tablespoon freshly grated lemon zest
$^3/_4$ cup freshly squeezed lemon juice
  5   pounds greengage or Santa Rosa plums
  1   tablespoon sugar
      Cold water
  1   cup dry white wine
  5   tablespoons olive oil or unsalted butter
      Salt and freshly ground white pepper
  2   tablespoons chopped fresh parsley
  2   tablespoons chopped fresh chives

1. Wash and dry the fish thoroughly and place it in a 9 × 13-inch flat baking dish. Sprinkle the lemon zest and pour the lemon juice over the fish. Cover the dish and marinate the fish in the refrigerator for at least 1 hour.
2. Place the plums in a saucepan and add the sugar and cold water to barely cover. Bring to a boil and reduce the heat to simmer. Simmer the plums until the fruit is cooked through and starts to disintegrate.
3. Pour the mixture through a sieve into a mixing bowl, pressing down hard on the fruit to remove all the fruit pulp. The skin and pits should remain in the sieve and a saucy puree of plum pulp should be in the bowl.
4. Pour the plum mixture back into the saucepan and add the wine and oil or butter. Bring to a boil and reduce the heat to simmer. Simmer until the mixture forms a sauce, about 20–25 minutes. Stir every once

in a while with a wooden spoon while the mixture cooks down. When the sauce has finished cooking, add the salt and white pepper to taste.

5. Preheat the oven to 350 degrees.

6. Remove the fish from the marinade and place the fillets side by side in another 9 × 13-inch baking dish. Pour the sour plum sauce over the fish and cover the pan with foil. Bake 20 minutes. Remove the foil cover and bake 10 minutes more.

7. The fish may be served immediately or left to cool and served at room temperature. It may also be chilled in the refrigerator and served cold. If serving chilled, use oil rather than butter in the sauce. Before serving, sprinkle the fish with the parsley and chives.

SERVING SUGGESTIONS:

Pescado ahilado con Abramela can be eaten as a main dish, an appetizer, or as part of a buffet. If serving as a main dish, accompany the fish with *Arroz Pilafi* (page 204), *Arroz de Sabato* (page 205), *Pilafi con Piniones* (page 205), or *Pilafi de Trahanas* (page 225). No vegetable accompaniment is necessary. Serve a salad before or after the main course. *Salata de Naranja y Verdura* (page 39) or *Salata de Verdura* (page 36) are both excellent choices. Conclude the meal with assorted fresh fruits, baklava or a Sephardic nut pastry like *Tishpitti* (page 260), and coffee.

Pescado Ahilado con Indivia

BAKED FISH WITH BITTER LETTUCES

 Variations on this dish are found throughout the Jewish Mediterranean. This is a robust dish best made with strong-tasting fish like fresh tuna or mackerel. Bitter lettuces, garlic, and white wine bring out the hearty flavors of the fish while sweet fennel and fresh tomatoes add softening tones.

PREPARATION TIME: 50–55 minutes
SERVINGS: 4–6

- 6 tablespoons olive oil
- 1 large onion, peeled and finely chopped
- 2 large cloves garlic, peeled and chopped (1 tablespoon)
- 4 stalks fennel, chopped, plus a handful of fennel leaves
- 2 tablespoons all-purpose flour
- 1 cup Vegetable Stock (page 299)
- $^1/_2$ cup dry white wine
- 3 large tomatoes, peeled, seeded, and chopped
- 3 cups finely shredded chicory
- 3 cups finely shredded endive lettuce
- 4 large fresh tuna steaks ($2^1/_2$–3 pounds)
- 8 anchovies, packed in olive oil, drained
- $^1/_2$ cup freshly squeezed lemon juice
- Freshly ground black pepper

1. Preheat the oven to 350 degrees. Oil a deep casserole that has a tight-fitting lid.
2. In a deep, wide sauté pan, heat 4 tablespoons oil over medium-high heat. Sauté the onion until soft and translucent (5–7 minutes). Reduce the heat slightly and add the garlic and chopped fennel stalks. Cook 4–5 minutes more or until the fennel stalks start to soften.
3. Sprinkle the vegetables with the flour. Cook 5 minutes longer, stirring constantly and regulating the heat to prevent scorching.
4. Slowly add the vegetable stock and stir constantly to prevent lumping. The mixture will thicken into a thin sauce. Add the white wine and tomatoes and cook another 7–8 minutes or until the tomatoes start to soften. Remove from the heat and set aside.
5. Combine the two lettuces and put half into the prepared casserole.
6. Place the tuna steaks on top of the lettuce. Lay two anchovies across each tuna steak. Place the fennel leaves over this. Ladle the sauce over the tuna, sprinkle with the lemon juice, and season all over with pep-

per. Top with the remaining lettuce, a few grinds of pepper, and the remaining 2 tablespoons oil.

7. Cover the casserole with foil and then with its cover. Braise in the oven 40–45 minutes. Remove from the oven and serve immediately.

SERVING SUGGESTIONS:

This is a filling entree and is accompanied only by crusty Mediterranean bread. Precede the entree with appetizers and salads like Roasted Eggplant Salad, Arabic Style (page 51), Cucumber Salad with Kasseri Cheese (page 32), marinated black olives (page 10), and sliced fresh tomatoes. Conclude the meal with assorted fresh fruit, Sephardic cookies or baklava, and coffee.

Pescado Ahilado con Legumbres or *Capama*

BAKED FISH WITH MEDITERRANEAN VEGETABLES

Many Mediterranean dishes feature fish baked with a variety of fresh vegetables. This version combines vegetables brought to Europe from America by the Spanish. The recipe caught on with Sephardic Jews long after the exile, when the New World products were marketed in the eastern Mediterranean. Jews in the Balkans made a similar dish without potatoes and substituted marjoram for the oregano.

PREPARATION TIME: 50–55 minutes
SERVINGS: 4–6

6 tablespoons olive oil
1 large onion, peeled and chopped
1 large clove garlic, peeled and chopped ($^1/_2$ tablespoon)
6 large fresh tomatoes, peeled, seeded, and chopped
1 teaspoon dried oregano
$^1/_2$ teaspoon dried thyme
1 teaspoon dried chervil
1 large green bell pepper, roasted, peeled, seeded, and cut into thin strips (for technique, see page 46)
1 teaspoon sugar
1 teaspoon salt
$^1/_4$ cup freshly squeezed lemon juice
2 large white baking potatoes ($1^1/_2$ pounds)
2 pounds cod or haddock, in 1 piece
Freshly ground black pepper

1. Heat 4 tablespoons olive oil in a sauté pan over medium-high heat and sauté the onion until soft and translucent (5–7 minutes). Reduce the heat to low and add the garlic and tomatoes. Partially cover the pot and cook 15 minutes or until the tomatoes begin to disintegrate.

2. Add the herbs and roasted pepper strips and cook 5 minutes longer. Remove from the heat and stir in the sugar, salt, and lemon juice. Set aside.

3. While the vegetable mixture is cooking, peel the potatoes and slice thinly.

4. Preheat the oven to 375 degrees.

5. Layer half the potatoes on the bottom of a 9 × 13-inch baking dish. Pour half the vegetables over the potatoes. Sprinkle pepper over this. Lay the fish on top of the vegetables and cover with the remaining vegetable mixture. Top with a few grinds of black pepper and the remaining potato slices. Sprinkle the remaining 2 tablespoons oil over the potatoes and sprinkle with more salt and pepper.

6. Place in the oven and bake 30–35 minutes or until the top is nicely browned. Cut into squares and serve immediately.

Pescado ahilado con legumbres needs no accompaniment other than good crusty bread. Precede the fish with a selection of appetizers and salads. *Toureto* (page 31), *Salata de Spinaca* (page 40), marinated green and black olives (page 9), and sliced fresh tomatoes are all good choices. Conclude the meal with an assortment of fresh fruit, Sephardic cookies, and mint or lemon verbena tea.

Pescado con Tarator

TURKISH-STYLE FISH WITH WALNUT SAUCE

This rich, complex dish is served at the Passover *seder* by the Sephardim of Turkey and Salonika, Greece. It is traditional among Sephardic Jews to eat foods composed of the same or similar ingredients as the ritual foods of the Passover *seder*. In this dish, the walnut paste resembles the *haroset* on the *seder* plate. Carp is usually the fish of choice. It is full-flavored and has a medium-heavy texture that will not be overwhelmed by the walnut sauce. If you are unable to get boned carp fillets, bluefish or halibut is a good second choice.

PREPARATION TIME: 25–30 minutes
SERVINGS: 8–10 as an appetizer, less as an entree

4 large fish fillets or steaks (boned carp, bluefish, halibut; about $1/2$–$2/3$ pound each)
2 large eggs, beaten
$1^1/_4$–$1^1/_2$ cups *matzoh* meal
Sunflower oil for frying
Salt and freshly ground black pepper
1 cup walnuts
$1/_2$ cup red wine vinegar
$1/_2$ cup cold water
$1/_4$ cup fresh mint leaves
Mint sprigs for garnish

1. Cut each fillet or steak in half or into quarters or fifths for appetizer-size pieces, one piece per diner. If using halibut steaks, remove the bone.
2. With the beaten eggs in a bowl and the *matzoh* meal on a plate, heat $1/2$ inch oil in a sauté pan over medium-high heat until just before it smokes.
3. Dip one piece of fish into the egg, let the excess drip off, and then gently roll it in the *matzoh* meal. Fry until golden brown and crisp on both sides. Drain on paper towels. Repeat this until all the fish is fried.
4. Place the drained fish on a platter and cover.
5. Put the remaining ingredients in a food processor or a blender and puree until smooth. This is the *tarator* sauce.
6. When ready to serve, just spoon some of the *tarator* sauce over the fish. Garnish with mint sprigs and serve.

SERVING SUGGESTIONS:

This fish is traditionally served as an appetizer. If serving as an entree, accompany with a green salad like *Salata de Verdura* (page 36) or *Salata de Naranja y Verdura* (page 39). Sautéed fresh spinach with garlic or sauteed green beans are also good as a side dish with this.

Keftedes de Pescado

SAUTÉED FISH PATTIES

 Sautéed fish patties are common to many different cuisines. This recipe is served as a Friday night appetizer with *agristada* or as a weekday entree with fresh lemon wedges. The herb seasoning comes from the culinary tradition of the Greek Romaniot Jews, who have resided in Greece since Roman times.

PREPARATION TIME: **40 minutes**
SERVINGS: **4–6 as an entree, 8–10 as an appetizer (makes 8–10 patties)**

$1^1/_2$ pounds cod or haddock
   2 scallions, finely chopped
$^1/_4$ cup chopped fresh parsley
   1 teaspoon dried oregano
$^1/_2$ teaspoon dried thyme
   2 thick slices French or sourdough bread, soaked in cold water and squeezed dry
   2 large eggs, beaten
$^1/_2$ cup bread crumbs
      Salt and freshly ground black pepper
      Sunflower or peanut oil for frying
      Lemon wedges for garnish or *Agristada* (page 305)

1. Place the fish in a food processor or meat grinder and coarsely grind. If using a food processor, pulse/chop the fish to achieve a coarse texture similar to that of coarsely ground hamburger meat. Put the fish into a mixing bowl.
2. Combine everything except the oil and the lemon wedges or *agristada* and form the mixture into 2-inch oblong or round patties. You will use a scant $^1/_2$ cup of the fish mixture for each patty.
3. In a deep, wide sauté pan, heat $^1/_2$ inch oil until just before it starts to smoke. Fry the patties until golden brown on both sides. Drain on paper towels and serve immediately, garnished with lemon wedges or with a sauceboat of *agristada* on the side.

SERVING SUGGESTIONS:

Keftedes de pescado and its variations (see below) can all be eaten as an appetizer or a main course. *Keftedes de pescado* should be accompanied by salads like *Salata Sepharadi* (page 34) if eaten as an entree. *Albondigas de pescado* should be accompanied only by crusty Mediterranean bread. An assortment of salads can precede the *albondigas*. *Salata de Spinaca* (page 40), *Borekas* (page 61) or *Buleymas* (page 71) with *Chandrajo* filling (page 65), Roasted Pepper Salad (page 46) with Paprika Vinaigrette (page 47), and marinated black and green olives (page 9) are all good choices.

VARIATIONS:

Albondigas de Pescado (Poached Fish Patties)

For an interesting variation on fried fish patties, shape the fish mixture into balls and poach them in Vegetable Stock (page 299). Serve the *albondigas* with *Agristada* (page 305).

Keftedes or *Albondigas de Pescado, Turkish Style*

Turkish Jews used parsley, dill, and chives rather than oregano and thyme to season the *keftedes* or *albondigas*. Substitute $1/_4$ cup chopped fresh dill and $1/_4$ cup snipped fresh chives for the oregano and thyme and follow the recipe given above.

Yuha and the Keftedes

A SEPHARDIC FOLK TALE

Yuha is a famous character in both Jewish and Muslim folklore. He is the proverbial fool who always manages to get himself into trouble. In this story, Yuha tackles the problem of *keftedes*.

Yuha and his mother went to a wedding where they served *keftedes* with rice pilav. Yuha gobbled up all the rice with his hands and then he ate the *keftedes* in one mouthful. "Yuha," said his mother, "you should be ashamed of yourself. Look at your manners! When you eat round things, you have to cut them into four pieces!"

A few days later at home, Yuha's mother served him some lentils. Yuha started to cut each lentil into four pieces. "What kind of stupid thing are you doing, Yuha?" said his mother.

"But, Mama," protested Yuha. "You told me that when you eat round things, you are supposed to cut them into four pieces!"

Poultry

Pollo al Forno (SEPHARDIC-STYLE ROAST CHICKEN)

Tunisian-Style Roast Chicken with P'kaila and Saffron

Braised Chicken with Tomatoes and Honey

Pollo con Berenjenna (BRAISED CHICKEN WITH EGGPLANT)

Pollo con Olivos y Limon (BRAISED CHICKEN WITH OLIVES AND PRESERVED LEMON)

Pollo con Apio (BRAISED CHICKEN WITH CELERY ROOT)

Arroz con Pollo (SAVORY CHICKEN WITH SAFFRON RICE)

   Arroz con Pollo, Southern Style

   Arroz con Pollo, Caribbean Version

Pollo Relleno con Trahanas (ROAST STUFFED CHICKEN, SEPHARDIC STYLE)

Pollo al Forno

SEPHARDIC-STYLE ROAST CHICKEN

Sephardic-style roast chicken is traditionally made in a clay pot. If you do not have a clay pot, this roast can be made in a tightly covered casserole but some of the special qualities that clay-pot cooking imparts to food are lost in a regular casserole.

Clay pots need to be soaked in hot water before they are put into the oven so that they do not crack and break during cooking. The moisture absorbed by the pot provides a rush of steam that is a primary element in cooking the meat. Despite the fact that steam is being used, meat roasted in a clay pot acquires a roasted rather than steamed texture. Steam coming out of the clay pot makes the meat exceedingly moist and tender but does not detract from the crispness desired in a roast. If nothing else containing moisture is added to the clay pot, the meat cooks in its own juices, receiving just enough moisture from the steam to give it a slightly crisp exterior. It is not as crisp as a regular roast but it contains a crispness that braised, and certainly steamed, meat generally lacks. To give clay-pot-roasted meat a crisper texture, it can be cooked uncovered at the end of the cooking cycle for 10 to 15 minutes.

Clay-pot roasting is easy since the meat does not have to be watched and basted. Because of the steam, the meat does not burn and because the pot is covered during most, if not all, of the cooking, there is no splattering of juices onto the walls of the oven.

Braised meats are also delicious cooked in a clay pot. This technique eliminates the need for browning the meat because it browns naturally in the covered clay pot. This, in turn, reduces the fat content of the dish. Besides reducing the fat, clay-pot cooking also reduces the amount of liquid needed for a braise. The steam from the presoaked pot provides most of the liquid required to cook the dish.

Clay pots need a fairly hot oven to cook in, at least at the beginning of cooking. The general rule of thumb is to increase the temperature by about 100 degrees. The meat also takes a little longer to cook than by regular roasting or braising. About 25–30 minutes of additional cooking time is necessary. Poultry is an exception to this rule. Poultry will often take less rather than more time to cook in a clay pot.

Clay is a fragile material. It is essential to begin clay-pot cooking in a cold oven. The utensil and the oven heat up gradually and at the same time. A rapid change in temperature might cause the pot to crack or break. For the same reason, it is a good idea to place a clay pot on a wooden board or a straw or fabric mat when removing it from the oven. A cold surface can also cause cracks or breaks in the pot.

To clean a clay pot, do not put it into the dishwasher. Use a plastic brush or scouring pad rather than a metal one. A paste made of baking soda and water does the best job of cleaning but a little gentle dishwashing liquid is also satisfactory. Allow the pot to dry in the open air before putting it away.

In this recipe, the chicken is moistened only by a small amount of lemon juice. The lemon gives a delicate taste to the finished dish and marries well with the garlic and the thyme. You may substitute 2 teaspoons dried thyme for the fresh if you cannot get fresh.

PREPARATION TIME: **2 hours**
SERVINGS: **4–6**

  1 whole 5-pound chicken
     Salt and freshly ground black pepper
  1 medium lemon
  6 sprigs fresh thyme or lemon thyme
  6 large cloves garlic, peeled and left whole
  3 tablespoons olive oil
 $2/3$ cup freshly squeezed lemon juice
     Fresh thyme sprigs for garnish

1. Presoak the top and bottom of the clay pot in hot water for 15 minutes. Remove from the water but do not dry. If not using a clay pot, skip this step.
2. Wash and dry the chicken and set aside the giblets for another purpose, such as making stock. Sprinkle the cavity of the chicken with

salt and pepper. Using a toothpick, poke holes in the lemon and gently squeeze it. This will soften it and help release the juices during cooking. Place the lemon in the cavity of the chicken.

3. Place two sprigs of thyme and one clove garlic in the cavity of the chicken. Truss it with kitchen string to help it keep its shape during cooking.

4. Salt and pepper the outside of the trussed chicken on all sides. Lay it in the clay pot. If using a casserole, put a rack in the bottom and lay the chicken on the rack.

5. Surround the chicken with the remaining thyme sprigs and garlic. Mix the olive oil and lemon juice and pour over the chicken.

6. If using a clay pot, cover it and put it into a cold oven. Turn the heat to 450 degrees and cook 15 minutes. Then turn the temperature of the oven down to 350 degrees. Roast for $1^1/_2$ hours. If using a casserole, preheat the oven to 450 degrees and put the chicken into the oven uncovered. Roast for 20 minutes. Reduce the heat to 350 degrees and cover the dish. Roast an additional 65 minutes. Uncover the pot and roast 20 minutes more.

7. Remove the chicken from the oven. If using a clay pot, you will be greeted with a heavenly aroma when you open it. The chicken will be golden brown all over but very moist and the pot will be full of a wonderful herb-scented sauce. As with any roast poultry, check for doneness by inserting a skewer or a toothpick into the thigh. If the juices run yellow, the roast is done. If you would like a crisper roast, put the pot back in the oven uncovered for 10–15 minutes. If roasting with a casserole, there will also be a great aroma and a nice sauce but the meat will not be as crisp and the texture of the meat will not be as soft and moist as with a clay pot. Either way the roast is delicious. Carve it into portions and decorate it with thyme sprigs before serving.

SERVING SUGGESTIONS:

This is a simple straightforward dish that goes well with rice or bulgur pilav. Any sautéed green vegetable can accompany the entree. Precede the main course with a selection of appetizers and salads. *Yaprakes de Oja* (page 19), *Humus* (page 7), *Anjinara* (page 28), Roasted Pepper Salad (page 46) with Bulgarian-Style Walnut Vinaigrette (page 48), and marinated olives (page 9) are good choices. Another interesting menu would be to start with a *Salata de Atun y Sardellas* (page 15) and serve the chicken with *Arroz de Sabato* (page 205) and a sautéed green vegetable like spinach. Conclude your meal with fresh fruit, Sephardic cookies, and mint or lemon verbena tea.

Tunisian-Style Roast Chicken with P'kaila and Saffron

 P'kaila is a North African herb and garlic condiment that has a heady aroma and a pungent flavor. When used in conjunction with saffron and hot paprika, it makes a rich, exotic dish. This dish, like *Pollo al Forno* (page 125), is traditionally prepared in a clay pot.

Clay-pot cooking is one of the most ancient and still one of the best methods of preparing food. It is considered to replicate the process of cooking something in a clay or brick oven. Clay-pot cookery is prevalent in Mediterranean cuisine, Jewish or non-Jewish, particularly in the North African countries, because the local soil is suitable to making ceramics. Clay has always been a cheap and plentiful material in this part of the world. Moroccan, Algerian, and Tunisian cooks make braised meat and fish dishes in a special clay pot called a *tajin*. A *tajin slaoui* is a *tajin* with a conical lid. Some are shallow and others are deep.

A clay pot has long been considered the ideal vessel for roasting or braising poultry because of the special qualities the technique imparts (see the recipe for *Pollo al Forno*).

PREPARATION TIME: $1^3/_4$ hours
SERVINGS: 8

3 tablespoons olive oil
1 large onion, peeled and finely chopped
$^1/_2$ teaspoon Hungarian hot paprika
$^1/_3$ or $^3/_4$ cup chicken stock
$^1/_4$ teaspoon saffron threads dissolved in $^1/_4$ cup Chicken Stock
1 cup *P'kaila* (page 302)
2 tablespoons freshly squeezed lemon juice
8 chicken quarters or 4 skinless, boneless chicken breasts, halved (about 2 pounds)

1. If using a clay pot, soak the pot in hot water for 15 minutes. Remove from the water but do not dry. While the pot is soaking, heat the oil in a skillet over medium-high heat. If using an ovenproof casserole, heat the oil in the casserole. Sauté the onion until soft and translucent (5–7 minutes).

2. Add the paprika to the onion, reduce the heat to low, and cook 5 minutes longer, stirring constantly.

3. Add $^1/_3$ cup stock to the skillet or $^3/_4$ cup stock to the casserole and scrape the bottom of the pan or pot with a wooden spoon to deglaze it.

4. If using a casserole, add the saffron mixture, *p'kaila,* and lemon juice to the pot at this point.

5. If using a clay pot, pour the contents of the skillet into the clay pot. Stir the saffron mixture, *p'kaila,* and lemon juice into the rest of the sauce ingredients. Lay the chicken pieces in the sauce. Cover the pot tightly.

6. Put the covered pot into a cold oven. Heat the oven to 450 degrees and cook 15 minutes for chicken quarters and 7 minutes for skinless, boneless chicken breasts. Then reduce the heat to 350 degrees and cook 1 hour longer. If using a casserole, preheat the oven to 375 degrees, cook for 10 minutes, and reduce the heat to 350 degrees. Cook chicken quarters an additional hour and cook skinless, boneless chicken breasts 40–45 minutes. Check for doneness by inserting a skewer or toothpick into a chicken thigh. If the juice runs yellow, it is

done. The same test can be done on skinless, boneless chicken breasts. Remove from the oven and serve immediately.

SERVING SUGGESTIONS:

This chicken dish is traditionally served with Couscous (page 216). Precede the main course with one of the Roasted Pepper Salads (page 46), meat-filled *Borekas* (page 63) or *Buleymas* (page 71), Hot and Savory Carrot Salad (page 45), black and green olives, and *Humus* (page 7). Conclude the meal with assorted fresh fruits, Sephardic sweets or baklava, and coffee or mint tea.

Braised Chicken with Tomatoes and Honey

 This dish is a specialty of the Moroccan Jews. The sweetness of the honey and the cinnamon strengthens the heady aroma of the saffron, which colors the sauce bright orange rather than red like the tomatoes. I use skinless, boneless chicken breasts, which is nontraditional, rather than a whole chicken in this recipe.

PREPARATION TIME: 1¹/₄ hours
SERVINGS: 8

- 4 tablespoons olive oil
- 4 skinless, boneless chicken breasts, halved (about 2 pounds)
- 1 large onion, peeled and finely chopped
- ¹/₂ cup chicken stock
- 10 large, meaty tomatoes, peeled and seeded, or two 24-ounce cans good quality tomatoes
- ¹/₄ teaspoon saffron threads dissolved in ¹/₄ cup boiling chicken stock
- ¹/₃ cup thick honey (preferably citrus flower honey)

2 sticks cinnamon
One 1-inch piece fresh gingerroot, peeled
$^1/_2$ cup toasted slivered almonds

1. Heat the oil over medium-high heat in a deep, wide sauté pan that has a tight-fitting lid. Brown the chicken breasts on both sides and set aside.

2. Sauté the onion in the same oil until soft and translucent (5–7 minutes). Reduce the heat and deglaze with the chicken stock, scraping up browned bits with a wooden spoon.

3. Add the tomatoes and cook until they begin to soften, stirring every once in a while. Add the saffron and honey. Stir well to dissolve. Add the cinnamon sticks and gingerroot.

4. Return the chicken breasts to the pot, making sure they are covered with sauce. Turn the heat down to simmer and cover the pan with foil. Then cover it with its lid. Cook 50 minutes. Test for doneness by inserting a skewer or toothpick into the meat. If the juice runs yellow, the meat is done.

5. While the chicken is cooking, toast the almonds by cooking them in a dry cast-iron skillet over medium heat or on a cookie sheet in a preheated oven at 350 degrees until nicely browned.

6. Remove the cinnamon sticks and gingerroot. The tomatoes will have dissolved into a nice sauce. Pass the sauce through a sieve to smooth it out before serving. If you used canned tomatoes, this has the added advantage of removing the seeds. Serve one piece breast per person, covered with some of the sauce and sprinkled with toasted almonds.

SERVING SUGGESTIONS:
Serve this dish with Couscous (page 215) or saffron rice pilav (page 205). Precede it with a selection of Moroccan salads and appetizers. Sweet Carrot Salad (page 44), Roasted Eggplant Salad, Arabic Style (page 51), Roasted Pepper Salad (page 46) with Simple Lemon Vinaigrette (page 47), and *Buleymas* (page 71) filled with spinach (page 64) are good

choices. Conclude the meal with assorted fresh fruit or Marzipan-Stuffed Dried Fruits (page 251), baklava or Sephardic cookies, and mint tea.

Pollo con Berenjenna

BRAISED CHICKEN WITH EGGPLANT

When I was a student in Jerusalem, I rented a room in an apartment owned by a family. The apartment building was a small one and had only eight units. During my two years in Israel, I got to know all eight families who lived in the building. One of them, the Ben David family, was from Turkey. Miri ben David was a fabulous cook who shared many of her family recipes and stories with me.

One Friday night when I was invited to dinner there, she served a dish of chicken cooked with eggplant in an intriguing tomato-based sauce. When I asked her what was in the sauce, she counted off the ingredients—eggplant, tomato, onion, a little garlic, cinnamon, and "some leaves from that plant that grows in front of the apartment building. The Ashkenazi next door wanted to burn it because she thought it was ugly. But I screamed and made a big fuss and I argued with them so much that they let me keep it. They call it 'Havatzelet ben David' [which means Ben David's rose, a play on the term 'Rose of Sharon' mentioned in the Song of Songs. The word *havatzelet* actually means 'lily']."

Ben David's rose turned out to be a rosemary plant. It was a beautiful specimen, full grown to a height of $4\frac{1}{2}$ feet and almost as wide as it was tall. The rosemary thrived on the warm Mediterranean sunlight and the cool, dry Jerusalem nights. The Ashkenazi neighbor next door loved to gossip to me about Miri ben David, saying that her cooking smelled bad because she put pieces of "that ugly weed" in her *cholent*. I don't believe I ever saw any of the Ashkenazim cook anything with this "weed." My landlady would not allow me to cook anything with it in her kitchen either, so I had to wait until I left Israel to try making anything with rosemary in it.

One of the criteria for being a good Sephardic homemaker is knowing how to cook eggplant. There are over one hundred different ways Sephardic Jews prepare this vegetable. In this recipe for *pollo con berenjenna*, my own variation on Miri ben David's recipe, herbs and spices combine to give the sauce a variety of taste and aroma sensations, including pungency from the rosemary and sweetness from the cinnamon.

SALTING TIME (EGGPLANT): **1 hour**
PREPARATION TIME: **$1^1/_2$ hours**
SERVINGS: **4–6**

  1 large eggplant (about $1^1/_2$ pounds)
     Coarse salt
  7 tablespoons olive oil plus 2 tablespoons more if needed
One $4^1/_2$–5-pound chicken, cut into eighths, or 4 skinless, boneless chicken
     breasts, halved (about 2 pounds)
  3 medium yellow or white onions, peeled and finely chopped
  1 large clove garlic, peeled and finely chopped ($^1/_2$ tablespoon)
  2 heaping teaspoons Hungarian sweet paprika
$^1/_2$ teaspoon Hungarian hot paprika
  1 cup chicken stock
$1^1/_2$ cups tomato puree (homemade or good quality canned)
  1 stick cinnamon
  1 bay leaf
  3 sprigs fresh rosemary
     Salt and freshly ground black pepper

1. Cut the eggplant, unpeeled, into 2-inch pieces. Layer the pieces in a colander, sprinkling each layer with coarse salt. Cover the top with plastic wrap and place several plates and cans of food on top of the eggplant in order to weight it down. Set aside for 1 hour. The salting and weighting draws out the eggplant's bitter juices. After 1 hour,

uncover the eggplant, rinse it, and gently squeeze the juices out. Dry the pieces on paper towels.

2. In a large, heavy sauté pan (enameled cast-iron works well), heat 4 tablespoons olive oil over medium heat. Brown the chicken pieces, remove, and set aside. The skinless, boneless chicken breasts are non-traditional but make a less fatty dish.

3. Add 3 tablespoons additional oil and sauté the eggplant pieces over fairly high heat. If the heat is high enough, the eggplant will cook well and quickly in less oil. If the eggplant starts to stick and burn during cooking, add a little more oil, but try to be sparing with it. When the eggplant is browned, remove it from the pan and set aside on paper towels.

4. If necessary, add 2 more tablespoons oil to the pan. Reduce the heat to medium and sauté the onions until soft and translucent (5–7 minutes), stirring constantly with a wooden spoon.

5. Stir in the garlic. After 1 minute, add the two paprikas and reduce heat again to low. Cook, stirring constantly, until paprika is mixed completely into the onion and garlic. Add 2 tablespoons chicken stock and stir in well. The liquid prevents the paprika from burning as it cooks. Cook, stirring constantly, for 5 minutes. If the liquid gets absorbed too quickly, continue to add stock by the tablespoonful. The preliminary cooking of the paprika brings its flavor out fully and is a necessary procedure when working with this spice.

6. When the paprika has finished cooking, slowly stir in the rest of the stock and deglaze the pan, scraping up any browned bits from the pan with the wooden spoon.

7. Stir in the tomato puree. Add the cinnamon stick, bay leaf, and rosemary. Return the eggplant and chicken to the pan together with any juices that have accumulated on the dish when they were set aside. Cover the pan tightly and simmer gently over very low heat for 45 minutes to 1 hour. If necessary, cover the pan with foil before covering it with its lid in order to tighten the seal. When the chicken is ready, remove and discard the cinnamon stick, bay leaf, and rosemary sprigs; season with salt and pepper; and serve immediately.

Pollo con berenjenna is traditionally served with *Arroz Pilafi* (page 204) or saffron rice pilav (page 205) but it may also be served on its own, accompanied by good country bread to soak up the rich sauce. Precede this dish with a selection of appetizers and salads, none containing either eggplant or tomatoes. *Ajada* (page 3), *Borekas* (page 61) or *Buleymas* (page 71) filled with meat (page 63) or spinach (page 64), and one of the Roasted Pepper Salads (page 46) are all good choices. Conclude the meal with assorted fresh fruits, Sephardic cookies, and coffee.

Pollo con Olivos y Limon

BRAISED CHICKEN WITH OLIVES AND PRESERVED LEMON

 This tangy, richly seasoned braised chicken is prepared with many variations throughout Morocco. The Sephardic Jews prefer a lighter touch with the spices than others. It is traditionally prepared in the Moroccan clay pot called a *tajin* but may also be cooked in a regular unglazed clay pot or in a casserole with a tight-fitting lid.

PREPARATION TIME: **1³/₄ hours**
SERVINGS: **4–6**

  3 cups boiling water
¹/₂ pound salty black olives, pitted (¹/₂ pound weight before pitting)
  2 tablespoons olive oil
  1 medium onion, peeled and finely chopped
  1 teaspoon Hungarian hot paprika
  1 teaspoon ground ginger
¹/₂ cup chicken stock
One 4¹/₂–5-pound chicken, cut in eighths
  6 large cloves garlic, peeled
  1 Salt-Preserved Lemon (page 288), cut into small pieces

1. If using a clay pot, soak it in hot water to cover for 15 minutes. Remove from the water but do not dry. If using a casserole, skip this step.

2. Pour the boiling water over the olives. Soak for 1 minute and drain. This removes excess salt from the olives.

3. If using a casserole, heat the oil in the casserole over medium-high heat and sauté the onion until soft and translucent (5–7 minutes). If using a clay pot, do this in a skillet.

4. Reduce the heat and add the paprika and ginger. Cook another 2 minutes, stirring constantly. Deglaze with chicken stock, scraping up any browned bits that cling to the pan. Remove from the heat.

5. If using a clay pot, place the chicken in the pot. Surround with the olives, garlic cloves, and the pieces of preserved lemon. Pour the onion mixture over the chicken. Cover the pot and place it in a cold oven. Turn the heat in the oven to 450 degrees and bake for 15 minutes. Then turn it down to 350 degrees and cook for $1\frac{1}{4}$ hours.

6. If using a casserole, preheat the oven to 375 degrees. Put everything in the casserole in which you cooked the onion mixture. Cover the casserole with foil and then with its cover. Cook at 375 degrees for 15 minutes then turn down the heat to 350 degrees. Cook an additional $1\frac{1}{4}$ hours. Serve immediately.

SERVING SUGGESTIONS:

This casserole is traditionally served with *Couscous* (page 215) or *Pilafi de Trahanas* (page 225). Precede it with a selection of salads and appetizers. Roasted Eggplant Salad, Arabic Style (page 51), *Ajada de Aves* (page 5) *Buleymas* (page 71) filled with meat (page 63) or spinach (page 64), and sliced cucumbers and tomatoes are all good choices. Finish the meal with assorted fresh fruits, baklava, and coffee or mint tea.

Pollo con Apio

BRAISED CHICKEN WITH CELERY ROOT

 Celery root, also called celeriac, is a favorite Sephardic winter vegetable. Celery root has an earthy taste and a faintly herbal aroma, which is heightened by the traditional *Agristada* (page 305), the egg/lemon sauce.

PREPARATION TIME: $1^1/_2$ hours
SERVINGS: **4–6**

4–6 tablespoons olive oil
One $4^1/_2$–5-pound chicken, cut in eighths
10 shallots, peeled and finely chopped
1 large clove garlic, peeled and chopped (1 tablespoon)
1 cup chicken stock
4 celery roots (about $2^1/_2$ pounds), peeled and cut into $^1/_2$-inch cubes
$^3/_4$ cup freshly squeezed lemon juice
2 large eggs, beaten
   Salt and freshly ground black pepper
$^1/_4$ cup finely chopped fresh parsley
$^1/_4$ cup finely snipped fresh chives

1. In a large sauté pan, heat 4 tablespoons oil over medium-high heat and brown the pieces of chicken. When browned on all sides, set the chicken aside on a platter.
2. If necessary, add more oil to the sauté pan and sauté the shallots until soft and translucent. Reduce the heat to medium and add the garlic. Cook 1 minute longer.
3. Add the stock and deglaze the pot, scraping up the browned bits with a wooden spoon.
4. Add the celeriac and half the lemon juice and bring to a boil. Return the chicken to the sauté pan, cover with foil, and then with the cover of the pan. Reduce the heat to a simmer and cook for 1 hour.
5. While the chicken is cooking, beat the eggs and remaining lemon juice together. When chicken is done cooking, uncover the pot. Test for

doneness by inserting a skewer or toothpick into a thigh or drumstick. If the juice runs yellow it is done. Ladle a little of the cooking liquid into the egg-lemon mixture, beating while you do so. Reduce the heat to the lowest simmer and slowly add the egg-lemon mixture to the pot, stirring well. Do not let the pot come anywhere near a boil or the eggs will curdle, ruining the sauce. Stir well until the sauce thickens, then remove from the heat.

6. Stir in the salt, pepper, and herbs and serve immediately. The sauce will thicken as it cools but the dish will still remain liquid like a stew. Serve in wide, deep soup bowls.

SERVING SUGGESTIONS:

This dish is traditionally served all by itself with crusty Mediterranean bread to go with the sauce. It may also be served like a gumbo, with a mound of boiled rice put into the stew, for an interesting nontraditional effect. Either way it is delicious. Precede the stew with a selection of appetizers and salads. *Salata de Panjar y Carnabeet* (page 43), Hot and Savory Carrot Salad (page 45), and *Borekas* (page 61) or *Buleymas* (page 71) with meat filling (page 63) are good choices. Finish the meal with assorted fresh fruits, a *Torta de los Reyes* (page 259), and coffee.

Arroz con Pollo

SAVORY CHICKEN WITH SAFFRON RICE

Arroz con pollo is an elegant and very old Jewish variation of Spanish *paella*. The main difference between the two dishes is that the Jewish dish leaves out the shellfish. Also *arroz con pollo* is baked in the oven rather than cooked in a *paella* pan on top of the stove. The only Sephardic Jews to preserve *arroz con pollo* in their culinary repertoire are those who settled in the countries of the West Indies (Curaçao, Barbados, Jamaica, and Cuba) and those who made their homes in the Southern United States, where Spanish influences were important in the cooking. Very few Jews live in the Caribbean Islands today, but there are historical landmarks like cemeteries and synagogues that record their presence in history.

Saffron provides the yellow color and distinctive heady aroma in both the Southern-style and the Caribbean-style *arroz con pollo*. The Southern style is closer to the Spanish original, where white rice and stock provide a subtle but flavorful backdrop to the saffron, which draws out the natural taste of the chicken and the vegetables. In the Caribbean version, lime juice adds a tart coolness and a dash of Tabasco or some other hot red pepper sauce gives the dish sharpness and bite.

Arroz con Pollo, Southern Style

PREPARATION TIME: $1^3/_4$ hours
SERVINGS: 4–6

4–6 tablespoons olive oil
One $4^1/_2$–5-pound chicken, cut in eighths
  1 large onion, peeled and finely chopped
  2 large cloves garlic, peeled and chopped (1 tablespoon)
  1 leek, white part only, carefully washed and thinly sliced
  2 cups long grain white rice, rinsed
  1 cup dry white wine
$1^1/_2$ cups chicken stock
  1 bay leaf
$^1/_4$ teaspoon saffron threads dissolved in $^1/_4$ cup boiling chicken stock
    Salt and freshly ground black pepper
  2 scallions, thinly sliced
One 10-ounce package frozen peas, defrosted
  1 cup fresh asparagus
  1 red bell pepper, roasted, peeled, cored, seeded, and cut into thin strips
    (for technique, see page 46)
$^1/_4$ cup finely chopped fresh parsley
    Sliced fresh tomatoes or oranges for garnish

1. Preheat the oven to 350 degrees.
2. In a deep, wide casserole with a tight-fitting lid, heat the olive oil over medium-high heat and brown the chicken pieces on all sides. When browned, remove the chicken from the casserole and set aside.
3. Sauté the onion in the same oil, adding more if necessary, until soft and translucent (5–7 minutes). Reduce the heat and add the garlic and leek. Cook an additional 3 minutes.
4. Add the rice to the casserole and stir well to cover all the grains with the oil.
5. Add the wine, stock, bay leaf, and saffron mixture to the casserole and stir well. Return the browned chicken pieces to the casserole together with any juices that have accumulated around them. Cover the casserole with foil and then with its lid. Put into the oven and bake for 1 hour.
6. Remove the casserole from the oven. There should still be a little liquid in it. Add the salt and pepper, scallions, peas, asparagus, and pepper strips to the casserole. Return the casserole to the oven and cook another 5–7 minutes. Remove the casserole from the oven and serve the *arroz con pollo* immediately, sprinkling each portion with fresh parsley and garnishing with slices of fresh tomato or orange.

Arroz con Pollo, Caribbean Version

MARINATING TIME (CHICKEN): **2 or more hours**
PREPARATION TIME: **1^3/$_4$ hours**
SERVINGS: **4–6**

One 5-pound chicken, cut in eighths
^{1}/$_3$ cup freshly squeezed lime juice
^{1}/$_2$ tablespoon finely grated lime zest
    Salt and freshly ground black pepper
  4 tablespoons corn or peanut oil
  1 large onion, peeled and finely chopped
  1 large green bell pepper, cored, seeded, and diced
  1 large red bell pepper, cored, seeded, and diced
  3 large cloves garlic, peeled and chopped (1^1/$_2$ tablespoons)

1 stalk celery, diced
2 cups long grain white rice, rinsed
$2^1/_2$ cups chicken stock
1 cup Fresh Tomato Sauce (page 300)
$^1/_4$ teaspoon saffron threads dissolved in $^1/_4$ cup boiling chicken stock
A few drops Tabasco or other hot pepper sauce
One 10-ounce package frozen peas, defrosted
$^1/_2$ cup cut-up pimento-stuffed green olives (cut in half widthwise)
$^1/_2$ cup finely chopped fresh cilantro

1. Put the chicken into a medium dish. Mix the lime juice, lime zest, salt, and black pepper in a small bowl. Mix together and pour over the chicken pieces. Marinate 2 or more hours in the refrigerator.
2. Preheat the oven to 350 degrees.
3. Bring the chicken to room temperature. Heat the oil in a deep, wide casserole over medium-high heat and sauté the onion until soft and translucent (5–7 minutes). Add the peppers, garlic, and celery and reduce the heat slightly. Continue to cook until the vegetables begin to soften.
4. Add the rice and stir well to cover well with the oil. Pour the stock, tomato sauce, saffron mixture, and Tabasco sauce into the casserole. Stir well and put the chicken and all the marinade into the casserole.
5. Cover the casserole with foil and then with its cover. Put the casserole in the oven and bake $1^1/_4$ hours.
6. Remove the casserole from the oven and add the peas and olives. Cover again and put back in the oven. Cook another 10 minutes and remove the casserole from the oven. Check chicken for doneness by inserting a skewer or toothpick into a thigh or drumstick. If juices run yellow, it is done. Serve *arroz con pollo* immediately and sprinkle each portion with cilantro.

SERVING SUGGESTIONS:
Arroz con pollo is a one-dish meal that needs no accompaniment. Precede the *arroz con pollo* with a green salad. *Salata de Maror* (page 37) or *Salata de Verdura* (page 36) are both good choices. *Impanadas*

(page 72) or *Borekas* (page 61) with meat filling (page 63) are good appetizers to serve with drinks before the meal. Conclude the dinner with fresh fruit, Sephardic cookies, or *Torta de los Reyes* (page 259) and coffee.

Pollo Relleno con Trahanas

ROAST STUFFED CHICKEN, SEPHARDIC STYLE

 This stuffing is versatile and works well with chicken, capon, squab, or cornish game hen. The mint and parsley provide a cool herbal accent that compliments the nutty flavor of the bulgur.

PREPARATION TIME: **2 hours**
SERVINGS: **6–8**

2 small chickens, $3^1/_2$–4 pounds each
Salt and freshly ground black pepper
1 cup bulgur
3 cups boiling chicken stock or water plus $^1/_2$ cup chicken stock, water, or dry white wine to deglaze (optional)
5 tablespoons olive oil
1 large onion, peeled and finely chopped
1 large clove garlic, peeled and finely chopped ($^1/_2$ tablespoon)
2 chicken livers, chopped
1 tablespoon chopped celery leaves
$^1/_4$ cup finely chopped fresh parsley
$^1/_4$ cup finely chopped fresh mint leaves
2 tablespoons freshly squeezed lemon juice

1. Wash and dry each chicken and set aside the giblets for another purpose, such as making stock. Season the cavity of both chickens with salt and black pepper and set aside.
2. Put the bulgur in a large bowl. Pour 2 cups boiling stock or water over the bulgur and allow it to sit, covered, for 15 minutes. Drain off any excess liquid not absorbed by the grain.

3. Preheat the oven to 350 degrees.

4. Heat 3 tablespoons oil over medium-high heat in a skillet and sauté the onion until soft and translucent (5–7 minutes). Reduce the heat and add the garlic and chopped chicken livers. Cook until no trace of pink remains in the meat, stirring constantly to prevent burning. Pour the contents of the skillet over the bulgur.

5. Add the celery leaves, parsley, mint, and lemon juice to the bulgur mixture and stir to combine everything thoroughly. Add salt and pepper to taste to the stuffing.

6. Stuff half the stuffing mixture into each of the chickens. Truss the opening of each bird with trussing needles or small skewers to prevent the stuffing from leaking out as the birds roast. Then tie and truss the birds with kitchen string.

7. Place the chickens on a rack in a roasting pan, breast side up. Pour 1 tablespoon olive oil over each chicken and sprinkle with salt and black pepper.

8. Roast 15 minutes. Pour $^1/_3$ cup of the remaining chicken stock over the chickens and reduce the oven temperature to 350 degrees. Roast 20 minutes longer.

9. Turn the chickens over, with the breasts facing downward and the backs up. Sprinkle this side of each chicken with salt and pepper and pour another $^1/_3$ cup of stock over the birds. Return to the oven and roast for another 20 minutes.

10. Turn the chickens over again and pour the remaining $^1/_3$ cup stock over the birds. Continue to roast another 25–30 minutes or until the chickens are golden brown. Baste every 7 or 8 minutes with the liquids that have accumulated at the bottom of the roasting pan. Test for doneness by inserting a skewer or toothpick into the place where the thigh and drumstick are joined. If the juices run yellow, the chicken is done.

11. When the chickens have finished roasting, remove them from the oven and transfer the birds to a platter. Untie and remove trussing string and needles. Pour the liquid from the roasting pan into a cup with a fat-skimming spout. Pour the liquid through the spout into a small saucepan. The fat will remain in the cup. If you wish, deglaze

the roasting pan with $^1/_2$ cup stock, water, or white wine by placing the pan over medium heat on the stove top and scraping up the browned bits from the pan. Add this to the liquid in the saucepan. Stir liquids together and pour into a sauceboat. This will be the gravy for the meat.

12. To serve, remove the stuffing from the cavities of the birds with a spoon. Carve each bird into four or five portions and serve each portion of meat with a little of the stuffing. Pour a little of the gravy over each portion of meat and serve the remainder in the sauceboat at the table.

SERVING SUGGESTIONS:

This roast chicken goes very well with any vegetable cooked in tomato sauce (page 300). Precede the entree with an assortment of salads and appetizers. *Anjinara* (page 28), *Yaprakes de Oja* (page 19), any of the Roasted Pepper Salads (page 46), marinated black or green olives (pages 10 and 11), and *Ajada de Aves* (page 5) are all good choices. Conclude the meal with fresh fruit, *Travados* (page 268), and mint tea.

VARIATION:

For a Greek Romaniot version of this dish, substitute $^1/_2$ cup dried currants for the mint leaves and add $^1/_4$ teaspoon dried thyme to the stuffing mixture.

Before the Holocaust, Sephardic Jews far outnumbered the Romaniot Jews in Greece, which had been part of the Ottoman Empire in 1492 when Jewish exiles from Spain were given sanctuary. Sephardic customs and traditions, as well as the Ladino language, dominated Jewish communities in Greece everywhere except in Ioannina, Larissa, Corfu—an island in the Adriatic—and Hania, a town on the island of Crete. Sephardic Jews drew their primary culinary influences from Spain, their ancestral homeland, and from Turkey, their host country after the exile. Romaniot Jews, on the other hand, spoke Greek, always followed Greek traditions in cooking, and used a different liturgy in their synagogues from that of the Jews of Spain and Portugal.

Roasted Snow

A MOROCCAN FOLK TALE

Once there was a tailor who had three daughters. He lived on a street through which the son of the King used to pass every day. The three girls used to look at the prince, who was very handsome, and dream about marrying him.

"I would love to marry the prince," said the first daughter, "so that I could eat the same bread the King eats."

"I would love to marry him in order to drink the same wine the King drinks," said the second daughter.

The third daughter said, "I would like to marry him just so that I could be his wife."

The prince overheard them talking and told every word to his father. The next day the King summoned the tailor to him. The tailor stood before him, shaking nervously. "Your Excellency, what can a poor humble tailor do for you?"

"I would like you to bring your three daughters to see me when they are pregnant," said the King.

The tailor could say nothing in response to the King's request except "Yes, your excellency."

The father returned home very sad and shaken. "What could the King want with the three of you?" he said to his daughters. "And why when you are pregnant?"

"Do not worry, Father," said the girls. "We will go and visit the King in nine months."

Nine months passed and when they did, the girls went to see the King. They put pillows into their stomachs underneath their dresses before they left the house. When the girls got to the palace, they were taken to the King's chamber. He greeted them with a smile. "What would you like as a gift before you give birth to your child?" he asked the first girl.

"I would like to have a piece of bread that is just like the kind the King eats," she said.

"And you?" he asked the second.

"I would like to have a drink of the same wine that the King drinks."

"And what about you?" he said to the third.

"I would like to eat some roasted snow."

The cook went into the kitchen and brought out some bread and some wine. "I tried to roast the snow but it melted and put out the fire, Your Excellency."

"Snow cannot possibly be roasted," said the King. "Ask me for something else."

The third daughter smiled and replied, "I know, Your Excellency. It is no more possible to roast snow than it is for the tailor's three honorable daughters to be pregnant when they are not married." With that, the three girls removed the pillows from underneath their cloaks to show that they were neither pregnant nor married.

The King then smiled at the girl and said, "Come with me into my garden." When he took her into his garden, the prince was waiting for her. He told her everything he had overheard from underneath their window when he had been walking in the street. Then he asked for her hand in marriage. The girl was overjoyed. She became the wife of the prince and her sisters got to enjoy all the bread and wine from the royal palace they desired.

Meats

Kodredo al Forno (ROAST LAMB)

Kodredo Relleno al Forno (ROAST STUFFED LAMB WITH EGG/LEMON CRUST)

Marinated Beef or Lamb Kebabs

    Greek-Style Marinade for Beef

    Turkish-Style Marinade for Beef

    Turkish-Style Marinade for Lamb

    Moroccan-Style Marinade for Lamb

Koftes (GROUND BEEF OR LAMB KEBABS)

    Balkan-Style Herb and Spice Mixture

    North African-Style Herb and Spice Mixture

Sopado (SEPHARDIC-STYLE BEEF STEW)

Sopado con Sedano (BRAISED BEEF WITH CELERY)

Sopado con Bamias (EGYPTIAN-STYLE BRAISED BEEF WITH OKRA)

Sopado de Kodredo à la Morisco (BRAISED LAMB, MOORISH STYLE)

Hamin

    Hamin, Salonika Style

    Moroccan S'kheena

    Loubia

Legumbres Yaprakes (SEPHARDIC-STYLE STUFFED VEGETABLES)

Kodredo al Forno

ROAST LAMB

When Sephardim think of meat, it is roast lamb that comes to mind. Lamb is the centerpiece of the Passover *seder* because it was used for the Passover sacrifice in the Hebrew Temple. In this way, Sephardic Jews keep the memory of their ancient history alive at Passover time. The Ashkenazim, on the other hand, maintain that the memory of the Temple sacrifices is kept alive by refraining from eating roasted lamb at the *seder* rather than making it the main item on the menu.

There are agricultural as well as spiritual reasons for the divergent customs. In Mediterranean countries, spring is the season when sheep are giving birth and lamb is therefore abundant at this time of year. Central and Eastern Europe were never sheep-producing regions so lamb was not readily available. It was also costly. So the Jews of these areas might have developed a rationale for not eating roasted lamb on Passover and therefore changing what may have been a more ancient and deeply ingrained Jewish tradition. The cost and difficulty involved in obtaining fresh lamb in Eastern Europe made the older practice prohibitive and impractical for Ashkenazic Jews.

Sephardic Jews do not restrict lamb to the *seder* on Passover either. The entire week of Passover is considered a time for feasting on lamb and many Passover lamb dishes have been created by them. Lamb appears in *Minas* (page 83), Passover *Borekas* (page 61), soups, and stuffed vegetables.

Not coincidentally, Greek Christians eat roasted lamb to celebrate Easter, which occurs at the same time as Passover. Like their Christian neighbors, Greek Jews created special dishes from the organs of the lamb—the heart, liver, and kidneys.

The recipe for roasted lamb below is simple, straightforward in typical Greek fashion, and absolutely delicious!

PREPARATION TIME: $2^{1}/_{2}$ to 3 hours
SERVINGS: 8–10

8–10 cloves garlic, peeled
 5–6 sprigs fresh rosemary
   1 teaspoon salt
 $^{1}/_{8}$ teaspoon freshly ground black pepper
 $^{1}/_{4}$ cup olive oil plus oil for rubbing
One 6–7-pound lamb shoulder, including ribs
 $^{1}/_{2}$ cup dry red wine mixed with $^{1}/_{2}$ cup cold water plus $^{3}/_{4}$ cup dry red
    wine to deglaze

1. Preheat the oven to 400 degrees. You will need a good roasting pan with a rack and a bulb baster to make this dish. You'll also need a meat thermometer.

2. In a food processor or blender, place the garlic, rosemary, 1 teaspoon salt, $^{1}/_{8}$ teaspoon black pepper, and $^{1}/_{4}$ cup olive oil and process until it becomes a paste. If necessary, add more oil to achieve correct consistency.

3. Make incisions all over the meat and, using a $^{1}/_{8}$ teaspoon measure, insert some of the garlic paste into each incision.

4. Rub the entire lamb shoulder with olive oil and sprinkle it with salt and black pepper.

5. Place the meat on the roasting rack and roast the meat for 25 minutes.

6. Turn the heat down to 325 degrees and roast for another 2–$2^{1}/_{2}$ hours. Baste frequently with the wine/water mixture. After you have used all the wine/water mixture to baste the meat, continue to baste it with the liquid that accumulates at the bottom of the roasting pan using a bulb baster.

7. The meat is ready when a meat thermometer is inserted and registers 140 degrees for rare, 150 degrees for medium, or 160 degrees for well done.

8. Allow the meat to rest for 15 minutes before carving. Meanwhile, deglaze the pan by pouring the $^{3}/_{4}$ cup dry red wine into it and putting it on an oven burner over medium heat. Scrape up the browned bits with a wooden spoon as you cook. Degrease using a bulb baster or a

degreasing cup with a special spout, which allows the juices to be poured out while holding in the fat. This type of cup is available in most cooking equipment stores.

9. Pour the degreased sauce into a sauceboat and serve with the roast. Carve the meat into portions before serving.

SERVING SUGGESTIONS:

Any sautéed, roasted, or grilled vegetables go well with this meat. I serve roasted potatoes and one or two green vegetables. Precede the meat with an assortment of salads and appetizers. *Anjinara* (page 28), Sautéed Eggplant Salad with Walnut Sauce (page 52), Roasted Pepper Salad (page 46) with Simple Lemon Vinaigrette (page 47), and *Borekas* (page 61) or *Buleymas* (page 71) filled with spinach (page 64) are good choices. Conclude the meal with fresh fruit, Sephardic cookies, and mint tea or coffee.

VARIATION:

This dish can also be prepared as a pot roast on top of the stove. Just brown the meat first in olive oil on all sides over medium-high heat. Then reduce the heat to its lowest simmer, cover the pot tightly, and cook without opening for $2^1/_2$–3 hours. Test for doneness, using a meat thermometer, as described above. Dried oregano ($1^1/_2$ tablespoons) can be substituted for the rosemary for a different flavor.

Kodredo Relleno al Forno

ROAST STUFFED LAMB WITH EGG/LEMON CRUST

 This variation on *Kodredo al Forno* (page 151) is one of the most elegant dishes in Sephardic cuisine. It is a splendid entree with or without the egg/lemon crust. I always prepare the stuffed roast the day before I plan to serve it because it can be cut into very attractive, thin slices after it is chilled. It also saves time to make this dish in two stages.

To make this dish, you must ask your butcher to prepare a half or a whole boned foresaddle of lamb. The foresaddle includes two shoulders, both racks of lamb, the entire breast, and the foreshanks. A foresaddle is very large, weighing 16–18 pounds, and it holds a very large amount of stuffing comfortably, usually between 5 and 6 cups. If preparing half a foresaddle, cut this amount in half. *Kodredo relleno al forno* is the perfect entree for your Passover *seder*. If you make the entire foresaddle, it will serve between 16 and 20 people easily.

PREPARATION TIME: $4^1/_2$–5 hours
SERVINGS: 16–20

  4 tablespoons olive oil plus oil for rubbing
  1 medium onion, peeled and finely chopped
  3 large cloves garlic, peeled and finely chopped ($1^1/_2$ tablespoons)
  2 pounds fresh spinach, chopped
  3 *matzot* or $1^1/_2$ cups *matzoh farfel*
$2^1/_2$ cups Vegetable Stock (page 299), warmed, plus additional stock if needed
  4 tablespoons pine nuts
$^1/_4$ cup finely chopped fresh parsley
$^1/_4$ cup finely chopped fresh dill leaves
$^1/_4$ cup finely chopped fresh mint leaves
$^1/_4$ cup finely chopped fresh chives
    Salt and freshly ground black pepper
  1 large egg, beaten
  1 foresaddle of lamb, rib bones removed and backbone left in
$^1/_2$ cup meat stock, dry red wine, or water for deglazing (optional)

For the Egg/Lemon Crust
$^1/_2$ cup freshly squeezed lemon juice
    Salt and freshly ground black pepper
$^1/_4$ cup finely chopped fresh dill leaves
  8 large eggs, well beaten

1. Start preparations a day before you plan to serve. To prepare the stuffing, heat the olive oil in a wide, deep sauté pan over medium-

high heat. Sauté the onion until soft and translucent (5–7 minutes). Add the garlic, reduce the heat slightly, and cook 2 more minutes. Add the chopped spinach and cook until the spinach leaves are wilted. Remove from the heat.

2. Break the *matzot* into small pieces and put them into a mixing bowl with the warmed stock. If using *matzoh farfel,* just pour the pieces of *farfel* into the bowl containing the stock. Allow this to rest 2 minutes. Drain whatever stock is not absorbed into another container. You should have a little more than $1^1/_4$ cups stock left. If you don't, add enough additional stock to make $1^1/_4$ cups.

3. Mix the soaked *matzoh,* spinach mixture, pine nuts, herbs, salt, pepper, and beaten egg together in the mixing bowl.

4. Preheat the oven to 450 degrees.

5. Lay the foresaddle of lamb flat on a board and place the stuffing in the cavity of the meat. Stuff the pockets that are opened under the ribs and distribute the stuffing evenly to either side of the backbone.

6. Thread a trussing needle with kitchen thread and sew up the cavity of the lamb wherever there are openings. After the cavity of the lamb is sewn, truss the meat and tie it with kitchen string.

7. Rub the lamb with olive oil and sprinkle it with salt and black pepper. Lay it on the rack of your roasting pan. Roast the meat for 25 minutes. Then reduce the heat to 325 degrees.

8. Roast the meat for $2^1/_2$–3 hours, basting it from time to time with the $1^1/_4$ cups stock. When you have used up all the stock, continue to baste the meat using a bulb baster with the pan juices that accumulate at the bottom of the pan.

9. Remove the lamb from the oven. Test for doneness with a meat thermometer. It registers 150 degrees for medium and 160 degrees for well done. Take it out of the pan and set it on a platter to cool. Remove the liquid from the roasting pan and set it aside in a container. If you wish, deglaze the pan with $^1/_2$ cup meat stock, dry red wine, or water by placing it on a burner on the stove over medium heat and scraping the browned bits with a wooden spoon. When the meat has cooled, cover it and refrigerate it until the next day.

Do the same with the pan liquid. It can be served as a gravy with the roast.

10. If you do not wish to serve *kodredo relleno al forno* with the egg/lemon crust, all you need to do is slice the meat into attractive thin slices and reheat it, covered, in a baking dish at 350 degrees. As this is a very large cut of meat, you will require at least two 9 × 13-inch baking dishes to hold all of it. Reheat the gravy as well and serve each slice of meat with the reheated gravy.

11. If you wish to serve it with the crust, preheat the oven to 350 degrees.

12. Bring the whole, uncut roast to room temperature. Remove all of the trussing strings, set it on the rack of the roasting pan, and warm in the oven for 15 minutes.

13. While the meat is warming, beat the lemon juice, salt, pepper, and chopped dill into the eggs.

14. Remove the meat from the oven and change the setting to broil, or preheat your broiler to 500 degrees.

15. Pour the egg/lemon mixture over the meat and put it under the broiler for 10–12 minutes or until the egg/lemon crust is golden brown. It will puff up slightly as it broils. The crust will be crisp on the outside and custardlike on the inside. Remove the meat from the oven and let it rest 15 minutes before carving. Serve in attractive slices, with a little of the reheated gravy poured over.

SERVING SUGGESTIONS:

This is a very visually appealing as well as tasty dish. It should be accompanied by simple grilled, roasted, or sautéed green vegetables and rice pilav or a vegetable cooked in tomato sauce (page 185). Simple sautéed vegetables like baby carrots, asparagus spears, and baby turnips are a very nice accompaniment. Precede the entree with *Anjinara* (page 28) or a green salad. For an elegant Passover *seder* menu featuring this dish, see page 326.

Marinated Beef or Lamb Kebabs

Grilled kebabs are as popular among Mediterranean Jews as they are among other ethnic communities in the region. The marinades vary from area to area but the method of preparing kebabs is the same throughout. The cubed meat is marinated for 2 or more hours, threaded on a skewer with a pearl onion on each end to hold it in place, and grilled, preferably outdoors. In Turkey, non-Jewish cooks marinate the meat with yogurt, which imparts its tangy flavor and softens the meat. Jews have devised alternative methods of achieving this without violating the laws of *kashrut* using wine, lemon juice, fresh tomato sauce, and pureed fresh herbs. Sephardic meat kebabs never include vegetables and meat on the same skewer. This makes sense, as vegetables have different cooking times than meat.

MARINATING TIME (LAMB OR BEEF): **2 or more hours**
PREPARATION TIME: **20 minutes to prepare marinade,**
15–20 minutes to grill meat
SERVINGS: **6–8**

1³/₄ cups marinade (see below)
   3 pounds lamb shoulder or beef flank steak, cut into 2-inch cubes
12–16 pearl onions

Marinate the cubes of meat, covered and refrigerated, for 2 or more hours. Meat can marinate as long as 24 hours. Preheat an outdoor grill or oven broiler. Discard the marinade. Thread the meat cubes on metal or wooden skewers. Put an onion at the beginning and at the end of each skewer to hold the meat in place as it grills. Grill each kebab for approximately 7–8 minutes on each side.

SERVING SUGGESTIONS:
Kebabs are always served with rice pilav. Any of the rice pilav recipes can be used as long as their flavors are compatible with the ingredients in the marinade but an *Arroz Pilafi* (page 204) or *Pilafi con Piniones* (page 205) is the most traditional. A *Salata Sepharadi* (page 34) is also a tradi-

tional accompaniment. While you are waiting for the kebabs to grill, serve a variety of appetizers. *Humus* (page 7) or Roasted Eggplant Salad, Arabic Style (page 51), marinated black or green olives (pages 10 and 11), *Yaprakes de Oja* (page 19), and one of the Roasted Pepper Salads (page 46) are all good choices. Conclude the meal with fresh fruit, Sephardic cookies, and coffee or mint tea.

Greek-Style Marinade for Beef

YIELD: $1^3/_4$ cups

- $^1/_3$ cup olive oil
- $^1/_2$ cup freshly squeezed lemon juice
- 1 small onion, peeled and quartered
- 2 teaspoons dried oregano
- $^1/_2$ cup Fresh Tomato Sauce (page 300)
- $^1/_4$ cup fresh parsley leaves, tightly packed
- 2 large cloves garlic, peeled
  Salt and freshly ground black pepper
- 2 bay leaves

Put everything except the bay leaves into a food processor or blender and puree until smooth. Pour over the meat cubes and add bay leaves to the bowl. Use as directed in the recipe.

Turkish-Style Marinade for Beef

YIELD: $1^3/_4$ cups

- $^1/_2$ cup olive oil
- $^2/_3$ cup Vegetable Stock (page 299)
- 1 medium onion, peeled and quartered
- 2 large cloves garlic, peeled
- $^1/_2$ teaspoon ground cinnamon
- 1 teaspoon coriander seeds, ground in a mortar
- $^1/_4$ teaspoon ground allspice
- $^1/_8$ teaspoon freshly grated nutmeg
  Salt and freshly ground black pepper

Place everything in a food processor or blender and puree until smooth. Use as directed in the recipe.

Turkish-Style Marinade for Lamb

YIELD: 1³/₄ cups

 1/3 cup olive oil
 1/2 cup dry red wine
   1 medium onion, peeled and quartered
   2 large cloves garlic, peeled
 1/3 cup fresh chervil leaves
 1/3 cup fresh parsley leaves
 1/4 cup fresh mint leaves
   1 tablespoon fresh thyme or lemon thyme leaves

Put everything into a food processor or blender and puree until smooth. Use as directed in the recipe.

Moroccan-Style Marinade for Lamb

YIELD: 1³/₄ cups

 1/3 cup olive oil
 1/3 cup plus 1 tablespoon freshly squeezed lemon juice
   1 medium onion, peeled and quartered
   1 clove garlic, peeled
 1/4 teaspoon ground cloves
   1 teaspoon ground ginger
 1/4 teaspoon ground cinnamon
   1 teaspoon Hungarian hot paprika
 1/4 cup fresh parsley leaves
 1/3 cup fresh cilantro leaves

Put everything into a food processor or blender and process until smooth. Use as directed in the recipe.

Koftes

GROUND BEEF OR LAMB KEBABS

Ground meat kebabs are another Mediterranean specialty. There are a variety of herb and spice mixtures that go into these kebabs. The two most important things to remember about preparing meat for *koftes* is that the meat must be very finely ground and that the mixture must be chilled for at least 90 minutes, both in a bowl and on a skewer before it is grilled. If you don't chill the meat, it might slip off the skewer as it cooks.

PREPARATION TIME: **15 minutes**
CHILLING TIME: $1^{1}/_{2}$ **hours or more**
SERVINGS: **6–8**

$2^{1}/_{2}$ **pounds lean ground beef or lamb**
$1^{1}/_{2}$ **cups herb and spice mixture (see below)**
$^{1}/_{4}$ **pound chopped beef or lamb marrow or** $^{1}/_{4}$ **cup olive or sunflower oil**
Cold water
Lemon wedges for garnish

1. Place the meat and the spice and herb mixture in a large mixing bowl. Add the marrow or oil and mix well with your hands so that everything is well incorporated.
2. Knead the meat with your hands. Cover the bowl and refrigerate the mixture for 30 minutes.
3. Remove the meat mixture from the refrigerator. Have a bowl of cold water and 6–8 metal skewers next to you while you work. Put the meat mixture onto a board and divide it into 6 or 8 portions.
4. Take one portion of meat and shape it around one skewer into a long sausage shape. The sausages will be 6–8 inches long and about $1^{1}/_{2}$ inches in diameter. Place this on a platter. Repeat with the remaining meat mixture.
5. Cover and refrigerate for 1 hour before grilling.

6. Preheat the outdoor grill or oven broiler to 500 degrees. Broil or grill meat kebabs 1 inch from the heat source for a total of 10–12 minutes, turning once halfway through the cooking. When done, *koftes* will be nicely browned and cooked completely through. Serve immediately, garnished with lemon wedges.

SERVING SUGGESTIONS:
The traditional accompaniment to ground meat kebabs is rice pilav and *Salata Sepharadi* (page 34). Precede the entree with a variety of appetizers and salads. Grilled Eggplant Salad, Balkan Style (page 49), Roasted Pepper Salad (page 46) with *Olivada* Vinaigrette (page 47), *Ajada de Aves* (page 5) or *Humus* (page 7), and *Buleymas* (page 71) filled with spinach (page 64) are all good choices. Complete the dinner with fresh fruit, Sephardic cookies, and coffee or mint tea.

Balkan-Style Herb and Spice Mixture

YIELD: 1$^{1}/_{2}$ cups

- 1 tablespoon Hungarian sweet paprika
- $^{1}/_{4}$ teaspoon Hungarian hot paprika
- 1 medium onion, peeled and quartered
- 2 cloves garlic, peeled
- $^{3}/_{4}$ cup fresh parsley leaves
- $^{1}/_{4}$ teaspoon ground allspice
- Salt and freshly ground black pepper

Place everything in a food processor or blender and puree until smooth. Use as directed in recipe above.

North African–Style Herb and Spice Mixture

YIELD: 1¹/₂ cups

- 1 medium onion, peeled and quartered
- 1 clove garlic, peeled
- 1 tablespoon Hungarian sweet paprika
- ¹/₄ teaspoon Hungarian hot paprika
- ¹/₂ cup fresh parsley leaves
- ¹/₂ cup fresh cilantro leaves
- ¹/₄ cup fresh mint leaves
- 1 teaspoon ground cinnamon
- Salt and freshly ground black pepper

Put everything into a food processor or blender and puree until smooth. Use as directed in recipe above.

Sopado

SEPHARDIC-STYLE BEEF STEW

The word *sopado* means "stewed" or "braised" meat. This spicy and sweet beef stew is a typical Sephardic dish that was popular throughout the Jewish Mediterranean. The seasoning varies from community to community. The recipe below is in the style of Salonika, Macedonia, and northern Greece. In the Balkans and Bulgaria, cinnamon would be left out. In Turkey and Rhodes, ground coriander seeds would be used instead of the cinnamon sticks and only hot paprika instead of both the sweet and hot. *Sopado* resembles Hungarian goulash and differs only in the quantity of onions and sweet paprika used in the dish. As Hungarian cuisine was influenced by Turkey during the Ottoman occupation of Hungary, it is very likely that *sopado* and goulash are related dishes.

6 tablespoons sunflower oil
$2^1/_2$ pounds stewing beef, cubed
8 shallots, peeled and chopped
2 teaspoons Hungarian sweet paprika
$^1/_2$ teaspoon Hungarian hot paprika
$^1/_2$ teaspoon ground allspice
$^1/_4$ teaspoon ground cloves
1 cup beef stock
1 pound pearl onions, peeled and left whole
4 large cloves garlic, peeled and left whole
1 stick cinnamon
2 bay leaves
1 tablespoon honey
2 cups Fresh Tomato Sauce (page 300)
1 cup dry red wine
Salt and freshly ground black pepper
$^1/_4$ cup freshly squeezed lemon juice

1. Heat the oil in a deep, large casserole over medium-high heat and brown the meat, a few pieces at a time. Transfer to a mixing bowl as it browns.

2. Reduce the heat to medium and add the shallots. Sauté until soft and translucent.

3. Reduce the heat to low and add the sweet and hot paprika. Cook 2–3 minutes, stirring constantly.

4. Add the allspice and cloves and cook 1 minute more.

5. Pour the stock into the pot and deglaze, scraping up all the browned bits with a wooden spoon.

6. Add all the remaining ingredients except for the lemon juice. Return the meat to the casserole and combine well. Cover the pot with foil and then with its lid. Cook undisturbed for 2 hours.

7. Uncover the pot and add the lemon juice. Partially cover the pot and cook another 15 minutes. The stew is ready when the meat is soft and tender and the remaining ingredients, except for the pearl onions, have

blended into a thinnish sauce. You may serve immediately or refrigerate for 1 day and reheat. Discard the bay leaves before serving. This stew tastes even better after it has been reheated and can be kept, refrigerated, for several days.

SERVING SUGGESTIONS:
Sopado may be served with rice pilav or all by itself with plenty of good crusty Mediterranean bread. Precede the *sopado* with *Ajada de Aves* (page 5) or *Humus* (page 7), *Salata de Panjar y Carnabeet* (page 43), *Borekas* (page 61) or *Buleymas* (page 71) filled with spinach (page 64) and marinated green or black olives (pages 10 and 11). Conclude the meal with a compote of dried fruits, baklava, and coffee.

Sopado con Sedano

BRAISED BEEF WITH CELERY

 This savory stew is a favorite throughout the Sephardic world. It can be enjoyed in every season.

PREPARATION TIME: $2^1/_2$ hours
SERVINGS: 6–8

  1 large bunch celery
4–6 tablespoons olive oil
$2^1/_2$ pounds stewing beef, cubed
  1 large onion, peeled and finely chopped
  2 large cloves garlic, peeled and chopped (1 tablespoon)
  1 teaspoon Hungarian sweet paprika
$^1/_4$ teaspoon Hungarian hot paprika
  1 cup beef stock

$1^1/_2$ cups Fresh Tomato Sauce (page 300)

    1 bouquet garni, consisting of 1 bay leaf, 8 sprigs fresh parsley, 6 sprigs fresh chervil (if available), and 4 sprigs thyme or lemon thyme, tied together with kitchen string

       Salt and freshly ground black pepper

       Finely chopped fresh parsley for garnish

1. Separate the celery into stalks. Finely chop the center of the head of celery and all of the end pieces of the stalks where leaves are attached. Finely chop the leaves. Cut the stalks into $1^1/_2$-inch-long pieces. (A bias cut is attractive.) Set aside.

2. Heat 4 tablespoons oil in a large, heavy casserole or Dutch oven over medium-high heat. Brown the meat a few pieces at a time; remove to a mixing bowl.

3. Reduce the heat slightly and, if necessary, add more oil. Sauté the onion until soft and translucent (5–7 minutes). Reduce the heat to low and add the garlic and paprikas. Cook, stirring constantly, for 4–5 minutes.

4. Add the finely chopped celery leaves and cook 5 minutes longer.

5. Preheat the oven to 350 degrees.

6. Pour in the stock and deglaze the pot, scraping up browned bits with a wooden spoon.

7. Add the tomato sauce, celery, and bouquet garni to the pot. Return the meat to the casserole together with any juices that have accumulated and stir well to combine.

8. Cover the casserole with foil and then with its cover. Braise in the oven for 2 hours.

9. Season the *sopado* with salt and black pepper to taste. The dish may be served immediately or it may be set aside and reheated later. Serve in deep, wide soup bowls. Before serving, remove the bouquet garni. Sprinkle each portion with fresh parsley.

SERVING SUGGESTIONS:

This *sopado* may be served with rice pilav or on its own with plenty of crusty bread. Precede the stew with Grilled Eggplant Salad, Balkan Style (page 49), any of the Roasted Pepper Salads (page 46), *Ajada* (page 3) or

Ajada de Aves (page 5), *Borekas* (page 61) or *Buleymas* (page 71) filled with spinach (page 64), and marinated black olives (page 10). Conclude the meal with fresh fruit, Sephardic cookies or *Travados* (page 268), and coffee or mint tea.

Sopado con Bamias

EGYPTIAN-STYLE BRAISED BEEF WITH OKRA

Okra is an African vegetable that moved north from West Africa into the Mediterranean region. There it entered the Sephardic kitchen. Okra was always much more popular among the Jews of North Africa and the Arab countries than it was in Turkey or Greece, although it appears occasionally in the dishes from these countries as well. Okra contains a viscous substance that is a natural thickening agent so a stew made with okra is usually quite thick after it is cooked. This vegetable has a natural affinity for tomato. This delicious *sopado*, hot, sweet, and tart, is topped traditionally with *taleya*, a spicy mixture of onion and garlic that is uniquely Egyptian.

PREPARATION TIME: $2^1/_2$ hours
SERVINGS: 6–8

4–6 tablespoons olive oil
$2^1/_2$ pounds stewing beef or lamb, cubed
1 large onion, peeled and finely chopped
2 large cloves garlic, peeled and finely chopped (1 tablespoon)
$1^1/_2$ teaspoons Hungarian hot paprika
1 cup beef stock
$1^1/_2$ pounds fresh okra, tops trimmed
2 cups Fresh Tomato Sauce (page 300)
$1/_3$ cup freshly squeezed lemon juice
2 tablespoons honey
Salt and freshly ground black pepper

For the Taleya

   3 tablespoons olive oil
   1 large onion, peeled and cut in very thin slices
   3 large cloves garlic, peeled and very finely chopped (1$^1/_2$ tablespoons)
   $^1/_4$ teaspoon Hungarian hot paprika

1. Preheat the oven to 350 degrees.
2. Heat 4 tablespoons oil in a large, heavy casserole over medium-high heat. Brown the meat, a few pieces at a time. Remove the meat to a mixing bowl after browning.
3. If necessary, add more oil. Sauté the onion until soft and translucent (5–7 minutes). Reduce the heat to low and add the garlic and paprika. Cook 3 minutes more, stirring constantly to prevent burning.
4. Deglaze the pan with the stock, scraping up browned bits with a wooden spoon.
5. Add the okra, tomato sauce, lemon juice, and honey to the pan. Return the meat to the casserole and stir well to combine.
6. Cover the pot with foil and then with its cover. Put the casserole in the oven and braise for 2 hours. Stew is done when the meat is soft and tender.
7. Prepare the *taleya* while casserole is cooking. Heat the oil over medium-high heat in a skillet. Add the onion and sauté until soft and translucent (5–7 minutes). Add the garlic and paprika, reduce the heat, and cook, stirring constantly, for 5 minutes. When *taleya* is browned it is done. Remove the casserole from the oven when the meat is ready. Sprinkle each portion of *sopado* with *taleya*.

SERVING SUGGESTIONS:
Pilafi de Trahanas (page 225) is the traditional accompaniment but rice pilav is also excellent. Precede the entree with Sweet Carrot Salad (page 44), *Olivada* with Black Olives (page 12), *Humus* (page 7), and *Buleymas* (page 71) filled with spinach (page 64). Finish the meal with fresh fruit, Sephardic cookies or baklava, and coffee or mint tea.

Sopado de Kodredo à la Morisco

BRAISED LAMB, MOORISH STYLE

This Moorish dish is very popular among Jews from Morocco and Algeria. It is spicy and sweet with the aroma of saffron and orange flower water. The saffron also imparts a warm golden glow to the sauce. The fruits used in the traditional recipe are prunes and dried quinces, which are not available in the United States. Dried pears make an excellent substitute. In Moroccan cooking, this dish is called a *tagine* and its usual method of cooking is in a clay pot. Lacking this, a heavy casserole with a tight-fitting lid will do nicely.

SOAKING TIME (FRUIT): **overnight**
PREPARATION TIME: $2^{1}/_{2}$ hours
SERVINGS: 6–8

    4 tablespoons olive oil
    1 large onion, peeled and very finely chopped
$1^{1}/_{4}$ or 3 cups beef stock
    $^{1}/_{2}$ pound pitted prunes and $^{1}/_{2}$ pound dried pears, soaked overnight in cold water
$2^{1}/_{2}$ pounds stewing lamb, cut into 1-inch cubes
    $^{1}/_{4}$ cup honey
One 1-inch piece fresh gingerroot, peeled
    1 stick cinnamon
$2^{1}/_{2}$ cups cubed, peeled pumpkin or Hubbard squash cut into 1-inch cubes
    $^{1}/_{4}$ teaspoon saffron threads dissolved in $^{1}/_{4}$ cup boiling water
        Finely grated zest of 1 orange
    1 tablespoon orange flower water
        Approximately 3–4 tablespoons toasted sesame seeds for sprinkling

1. If using a clay pot, soak the top and bottom in hot water to cover for 15 minutes. Remove the pot from the water but do not dry. If using a casserole, skip this step.

2. If using a clay pot, heat the oil in a skillet over medium-high heat. If using a casserole, heat the oil in the casserole. Sauté the onions until soft and translucent (5–7 minutes).

3. Deglaze the skillet or the casserole with $1/2$ cup stock, scraping up the browned bits with a wooden spoon. Remove from the heat.

4. If using a casserole, preheat the oven to 350 degrees. Add $2^1/2$ cups stock and bring to a boil. Drain the prunes and pears and add them to the casserole. Add the meat and the remaining ingredients except the sesame seeds. Cover the pot with foil and then with its lid and braise in the oven for 2 hours.

5. If using a clay pot, put the drained fruit, the meat, and the remaining ingredients except for the stock and sesame seeds in the bottom half of the pot. Pour the onion mixture from the skillet over this and add $3/4$ cup additional stock. Cover the clay pot with its top and put it into a cold oven. Turn the oven up to 450 degrees and cook for 25 minutes. Then turn the oven down to 375 degrees. Cook an additional $1^3/4$ hours. Stew is done when the meat is soft and tender.

6. To serve the stew, remove the pot from the oven and serve immediately in deep, wide soup bowls. Sprinkle with toasted sesame seeds before serving.

SERVING SUGGESTIONS:

This dish is traditionally served by itself with spicy Moroccan bread. Precede the stew with *Buleymas* (page 71) filled with spinach (page 64), Sweet Carrot Salad (page 44), Roasted Pepper Salad (page 46) with Simple Lemon Vinaigrette (page 47) and *Humus* (page 7) or *Olivada* (page 12). Conclude the meal with a delicious Moroccan-style Sweet *Couscous* Pudding (page 255) and coffee.

Hamin

Hamin is the most ancient of all Jewish dishes. It is a stew containing meat, beans, grains, and vegetables cooked for a very long time in a very slow oven. *Hamin* is prepared specially for the Sabbath afternoon meal. Because cooking is forbidden on the Sabbath, the stew is put into the oven set at the lowest possible temperature on Friday before sundown and left there until Saturday afternoon, when it is taken out of the oven and eaten as a hot meal. Since the cooking of the *hamin* was begun before the Sabbath, it is permissible to allow it to continue to cook until it is ready to eat on Shabbat afternoon.

Hamin is mentioned by name in the *Talmud* and in various other places in Rabbinic literature. Jews around the world have created many variations on the theme of *hamin* using the meats, grains, and legumes available to them. In Greece, Turkey, the Balkans, and the Arabic countries, the dish is called by its oldest name, *hamin*. In North Africa, it is called *adafina*, or *s'kheena*. Tunisian and Lybian Jews prepare a variation called *loubia*, which traveled to Egypt and from there to other parts of the Mediterranean. The Asheknazic dish *cholent* is a variation of *hamin*. Sephardic *hamin* differs slightly from *cholent* in that it almost always contains whole, unbroken eggs called *haminados* that cook together with the meat and absorb all the other flavors, turning a rich golden brown and creamy smooth in texture. Hungary is the only country whose Ashkenazic Jewish cuisine includes recipes for *cholent* containing whole unbroken eggs. This was probably due to its occupation by Turkey, which had a significant impact on the cuisine of the country.

Old cookbooks and historic literature mention a wide variety of *hamin*-type dishes. Winter *hamin* features meat, *Huevos Haminados* (page 231), marrow bones or calves' feet, beans, potatoes, rice, and dumpling-like puddings called *koklas*. *Hamin* is also made with pearl barley, wheat berries, and cracked wheat. In Turkey and Italy, *hamin* recipes sometimes include greens like Swiss chard or kale. Autumn *hamin* invariably includes *kalabasa* (pumpkin, Hubbard, butternut, or some other type of winter squash).

For Sephardic and other Mediterranean Jews, *hamin* is considered cool- or cold-weather fare. During the warm days of spring, summer, and early autumn, *huevos haminados* become the *hamin*. A light dairy or vegetarian meal called *desayuno* is served in the warm weather, which features warm *huevos haminados*, *Borekas* (page 61), *Boyos* (page 66), or *Buleymas* (page 71), and a variety of salads and fresh vegetables. The savory pastries are cooked before Shabbat and warmed on a tin tray called a *tafsin* before serving. This warming of the pastries is not considered cooking on Shabbat because the *tafsin* is placed on top of a metal sheet that covers the heat source of the stove and does not touch it directly. *Kiddush,* the blessing over wine, and *hamotzi,* the blessing over bread, are made before the *desayuno* is eaten. When the weather is cooler, *desayuno* is served in the early afternoon and a *hamin* is served in late afternoon. The *kiddush* and *hamotzi* are saved for late afternoon, when the *hamin* is eaten.

There are special *hamin* for special Sabbaths. For *Shabbat Bereshit* ("Genesis" Sabbath, which immediately follows Simchat Torah in the Jewish calendar and which is the Sabbath when the first chapters of the Book of Genesis are read from the *Torah* scroll in the synagogue) a seven-layered *hamin* is prepared by some Sephardic Jews. The seven layers symbolize the Seven Days of Creation. For *Shabbat Shira* (the "Sabbath of Song," when the song sung by Moses as the Hebrews crossed the Red Sea during the Exodus from Egypt is read from the *Torah,* and which occurs during the week Tu B'Shevat is celebrated) a special *hamin* made with cracked wheat is prepared.

No Jewish dish has had more of an influence on other cuisines than *hamin*. French *cassoulet* and Spanish *cocido madrileno,* which contain a variety of meats braised with beans and sometimes other vegetables and grains, are both variations of *hamin*.

My friend Avner and I had a Sephardic Jewish friend in Israel named Nissim, who would invite us very often to his home for the Sabbath. His mother was an excellent cook but, unlike me, Avner had a conservative and unadventurous palate and found the Sephardic food in Nissim's home too strange and exotic for his taste. Whenever we went to Nissim's, Avner would timidly pick at his food, telling the hosts that he had a bad stomach that day and hoping that he was not giving offense. After this happened four or five times, Nissim's mother surprised us with an "Ashkenazi *hamin*," which she was sure would please the finicky Avner.

An Ashkenazi *cholent* in Israel typically tastes nothing like its American or European counterpart. Because Israel is a tiny country, it has very little grazing land and, therefore, very little home-grown beef. The small amount that is available is imported and expensive, so Ashkenazi Israelis have developed a habit of preparing *cholent* with chicken or turkey, which is cheap and plentiful. The heavy, stick-to-your-ribs combination of beans, potatoes, and barley does not go well with the delicate meat of poultry. Avner and I had developed a loathing for Israeli *cholent* long before we met Nissim. We could think of nothing worse to sit down to on a Shabbat afternoon than a meal made of this combination of ingredients. Nissim's mother, herself unused to Ashkenazic cooking, served her "Ashkenazi *cholent*" with a side dish of the saffron rice pilav. That Shabbat, Avner and I both ate heartily of the *borekas* and salads and rice. Avner, for his part, proclaimed himself happy to be free enough of his stomach problems that he could finally enjoy the taste of "real Sephardic cooking." To the relief of both of us, Nissim's mother never again tried to cook Ashkenazi.

Here are three different versions of *hamin* from three different regions of the Jewish Mediterranean. *Hamin* Salonika style is typical of the kinds of *hamin* dishes prepared by Jews from the countries of the Ottoman Empire. Its seasoning is simple—nothing more than onions, garlic, paprika, and a bouquet garni of fresh herbs. It is the Sephardic *hamin* dish that most resembles Ashkenazic *cholent*. Moroccan *s'kheena* is made with chick-peas and potatoes and is flavored with saffron and sweet spices like ginger, cinnamon, and cloves in the Moorish fashion. *Loubia* is an altogether different type of North Africa *hamin*. Its savory taste comes from *P'kaila* (page 302), a seasoning mixture of spinach, cilantro, and other fresh green herbs.

Hamin, Salonika Style

SOAKING TIME (BEANS): **overnight**
ASSEMBLY TIME: **20 minutes**
COOKING TIME: **12 or more hours**
SERVINGS: **8–10**

- 1 pound dried white kidney beans
- 8–10 beef marrow bones, with plenty of marrow in them
- 6 tablespoons olive oil
- $2^1/_2$ pounds beef flank steak or skirt steak, in 2 or 3 pieces
- 2 large onions, peeled and finely chopped
- 3 large cloves garlic, peeled and chopped ($1^1/_2$ tablespoons)
- 2 heaping teaspoons Hungarian sweet paprika
- $1/_4$ teaspoon Hungarian hot paprika
- 6 cups beef stock
- 2 cups long grain white rice, tied loosely in a double layer of cheesecloth
- 8–10 large eggs
- 1 bouquet garni, consisting of 6 sprigs fresh parsley, 1 bay leaf, 2 sprigs fresh thyme, and 3 sprigs fresh marjoram, tied together with kitchen string
  Salt and freshly ground black pepper

1. Soak the beans overnight in cold water to cover by 1 inch. Drain and rinse.
2. Bring a large ovenproof casserole (enameled cast iron is best) of salted water to boil. When the water is boiling, plunge in the marrow bones and parboil them for 5 minutes. Remove them with a slotted spoon and set on a platter. Discard the water. This rids the bones of scum without actually cooking them.
3. Heat the oil in a large, heavy casserole or Dutch oven with a tight-fitting lid over medium-high heat. Brown the meat one piece at a time. Remove it to a platter after it is browned.
4. Sauté the onions in the same oil until soft and translucent (5–7 minutes). Reduce the heat, add the garlic and the sweet and hot paprika. Cook, stirring constantly, for 5 minutes. Regulate the heat to prevent scorching.
5. Preheat the oven to 175 degrees.

(continued)

6. Deglaze the pan with the stock, scraping up the browned bits with a wooden spoon.

7. Put the beans, marrow bones, browned meat, package of rice, unshelled eggs, and bouquet garni in the pot. Cover tightly with foil and then with the cover of the pot. Cook undisturbed for 12 or more hours. Remove the bouquet garni and add salt and freshly ground black pepper to taste before serving.

SERVING SUGGESTIONS:

Hamin is served all on its own in deep, wide soup bowls together with bread, pickled vegetables, and good red wine. Most of the liquid will have been absorbed by the beans and meat during the long slow cooking. If there is any left, use it as a sauce for the *hamin*. Serve one marrow bone and one egg per portion of *hamin* together with some of the meat and the beans. Precede the meal with a variety of salads and appetizers. My favorites are marinated black and green olives (page 9), *Toureto* (page 31), one of the Roasted Pepper Salads (page 46), and *Borekas* (page 61) or Buleymas (page 71) with spinach filling (page 64). Conclude the meal with fresh fruit, Sephardic cookies, and coffee or mint tea.

Moroccan S'kheena

SOAKING TIME (CHICK-PEAS): **overnight**
ASSEMBLY TIME: **20 minutes**
COOKING TIME: **12 or more hours**
SERVINGS: **8–10**

$^1/_2$ pound dried chick-peas
6 tablespoons olive oil
One 3$^1/_2$-pound brisket of beef
1 large onion, peeled and finely chopped
8 large cloves garlic, peeled and left whole
5$^1/_2$ cups beef stock
$^1/_4$ teaspoon saffron threads dissolved in 1$^1/_4$ cups boiling water
One 1-inch piece fresh gingerroot, peeled
1 stick cinnamon
1 bay leaf

6 whole cloves
8 medium red boiling potatoes (about 3$^{1}/_{2}$ pounds),
   peeled and cut in half
8 eggs
   Salt and freshly ground black pepper

1. Soak the chick-peas in cold water overnight to cover by 1 inch. Drain and rinse.

2. Heat the oil in a large casserole or Dutch oven with a tight-fitting lid over medium-high heat. Brown the meat on all sides and then remove it to a platter.

3. Sauté the onion in the same oil until soft and translucent (5–7 minutes). Reduce the heat slightly and add the garlic cloves. Cook 1 minute longer and then deglaze the pot with the stock, scraping up the browned bits with a wooden spoon.

4. Preheat the oven to 175 degrees. Add the spices and chick-peas to the casserole. Return the meat and any juices that have accumulated around it. Add the potatoes and the whole, unshelled eggs. Cover the pot tightly with foil and then with its cover. Place in the oven and let it cook undisturbed for 12 or more hours. Season with salt and black pepper and discard the bay leaf before serving.

SERVING SUGGESTIONS:
S'keena is served on its own with Moroccan-style bread, pickled vegetables, and red wine. Precede the entree with a variety of Moroccan-style salads. Hot and Savory Carrot Salad (page 45), Roasted Eggplant Salad, Arabic Style (page 51), Roasted Pepper Salad (page 46) with Simple Lemon Vinaigrette (page 47), and *Toureto* (page 31) are good choices. Conclude the meal with fresh fruits, baklava, and coffee or mint tea.

Loubia

Loubia is an aromatic and spicy meat and bean stew seasoned with *p'kaila* and fresh tomato sauce. It is one of the most delicious of the *hamin* dishes and the only one I know of in Sephardic cooking that does not include *haminados* ("eggs").

SOAKING TIME (BEANS): **overnight**
ASSEMBLY TIME: **20 minutes**
COOKING TIME: **12 or more hours**
SERVINGS: **8–10**

- 1 pound dried white kidney beans
- 6 tablespoons olive oil
- 3 pounds beef skirt steak, in 2 or 3 pieces, or plate brisket, in 1 piece
- 1 large onion, peeled and finely chopped
- 4 shallots, peeled and finely chopped
- 2 cups beef stock
- 4 heaping tablespoons *P'kaila* (page 302)
- 4 cups Fresh Tomato Sauce (page 300)
- 1 teaspoon sugar
- $1/2$ teaspoon cayenne pepper
- Salt and freshly ground black pepper

1. Soak the beans overnight in cold water to cover by 1 inch. Drain and rinse.
2. Heat the oil in a large casserole or Dutch oven over medium-high heat. Brown the meat on all sides; set on a platter until all the pieces are browned.
3. Cook the onion and shallots in the same oil until soft and translucent (5–7 minutes). Deglaze the pot with the stock, scraping up the browned bits with a wooden spoon.
4. Preheat the oven to 175 degrees.
5. Add the *p'kaila,* tomato sauce, sugar, and cayenne to the pot. Return the meat and add the beans to the pot. Cover tightly with foil and then with the cover of the pot. Place in the oven and cook undisturbed for 12 or more hours. Season with salt and black pepper before serving.

SERVING SUGGESTIONS:

Serve *loubia* with plenty of good crusty bread. Precede the entree with a variety of salads and appetizers. *Salata de Haminados* (page 8), *Toureto* (page 31), Roasted Pepper Salad (page 46) with Simple Lemon Vinaigrette (page 47), and *Buleymas* (page 71) filled with spinach (page 64) are good choices. Conclude the meal with fresh fruits, baklava, and coffee or mint tea.

Legumbres Yaprakes

SEPHARDIC-STYLE STUFFED VEGETABLES

Stuffed vegetables are among the most festive Sephardic dishes. They are served on many different special occasions, like circumcisions, bar mitzvahs, and weddings. During the holiday of Sukkot, when the autumn harvest is in and the countries of the Mediterranean abound in beautiful fresh vegetables and fruits, *legumbres yaprakes* are the main event. The recipe for the stuffing is fairly uniform throughout the region, with herbs and spices varying from country to country.

The word *yaprakes*, which means "leaves," literally should apply only to stuffed grape leaves, cabbage leaves, and lettuces but Sephardic cooks use the word to name all stuffed vegetables in their cuisine, including those that are the fruits rather than the leaves of plants.

One of the Yiddish words for stuffed cabbage, *prakkes*, is derived from the Sephardic word *yaprakes*. It is possible that this came about because of trade between Jewish merchants from Russia and Turkey. Many other dishes of Middle Eastern or Mediterranean origin, like *halva* and macaroons, came into the cuisine of Yiddish-speaking Jews via this route. There were also small numbers of Jews who migrated northward from Mediterranean countries into Poland and settled there just as there were Ashkenazic Jews who established homes in the countries of the Mediterranean region. Salonika and Venice had Ashkenazic communities large enough to support their own synagogues. However, the Jews of Mediterranean origin were never numerous enough in Eastern Europe to have had much of an impact on how Judaism was practiced in those countries. Still, it is likely that these Jews brought recipes with them that, over time, found their way into Yiddish cuisine.

When Sephardic cooks prepare stuffed vegetables they use a minimum of three kinds of vegetables and often more than this. This recipe for *legumbres yaprakes* contains several different examples.

PREPARATION TIME: $3^1/_2$–4 hours
SERVINGS: 8–10

4 each of the following vegetables: small eggplants (3 inches in length, 1–2 inches in width), small zucchini (each 4 inches in length), medium onions (about $1^1/_2$-inches in diameter), medium tomatoes ($1^1/_2$-inches in diameter)
8 small green bell peppers, each 3 inches long and 1 inch wide
8–10 large cabbage leaves
16–18 grape leaves
12 cups stuffing (see below)
Olive oil
Approximately 4 cups Vegetable Stock (page 299)
$1/_3$ cup freshly squeezed lemon juice
Sauces (see below)

1. Cut the eggplants in half. Remove the pulp from the center of the vegetable, chop it, and set aside. Leave enough pulp attached to the skin to create a nice shell.
2. Cut the zucchini in half and remove the pulp from the center, leaving enough of the vegetable to make a shell for stuffing. Chop the pulp and set it aside.
3. Cut the onions in half and scoop out enough of the centers to make an attractive shell. Chop the onion pulp and set it aside.

4. Cut the tomatoes in half and scoop out the centers. Leave enough to make an attractive shell. Chop the tomato pulp and set it aside.

5. Cut around the top of each green bell pepper and remove this cap. Then remove the core and seeds of the peppers. Set each cap on top of the pepper to which it belongs.

6. Bring a large pot of salted water to boil on top of the stove. Blanch the cabbage leaves by cooking them in the salted water for 2–3 minutes or until they soften enough to be able to be used as a wrapping for stuffing. Remove with a slotted spoon and set aside on paper towels to dry.

7. Follow the directions on page 19 for preparing grape leaves for stuffing. Set these aside.

8. Prepare the stuffing for the vegetables according to the directions below. Fill the eggplant halves, zucchini halves, onion halves, and tomato halves full to the top with stuffing. To stuff the peppers, fill them three-fourths of the way with stuffing and place the caps on top of them. Prepare the cabbage leaves by filling each with 2 table-spoons stuffing at the stem end. Fold the ends of the cabbage leaves over the stuffing and roll them into a cylinder shape. To stuff the vine leaves, follow the directions on pages 20–21. Cabbage leaves are rolled the same way vine leaves are rolled but they contain a little more filling. The vegetables will be cooked separately but served all together as a main dish with different sauces.

9. Place the stuffed eggplant halves, zucchini halves, and onion halves in 9 × 13-inch baking pans. Cover the baking pans with foil.

10. Place the tomatoes in their own separate 9 × 12-inch baking pan. Pour enough olive oil into the pan to come halfway up the sides of the tomatoes.

11. Place the peppers into a 2-quart saucepan or casserole in which they will all fit snugly side by side. Put 1 cup vegetable stock into this pot and cover it tightly.

12. In a small $1^1/_2$-quart casserole place the cabbage leaves side by side and add 1 cup vegetable stock to the casserole. Cover tightly.

13. Place the vine leaves in a 2-quart pot. Mix 2 cups stock with the

lemon juice and pour it over the grape leaves. Weight the grape leaves down with several plates.

14. Preheat the oven to 350 degrees. It helps if you have two ovens because you can bake the tomatoes in a separate oven. The tomatoes are cooked separately from the other vegetables because the olive oil prevents them from breaking apart as they cook. Otherwise they will have to be cooked after the other vegetables have finished cooking. Put the stuffed eggplants, zucchini, and onions into the oven and bake for 1 hour. Remove the cover and return to the oven to brown for 15 minutes. Bake the tomatoes uncovered for 1 hour in the oven.

15. While there are vegetables baking in the oven, there will also be some cooking on top of the stove. Bring the three pots containing the stuffed peppers, cabbage leaves, and grape leaves to a boil over medium-high heat. Reduce the heat to simmer and simmer the peppers and cabbage for 1 hour and the grape leaves for $1^1/_2$ hours. The cabbage and peppers could also be cooked inside the oven if there is room for them. Cooking time in the oven would be the same as on top of the stove. The grape leaves are best cooked on top of the stove because they are cooked uncovered. They may be cooked, covered, in the oven if the weights used to weigh them down are ovenproof. Cooking time will be $1^1/_2$ hours.

16. All the stuffed vegetables can be prepared ahead of time and reheated just before serving. They are served warm or at room temperature. Serve the stuffed grape leaves with *agristada* poured over them. The other stuffed vegetables (except for the tomatoes) can be served with either *agristada,* with the sauce made of fresh tomatoes and dill that follows below, or just as they are, unsauced. Do not serve the stuffed tomatoes with the tomato/dill sauce.

SERVING SUGGESTIONS:

Serve the vegetables on platters and put the sauces in sauceboats on the table. Let every diner help himself or herself. Serve the stuffed vegetables with bread. Precede the stuffed vegetables with a selection of appetizers and salads. The following are all good choices: *Borekas* (page 61) or *Buleymas* (page 71) filled with spinach (page 64), *Humus* (page 7), Turkish chopped egg and potato salad (page 8), *Toureto* (page 31), and marinated black and green olives (page 9). Conclude the meal with fresh fruit, a special holiday sweet like *Tishpitti* (page 260), and coffee or mint tea.

Stuffing for Legumbres Yaprakes

PREPARATION TIME: **25 minutes**
YIELD: **12 cups stuffing**

6 tablespoons olive oil
1 large onion, peeled and finely chopped
All of the vegetable pulp saved from preparing the vegetables for stuffing
2 large cloves garlic, peeled and chopped (1 tablespoon)
2 cups long grain white rice, parboiled for 6 minutes
2 pounds lean ground beef
$1/_3$ cup chopped fresh parsley
$1/_4$ cup chopped fresh mint leaves
$1/_2$ cup pine nuts
Salt and freshly ground black pepper

1. In a deep, wide sauté pan, heat the oil over medium-high heat. Sauté the onion until soft and translucent (5–7 minutes).
2. Reduce the heat slightly and add all the vegetable pulp and the garlic. Cook until the vegetables begin to soften. Remove from the heat.
3. Add the rice and meat to the vegetables. Mix together well. Then add the herbs, pine nuts, salt, and pepper. Use as directed in the recipe above.

Sauces for Legumbres Yaprakes

Legumbres yaprakes are served with a fresh tomato sauce with dill, and with *Agristada* (egg/lemon sauce; page 305). To make fresh tomato sauce with dill, heat 2 cups Fresh Tomato Sauce (page 300) and put $1/_4$ cup chopped fresh dill leaves into it. Pour the sauces into sauceboats and serve as directed in the recipe.

Why the Jewish Girl Became a Muslim

A LADINO POEM

Judia? Mas que Judia!
Turca se fue aboltar,
   Por unos negros yaprakitos
Que non los supo bien guizar!

Jewish? She was very Jewish!
   She became a Turk [Muslim]
Only because of some burned *yaprakes*
   That she did not cook very well!

Vegetables
and
Vegetarian
Dishes

Legumbres en Salsa de Tomate (VEGETABLES IN TOMATO SAUCE)

    Eggplant Cooked in Tomato Sauce

Apio (BRAISED CELERY ROOT AND CARROTS)

Anjinara con Aves (BRAISED ARTICHOKES AND FAVA BEANS)

Berenjenna Imam Bayildi or *Berenjenna Rellena* (BAKED STUFFED BABY EGGPLANTS WITH HERBS)

Almadrote de Berenjenna (BAKED EGGPLANT WITH CHEESE)

Keftedes de Prasa (LEEK FRITTERS)

Patata y Sedano (BRAISED POTATOES WITH CELERY)

Braised Chick-Peas with Spinach

Legumbres en Salsa de Tomate

VEGETABLES IN TOMATO SAUCE

 This is a classic Sephardic method of preparing vegetable side dishes. The same sauce is used for a variety of different vegetables including green beans, celery, fennel, leeks, spinach, and zucchini. This method of cooking vegetables also entered the cuisine of Yiddish-speaking Jews via Hungary and Romania, whose cuisines were influenced by Turkey. In the Balkans, paprika is added to the dish and sometimes replaces the chopped parsley. The same method is used for cooking one kind of vegetable or for a combination of fresh vegetables.

PREPARATION TIME: **20–25 minutes**
SERVINGS: **8–10**

1 pound fresh vegetables (green beans, celery, fennel, zucchini, pattypan squash, yellow summer squash, leeks, fresh fava beans, okra)
3 tablespoons olive oil
1 medium onion, peeled and finely chopped
1 large clove garlic, peeled and finely chopped ($^1/_2$ tablespoon)
1 large fresh tomato, peeled, seeded, and finely chopped
$^1/_2$ cup Fresh Tomato Sauce (page 300)
Salt and freshly ground black pepper
Chopped fresh parsley for garnish

1. Prepare the vegetables for cooking. If using green beans, trim the ends. Cut the celery or fennel bulb into $^1/_2$-inch pieces. Cut the zucchini, pattypan, or yellow squash into rounds but do not peel. Trim the leeks of all but 1 inch of the greens and cut in half, washing carefully to remove any sand that is trapped between layers. Fresh fava beans must be shelled and peeled. The stem tips of okra must be cut off but not all the way. If the pod is opened to expose the seeds a viscous liquid will leak out during cooking, which will thicken the sauce and deflate the okra pods.

(continued)

2. Heat the oil in a sauté pan over medium-high heat. Sauté the onion until soft and translucent (5–7 minutes). Reduce the heat slightly and add the garlic. Cook 1 minute more, stirring constantly.

3. Add the chopped fresh tomato and cook 5 minutes more, or until the tomato starts to soften.

4. Add the tomato sauce and mix well. Bring to a boil.

5. Add the vegetable(s) of your choice, combine everything well, and cover the pot. Reduce the heat to simmer and cook 20 minutes or until the vegetables are tender.

6. Sprinkle with salt and black pepper and mix well. Serve the vegetables immediately, sprinkled with chopped parsley.

SERVING SUGGESTIONS:
Serve vegetables cooked in tomato sauce with meats that have been grilled or roasted and do not have a sauce.

VARIATION:
Eggplant Cooked in Tomato Sauce
Use 4 cups cubed, unpeeled eggplant. To prepare it, follow the directions on page 65. Rinse and dry the cubes. Sauté the eggplant quickly in 4–6 tablespoons olive oil before preparing the tomato sauce. Set it aside and proceed with the above recipe, beginning with step 2. Add the sautéed eggplant as directed in step 5.

Apio

BRAISED CELERY ROOT AND CARROTS

 Celery root is a favorite winter vegetable among Greek and Turkish Jews. It is braised in lemon juice, which adds tartness and brings out the natural flavor of the vegetable.

PREPARATION TIME: **40 minutes**
SERVINGS: **8–10**

   5 tablespoons olive or sunflower oil
   2 large celery roots, peeled and cut into $1/_2$-inch cubes (about 4 cups)
   4 cups cut-up, peeled carrots (cut in $1/_2$-inch rounds)
$1/_3$ cup freshly squeezed lemon juice
$1/_3$ cup Vegetable Stock (page 299)
     Salt and freshly ground black pepper
$1/_4$ cup finely chopped fresh parsley

1. In a large, deep sauté pan, heat the oil over medium heat. In batches, sauté the cubes of celery root and the carrots until brown on all sides. Remove to a mixing bowl.
2. When all of the celery root and carrots have been browned, deglaze the pan with the lemon juice and stock, scraping up browned bits with a wooden spoon.
3. Return the vegetables to the pan, cover, turn the heat down to the lowest simmer, and cook $1/_2$ hour.
4. Remove the cover. Most of the liquid will have been absorbed and the vegetables should be well cooked but not mushy. Season with salt and pepper and serve immediately, sprinkled with chopped parsley.

SERVING SUGGESTIONS:

Apio is delicious with roasted or grilled meats. Try it with *Pollo al Forno* (page 125), with either of the roast lamb dishes (pages 151 and 153), or plain roast beef.

VARIATIONS:

The same recipe can be made with other root vegetables such as turnips, rutabagas, parsnips, kohlrabi, or Jerusalem artichokes combined with the carrots. A combination of carrots and celery is also excellent prepared this way.

Anjinara con Aves

BRAISED ARTICHOKES AND FAVA BEANS

 This dish is traditionally prepared with the first fava beans of the season and tiny new artichokes. It is popular in Sicily but its origin is most likely Sephardic, as it is prepared by the Jews of Greece, Turkey, and Egypt. Frozen baby lima beans make an excellent substitute for the fava beans.

This is a seasonal spring dish, sweet with the aroma of fresh dill and garlic. Sephardic Jews traditionally serve it with the roast lamb at the Passover *seder*.

PREPARATION TIME: **1 hour**
SERVINGS: **8–10**

- $^1/_2$ cup cold water
- $^1/_3$ cup freshly squeezed lemon juice
- 1 teaspoon sugar
- 1 large clove garlic, peeled and very finely chopped ($^1/_2$ tablespoon)
- 4 tablespoons olive oil
- 8 small young artichokes, prepared as directed on page 29 and cut in half
- 1 pound fresh fava beans or frozen baby lima beans, thawed
- $^1/_4$ cup finely chopped fresh dill leaves
  Salt and freshly ground black pepper

1. Mix the water, lemon juice, sugar, garlic, and olive oil in a pot that will hold all the vegetables. Bring to a boil and reduce the heat to simmer.
2. Add the artichokes and fresh beans, if using them. Partially cover the pot and cook 45 minutes. If using frozen baby lima beans, add them to the pot after the artichokes have cooked 25 minutes.
3. When the vegetables finish cooking, the liquid in the pot will be considerably reduced. Stir in the dill, salt, and pepper and serve immediately.

SERVING SUGGESTIONS:

This is a perfect vegetable side dish for the roasted lamb recipes on pages 151 and 153.

Berenjenna Imam Bayildi
or Berenjenna Rellena

BAKED STUFFED BABY EGGPLANTS
WITH HERBS

This dish has both an Arabic and a Ladino name. The Ladino name, *berenjenna rellena* (stuffed eggplant), is nondescript. But the Arabic name, *Imam bayildi,* which means "swooning Imam," is rather colorful. An Imam is the spiritual head of the Islamic community. There are different folk tales told about what made the Imam swoon when he tasted this dish. The first theory is that he went into raptures about how exotic the dish appeared and tasted. The second implies that he fainted when he learned how expensive its ingredients were. Both of these theories are ludicrous. The ingredients for *berenjenna Imam bayildi* are simple, basic, and quite inexpensive. In Mediterranean countries the eggplant is as ubiquitous as the potato in Ireland. *Imam bayildi* is, indeed, delicious but hardly exotic. I also suspect that if the first Imam who tasted *berenjenna Imam bayildi* swooned over the price of his dinner, it is probably because he was wondering how a dish this good could be made from ingredients so ordinary and cheap.

I have my own theory about what made the Imam swoon: His manservant got drunk one day on arak (which Muslims are absolutely forbidden to do) and he forgot to go to the market and buy food for his master's dinner. The cook, who was also the manservant's wife, went into a panic—what could she possibly serve that would taste so good the master would never suspect what had happened. She searched through the pantry and found, to her delight, a few little eggplants that were too small to do anything with and too large to pickle, some onions, some garlic, a lemon, and plenty of olive oil. She ran out to the garden and picked some tomatoes. "Oh, phooey!" she muttered. "Not enough ripe ones to make a good sauce . . ." She snipped a few sprigs of parsley. "What can I do with such little eggplants? No sense in slicing them.

There isn't even enough to cover the bottom of a baking dish. Can't peel them. Half the vegetable would end up in the garbage. Can't stuff them with meat. There isn't any." And then came a moment of revelation. A stuffing of vegetables and herbs! "I'll cut them into attractive fan shapes, fill the cracks with vegetables and herbs and make them into delicate little surprise packages. What they lack in substance will be made up by their beautiful appearance!" And so she set to work, creating the eggplant dish that would win such praise from her master that he would swoon with delight! And from that day on, she called it *berenjenna Imam bayildi*, a pantry-shelf-throw-together dish that saved the cook's job and which is sure to win the devotion of any aesthetically inclined gourmet!

SALTING TIME: $1^1/_2$ hours
PREPARATION TIME: 1 hour
SERVINGS: 6–8

10–12 very small eggplants, no more than 6 inches long and no more than $2^1/_2$ inches wide ($1^1/_2$–2 pounds)
Coarse salt
4 tablespoons plus $^1/_2$ cup olive oil
3 medium onions, peeled and very finely chopped
3 large cloves garlic, peeled and finely chopped ($1^1/_2$ tablespoons)
4 medium tomatoes, peeled, seeded, and finely chopped
$^1/_2$ cup finely chopped fresh parsley
Salt and freshly ground black pepper
$^1/_3$ cup freshly squeezed lemon juice
$1^1/_2$ teaspoons sugar
$^1/_3$ cup cold water

1. Cut the eggplants in half and cut slits across the length of each vegetable. Starting at the crown end of the eggplant, cut almost but not quite all the way through the vegetable, leaving $^1/_4$ inch uncut. After the eggplants are cooked, they will be opened up on the stem end into a fan shape.
2. Sprinkle the eggplants with coarse salt on the cut side and lay them, facedown, in a colander in the sink. Cover the top with plastic wrap and lay several plates and cans of food on top to weight down the vegetables. Allow them to rest $1^1/_2$ hours.

3. After the eggplants have rested, remove the plates, cans, and plastic wrap. Rinse and then squeeze them gently to remove the bitter juices. Dry carefully and set aside.

4. While the eggplants are being salted, prepare the stuffing.

5. Preheat the oven to 350 degrees.

6. Heat 4 tablespoons of the oil in a skillet over medium-high heat and sauté the onions until soft and translucent (5–7 minutes). Reduce the heat slightly and add the garlic. Cook 1 minute longer and remove from the heat.

7. Combine the onion and garlic in a mixing bowl with the tomatoes, parsley, salt, and black pepper.

8. Stuff the slits of each eggplant half with the stuffing mixture. Press each stuffed eggplant together and lay it in a 9 × 13-inch baking pan. The stuffed eggplants should all fit snugly in one layer.

9. Whisk together the remaining olive oil, lemon juice, sugar, and water in a bowl and pour it over the eggplants. Bake, uncovered, in the oven for 40–45 minutes or until the eggplants are well cooked and browned. The eggplants may be served hot or at room temperature. Serve one or two stuffed eggplants per person. When serving, gently open up the crown end and arrange the eggplant spread out like a fan.

SERVING SUGGESTIONS:

Berenjenna Imam bayildi can be served as an entree with *Pilafi de Spinaca* (page 208) or as a vegetable side dish with roasted or grilled meat. *Kodredo al Forno* (page 151) and meat kebabs (page 157) are good choices. It is also excellent as part of a vegetarian buffet.

Almadrote de Berenjenna

BAKED EGGPLANT WITH CHEESE

This vegetarian entree has many variations. In some, the eggplant is baked and then peeled and mixed with eggs, onions, tomatoes, cheese, and herbs and then baked again into a kind of quiche. In other recipes, the cheese and eggs are used to make a stuffing mixture for eggplant halves. This version is light, does not require a great deal of oil for frying, and makes attractive individual portions. It is also one of the few eggplant recipes that does not require preliminary salting.

PREPARATION TIME: **50 minutes**
SERVINGS: **6–8**

- 3 large, round-shaped eggplants (about 1 pound each)
  Oil for brushing plus 4 tablespoons olive oil
- 1 large onion, peeled and finely chopped
- 2 large cloves garlic, peeled and finely chopped (1 tablespoon)
- 1 cup freshly grated imported Parmesan cheese
- 1 cup crumbled feta, soft, white kasseri, or brynza cheese
- 1 cup grated kashkaval cheese
- $1/3$ cup finely chopped fresh parsley
- $1/4$ cup finely chopped fresh mint leaves
  Salt and freshly ground black pepper
- 3 large eggs, beaten
- 1 cup Fresh Tomato Sauce (page 300)

1. Preheat the broiler.
2. Remove the stem end of the eggplants and slice widthwise into $1/4$-inch slices. Place the eggplant slices on a broiler rack and brush the tops with olive oil. Broil 5 minutes. Turn slices over and brush again. Broil another 5 minutes. Repeat this step with all the eggplant slices until all of them are browned.
3. Heat 4 tablespoons olive oil in a skillet over medium-high heat. Sauté the onion until soft and translucent (5–7 minutes). Add the garlic, lower the heat slightly, and cook 2 minutes longer. Remove from the heat.

4. Combine the cheeses, parsley, mint, onion mixture from skillet, salt, and black pepper together in a mixing bowl. Add two beaten egg and mix again.

5. Preheat the oven to 350 degrees.

6. Lay half the browned eggplant slices in a baking dish. Spread some of the cheese mixture on top of each slice and top with the remaining slices, making eggplant sandwiches.

7. Beat the tomato sauce together with the two remaining eggs and pour over the eggplant.

8. Bake the stuffed eggplant sandwiches in the oven for 30–35 minutes or until the top is nicely browned and the eggs are set. Serve immediately.

SERVING SUGGESTIONS:

This delicious vegetarian entree is usually served all by itself with crusty Mediterranean bread. A tossed green salad can precede or be served together with the entree. *Salata de Verdura* (page 36) is a good choice. Precede the dinner with *Olivada* (page 12), *Ajada* (page 3), or *Ajada de Aves* (page 5) accompanied by crisp raw vegetables for an appetizer. Conclude the dinner with baklava, fresh fruit, and coffee.

Keftedes de Prasa

LEEK FRITTERS

 The ancient Hebrews learned about leeks, cucumbers, onions, and garlic from the ancient Egyptians and, in their migrations, brought these vegetables to Iberia and other parts of the Mediterranean. Garlic and onions were so loved by Jewish cooks that they came to be associated with Jewish cooking in many parts of Europe. In Eastern and Central Europe, where garlic was disdained and onion used sparingly, these plants were called "Jewish" plants because Jewish cooks continued to use them lavishly.

Keftedes de prasa is a traditional Passover dish in both Greek and Turkish Sephardic communities. Fritters made of various kinds of herbs and aromatic vegetables are loved by the Sephardic Jews for their clean, fresh taste. These leek fritters are very delicate.

PREPARATION TIME: **25 minutes**
SERVINGS: **8–10**

- 2 pounds leeks (whites and first 2 inches of greens)
- 4 large eggs
- 1 cup mashed boiled potatoes
- $1/2$ cup *matzoh* meal or $1/4$ cup *matzoh* meal and $1/4$ cup grated pecorino cheese
- 1 teaspoon salt
  Freshly ground black pepper
  Peanut oil for sautéing
  Lemon wedges for garnish

1. Trim and carefully wash the leeks, going between the layers to remove all the sand and dirt. Slice the leeks thinly.
2. Bring 2 quarts salted water to a boil. Parboil the leeks for 3 minutes. Drain and place the leeks in a mixing bowl. The leeks can also be parboiled in the microwave in just enough salted water to come to the top of the vegetables. Cook covered in microwave for $2^1/2$ minutes. Drain and put into the bowl.
3. Combine all the remaining ingredients except the oil and lemon wedges with the leeks.
4. Heat $1/4$ inch oil in a 12-inch skillet. Form a patty out of $1/4$ cup of the leek mixture. Place in the sizzling oil. Repeat until you have three or four fritters cooking. Sauté on both sides until golden brown, turning only once during cooking. Drain the fritters on paper towels after removing them from the oil. Serve garnished with lemon wedges.

Keftedes de prasa make a delicious appetizer. They go well with simple grilled or roasted meats or fish or with dishes that are cooked in tomato-based sauces. *Pescado Ahilado con Tomate* (page 108), *Pollo con Berenjenna* (page 132), *Sopado con Bamias* (page 166), or *Sopado de Kodredo à la Morisco* (page 168) are all good choices. Do not use cheese in the fritters if serving them with a meat entree.

Patata y Sedano

BRAISED POTATOES WITH CELERY

In this dish, the tomato-based braising stock brings out a subtle, earthy freshness in both the potatoes and the celery. Celery contains a lot of natural sodium, which enhances the smooth, mellow taste of the potatoes and, at the same time, is softened and balanced by it.

PREPARATION TIME: **35 minutes**
SERVINGS: 8–10

4 tablespoons olive oil
1 small onion, peeled and finely chopped
6 large stalks celery, cut into 1-inch chunks
2 cups Vegetable Stock (page 299)
$1/_2$ cup Fresh Tomato Sauce (page 300)
1 bay leaf
3 large red boiling potatoes (2 pounds), peeled and cut into small chunks
Salt and freshly ground black pepper
$1/_4$ cup finely chopped fresh parsley

1. In a deep, wide saucepan, heat the oil over medium-high heat. Sauté the onions until soft and translucent (5–7 minutes).
2. Reduce the heat slightly and add the celery pieces. Sauté another 2 minutes, stirring constantly.
3. Add the stock to the pan, scraping up any browned bits that cling to the bottom with a wooden spoon.
4. Add the tomato sauce, bay leaf, and potatoes. Bring to a boil and reduce the heat to the lowest simmer. Partially cover the pot and simmer gently for 20–25 minutes or until the potatoes are done.
5. Stir in the salt and black pepper and discard the bay leaf before serving. Serve sprinkled with chopped parsley.

SERVING SUGGESTIONS:

This is one of the most delicious side dishes to accompany roasted or grilled meats. Try it with *Pollo al Forno* (page 125), *Pollo Relleno con Trahanas* (page 142), or *Kodredo al Forno* (page 151).

VARIATIONS:

Substitute two fennel bulbs for the celery in this dish. Cut the fennel bulb into 1-inch slices and cook as directed above. Fennel is sweetly aromatic and a lovely foil for the mellow potatoes. Add $^1/_4$ cup chopped fennel leaves during the last 5 minutes of cooking. Another variation is to substitute for the celery 2 cups Swiss chard stalks cut into 1-inch pieces. Cook as directed above.

Braised Chick-Peas with Spinach

 This vegetable dish is popular in Turkey and Syria. It is eaten as a main dish stew together with rice pilav. Swiss chard leaves or any of the Southern greens such as collards, mustard greens, or turnip greens can be substituted for the spinach in this recipe for an interesting, if nontraditional, variation. If using the Southern greens, they must first be chopped and cooked before being added to the chick-peas. Swiss chard leaves can be treated exactly like spinach.

SOAKING TIME (CHICK-PEAS): **12 hours or overnight**
PREPARATION TIME: **2 hours**
SERVINGS: **8–10**

- 1 pound dried chick-peas
- 4 tablespoons olive oil
- 1 large onion, peeled and finely chopped
- 1 large clove garlic, peeled and finely chopped ($^1/_2$ tablespoon)
- $^1/_2$ teaspoon Hungarian hot paprika
- 1 teaspoon ground cumin
- 2 pounds fresh spinach
- 1 teaspoon sugar
   Salt and freshly ground black pepper
   Leftover *Huevos Haminados* (page 231) or hard-boiled eggs, sliced into wedges for garnish

1. Soak the chick-peas in water to cover by 1 inch overnight. Drain, rinse, and put into a stockpot. Cover with fresh cold water by 1 inch and bring to a boil. Reduce heat to simmer and cook chick-peas, partially covered, for $1^3/_4$ hours.

2. When the chick-peas have 20 minutes left to cook, heat the oil over medium heat in another stockpot. Sauté the onion until soft and translucent (5–7 minutes). Reduce the heat slightly and add the garlic, paprika, and cumin. Cook, stirring constantly until the spices start to give off an aroma (about 2 minutes).

3. Add 1 ladleful of the water in which the chick-peas are cooking to this stockpot and deglaze, scraping up any browned bits with a wooden spoon.

4. Add the spinach to the pot and cover. Reduce the heat to the lowest simmer.

5. Drain the chick-peas and add them to the pot in which the spinach is cooking. By this time the spinach leaves should be wilting. Stir everything well to combine and, as soon as the spinach leaves have wilted,

remove the pot from the heat. Season with salt and black pepper to taste and serve immediately, garnished with sliced *huevos haminados* or hard-boiled eggs.

SERVING SUGGESTIONS:

Serve chick-peas and spinach with *Arroz Pilafi* (page 204) or saffron rice pilav (page 205). Serve *Ajada* (page 3), *Olivada* (page 12), or *Toureto* (page 31) accompanied by raw vegetables to dip as an appetizer before the entree. Finish the meal with baklava and coffee.

Okra? Phew . . . !!

A SEPHARDIC FOLK TALE

Once there was a vegetable merchant from Istanbul who did business all over Turkey and its provinces. One day he got a telegram from one of his customers in Cairo asking the price of vegetables. He dictated prices to his clerk—zucchini, twenty dinars; tomatoes, thirty dinars; spinach, forty dinars; eggplant, fifteen dinars. As he dictated, his clerk wrote. When the merchant finished, his clerk asked him, "And what is the price of okra?"

"Okra? Phew . . . !!"

The clerk wrote it all down and sent a telegram down to Cairo. A few days later a purchase order came in from Cairo. It listed every price but the price of okra. Next to the word "okra," it said, "You did not give me the price of okra. What does it mean, 'Okra? Phew . . . !!'"

The merchant called in his clerk and asked, "What kind of a stupid thing did you write down in the telegram?"

"When I asked you what the price of okra was, all you said was, 'Okra? Phew . . . !!'"

"Stupid idiot! Okra is expensive, but it has a price, just like everything else. Now you have to send another telegram to Cairo to give them the price of okra!"

From that day on, "Okra? Phew . . . !!" has been used by merchants in Turkey to state the value of okra.

Rice and Grain Dishes

Pilafi (SEPHARDIC-STYLE RICE PILAV)

    Arroz Pilafi (PLAIN RICE PILAV)

    Pilafi con Piniones (RICE PILAV WITH PINE NUTS OR ALMONDS)

    Pilafi con Cibollas Fritas (ONION RICE PILAV)

    Arroz de Sabato (SABBATH RICE PILAV WITH SAFFRON)

    Pilafi con Berenjenna (EGGPLANT RICE PILAV)

    Pilafi con Tomata (TOMATO RICE PILAV)

    Pilafi de Spinaca (SPINACH RICE PILAV)

Mujeddra (ARABIC-STYLE RICE PILAV WITH LENTILS)

Carolina Perloo

Arroz con Fidellos (RICE PILAV WITH ANGEL HAIR PASTA)

Fidellos Tostados (TOASTED FIDELLOS)

Couscous

    Basic Couscous

    Couscous con Siete Legumbres (COUSCOUS WITH SEVEN VEGETABLES)

    Couscous à la Mode du Tangier (COUSCOUS, TANGIER STYLE)

    Cuscussu (TUNISIAN-STYLE COUSCOUS WITH FISH)

Pilafi de Trahanas (BULGUR PILAV)

Pilafi

SEPHARDIC-STYLE RICE PILAV

Rice is one of the three standard grains of Sephardic cooking and by far the most popular and widespread. The other two are bulgur and couscous, both forms of wheat. Rice dishes were brought from Spain into the Ottoman Empire, Italy, and Egypt. Morocco, Algeria, Tunisia, and Lybia are the only countries settled by Sephardic Jews where another grain, couscous, was more important than rice. In these countries as well, rice was prepared by Jewish cooks.

The favorite method of cooking rice in the Sephardic kitchen is a pilav. Food historian Karen Hess devotes three chapters in *The Carolina Rice Kitchen* (University of South Carolina Press, 1992) to the subject of pilav and its variations. She states that Persian and later Sephardic Jews were most likely responsible for popularizing rice pilav dishes throughout Europe and the Americas. Hess also offers two Jewish recipes for "rice pilau," both of which contain saffron and aromatic spices like nutmeg and bay leaves.

While the classic method of cooking the rice is on top of the stove, I prefer to bake my *pilaf* or *pilafi* in the oven. The aroma of the dish is heightened and the flavors are strengthened by this method of preparation.

Good *pilaf* contains four basic ingredients—rice, stock, oil, and salt. Other things can be added for variety, like saffron, pine nuts, or vegetables. Cooks disagree on when to add the oil to the *pilaf*. Some put it in when the liquid is added. Others pour it in at the end, just before all the liquid has been absorbed by the grain. Others sauté the grains in the oil at the beginning, just before adding the liquid. All three methods work well.

There is also considerable disagreement among Sephardic cooks as to whether or not the grains need to be washed before cooking to remove the excess starch. Washing the grains before cooking them will result in a *pilaf* in which every grain is separate and none stick together.

However, this applies only to white rice. Brown rice contains bran as well as starch and it makes no sense to wash the grain and remove the bran along with the starch.

Here are several kinds of rice pilav, which I hope you will enjoy. The first dish is the most basic rice pilav, made only with rice, olive oil, stock, and salt. The second and third are variations of the first and add the flavors of nuts or sautéed onions. *Arroz de Sabato* is the classic saffron rice that has been served for centuries by Sephardic Jews for the Sabbath.

Arroz Pilafi
(Plain Rice Pilav)

DRYING TIME (RICE): **20 minutes**
PREPARATION TIME: **1 hour**
YIELD: **4 cups cooked rice**
SERVINGS: **6–8**

2 cups long grain white or brown rice
3 tablespoons olive oil
1 scant teaspoon salt
4–5 cups chicken stock or Vegetable Stock (page 299)

1. Preheat the oven to 350 degrees.
2. If using white rice you will need 4 cups stock. If using brown rice, you will use 5 cups stock.
3. If using white rice, place the rice in a colander and rinse it in the sink in cold water until the water runs clear. Allow the rice to drain and dry for 20 minutes. If using brown rice skip this step.
4. Over medium heat, heat the olive oil in a casserole with a tight-fitting lid. Sauté the rice in the oil until it starts to brown.
5. Sprinkle the salt over the rice and pour in the stock. Cover tightly and place in the oven. Bake for 35–40 minutes (white rice) to 1 hour (brown rice). When the *pilaf* is done, all of the liquid will have been absorbed. A lovely earthy aroma will fill the room when you open the lid of the pot. Serve immediately as a side dish with a meat, fish, or vegetarian entree.

Pilafi con Piniones
(Rice Pilav with Pine Nuts or Almonds)

> DRYING TIME (RICE): **20 minutes**
> PREPARATION TIME: **1 hour**
> YIELD: **4 cups cooked rice**
> SERVINGS: **6–8**

Toast $^1/_3$ cup pine nuts or slivered blanched almonds on a cookie sheet in a 350-degree oven for 10–12 minutes or in a dry skillet on top of the stove for 12–15 minutes. Prepare rice pilav as directed above. Add the nuts to the casserole together with the stock before baking in the oven. Serve as a side dish with a meat, fish, or vegetarian entree.

Pilafi con Cibollas Fritas
(Onion Rice Pilav)

> DRYING TIME (RICE): **20 minutes**
> PREPARATION TIME: **1 hour**
> YIELD: **4 cups cooked rice**
> SERVINGS: **6–8**

In a casserole, sauté 1 medium onion, peeled and thinly sliced, in the olive oil until golden brown. Do not sauté the rice in the oil for this recipe. Add the stock and salt before adding the rice. Bake in the oven as directed above. Serve as a side dish with a meat, fish, or vegetarian entree.

Arroz de Sabato
(Sabbath Rice Pilav with Saffron)

> DRYING TIME (RICE): **20 minutes**
> PREPARATION TIME: **1 hour**
> YIELD: **4 cups cooked rice**
> SERVINGS: **6–8**

Add 1 bay leaf and $^1/_4$ teaspoon saffron threads dissolved in $^1/_4$ cup boiling water to the rice together with the stock. Cook as directed above. The rice gets a beautiful yellow color and a heady aroma from the saffron and bay leaf. The bay leaf will be resting on top of the rice at the end of cooking. Remove and discard it before serving. Serve as a side dish with a meat, fish, or vegetarian entree.

Pilafi con Berenjenna
(Eggplant Rice Pilav)

This is the only rice pilav recipe I never make in the oven. I do it on top of the stove because of the special steaming process at the end. I also make this one only with white rice because it looks more appealing than brown rice.

SALTING TIME (EGGPLANT): **$1^1/_2$ hours**
PREPARATION TIME: **1 hour**
YIELD: **$5^1/_2$ cups cooked pilav**
SERVINGS: **6–8**

1 medium eggplant ($^3/_4$ pound)
  Coarse salt
  Olive oil
2 cups long grain white rice
  Salt
  4 cups chicken stock or Vegetable Stock (page 299)

1. Cut the unpeeled eggplant into 1-inch chunks. Place them in a colander and sprinkle with the coarse salt. Cover with plastic wrap and weight the eggplant down with several plates. Allow it to rest $1^1/_2$ hours. While the eggplant is resting, place the rice in another colander and rinse it with cold water until the water runs clear. Leave it to drain and dry over the sink.

2. Remove the plates and plastic wrap and rinse the eggplant. Gently squeeze to remove the bitter juices and dry on paper towels.

3. Heat $^1/_4$ inch olive oil in a 4-quart pot in which you will cook the pilav and sauté the eggplant cubes, a few at a time, over medium-high heat until browned. Put the eggplant on paper towels to dry.

4. Add the rice to the oil that remains in the pot and cook over medium-high heat for 2 minutes.

5. Sprinkle the rice with the salt and add the stock. Reduce the heat to simmer and cook the rice 12 minutes. The rice will be partially cooked and some liquid will be left in the pot.

6. Add the eggplant and push it down into the rice. Place a clean cloth on top of the pot. Cover the pot and drape the overhanging ends of the cloth over the cover. Turn the heat down to the lowest simmer and

steam the rice for 15 minutes. The cloth will absorb all of the moisture that the rice doesn't. The eggplant will add its moisture and flavor to the rice. The result will be a pilav where every grain is puffed out and separate. A most interesting and tasty dish!

SERVING SUGGESTIONS:
This dish may be served alongside plain grilled or roasted meats or fish or as a main dish accompanied by yogurt and a legume puree like *Ajada de Aves* (page 5).

Pilafi con Tomata
(Tomato Rice Pilav)
In this dish, the pilav cooks in a mixture of fresh tomato sauce, herbs, and stock.

> PREPARATION TIME: **1 hour**
> YIELD: $4^1/_2$ cups cooked pilav
> SERVINGS: **6–8**

>   3 tablespoons olive oil
>   1 medium onion, peeled and thinly sliced
>   1 large clove garlic, peeled and finely chopped
>   2 cups long grain white or brown rice
> $^1/_2$ teaspoon salt
> 2 or $2^1/_2$ cups Vegetable Stock (page 299)
> 2 or $2^1/_2$ cups Fresh Tomato Sauce (page 300)
>   1 bay leaf

1. Preheat the oven to 350 degrees.
2. Heat the oil in a casserole with a tight-fitting lid over medium-high heat. Sauté the onion until soft and translucent (5–7 minutes).
3. Reduce the heat slightly and add the garlic and rice. Sauté for 2 minutes longer.
4. Add the salt, stock and tomato sauce (2 cups if using white rice, $2^1/_2$ cups if using brown rice), and bay leaf. Cover the pot and place in the oven. Bake 35–40 minutes for white rice or 1 hour for brown. Remove from the oven, discard the bay leaf, and serve immediately. The rice pilav will have a beautiful red color, and all of the liquid will have been absorbed.

This rice pilav goes particularly well with an entree that is cooked with green vegetables like spinach, zucchini, or green herbs like dill and fennel.

Pilafi de Spinaca
(Spinach Rice Pilav)

DRYING TIME (RICE): **20 minutes**
PREPARATION TIME: **1 hour**
YIELD: **4^1/$_2$ cups pilav**
SERVINGS: **6–8**

- 2 cups long grain white rice
- 3 tablespoons olive oil
- 1 small onion, peeled and chopped
- 1 pound finely shredded fresh spinach
- 4 cups chicken stock or Vegetable Stock (page 299)
  Salt

1. Place the rice in a colander and rinse it over the sink with cold water until the water runs clear. Allow to drain and dry 20 minutes.
2. Preheat the oven to 350 degrees.
3. Over medium heat, heat the oil in a casserole with a tight-fitting lid. Sauté the onion until soft and translucent (5–7 minutes).
4. Add the rice and reduce the heat slightly. Cook 2 more minutes.
5. Stir in the shredded spinach and pour in the stock and salt. Cover the casserole and place it in the oven. Bake 35–40 minutes. Remove from the oven and serve immediately. The rice will be flecked with bits of cooked spinach and all of the liquid will have been absorbed. Because of the long cooking time, the spinach will not have a bright green color. It will be dark green.

SERVING SUGGESTIONS:
This pilav is good with dishes cooked in tomato-based sauces and fish dishes served with *Agristada* (page 305). The spinach adds a savory accent to the oven-roasted grains.

Mujeddra

ARABIC-STYLE RICE PILAV WITH LENTILS

 Mujeddra is an Arabic dish that is much loved by the Jews of Egypt, Syria, and Lebanon. It is a traditional Thursday night dish in many Middle Eastern Jewish homes because it is filling and easy to prepare, freeing the cook to work on preparing the food for the Sabbath. *Mujeddra* is very healthy as well as flavorful because the lentils provide protein and the brown rice, fiber.

PREPARATION TIME: $2^1/_2$ hours
SERVINGS: 6–8

10	cups cold water
1	pound dried brown lentils
6	tablespoons olive oil
1	large onion, peeled and finely chopped
1	medium carrot, peeled and grated
1	large clove garlic, peeled and finely chopped ($^1/_2$ tablespoon)
$^1/_4$	teaspoon ground coriander seeds
$^1/_4$	teaspoon ground allspice
$^1/_4$	teaspoon ground cinnamon
2	cups long grain brown rice
1	bay leaf
	Salt and freshly ground black pepper
2	medium sweet red onions, peeled and very thinly sliced
$^1/_4$	cup finely chopped fresh parsley for garnish

1. Bring 6 cups cold water to a boil in a large stockpot over high heat. Add the lentils, reduce the heat to simmer, and cook for 45 minutes.

2. While the lentils are cooking, heat 3 tablespoons olive oil in a skillet over medium-high heat. Sauté the onion until soft and translucent (5–7 minutes).

3. Add the grated carrot and cook 5 minutes, stirring constantly.

4. Add the garlic, coriander, allspice, and cinnamon. Cook 5 minutes, stirring constantly. Remove from the heat. When the lentils have cooked 45 minutes, add this mixture to them.

5. Add the rice, bay leaf, and 4 cups more water to the lentil mixture. Reduce the heat to simmer and cover the pot tightly. Cook $1\frac{1}{4}$ hours.

6. While the rice and lentils are cooking, heat the remaining oil in a skillet over medium-high heat. Sauté the thinly sliced red onion until golden brown. Remove from the heat.

7. When the rice has finished cooking, add the salt and pepper. Allow the dish to rest 10 minutes so that all liquid will be absorbed before it is served. Remove and discard the bay leaf, which will be resting on top of the *mujeddra,* and serve, sprinkled with the golden brown sautéed onions and finely chopped parsley.

SERVING SUGGESTIONS:

This delicious one-dish casserole should be served with thick yogurt and sliced tomatoes and cucumbers or a green salad. Conclude the meal with fresh fruit, Sephardic cookies, and mint tea or coffee.

VARIATION:

For a variation in seasoning, replace the coriander, allspice, and cinnamon with 1 teaspoon roasted, ground cumin seeds and $\frac{1}{4}$ teaspoon cayenne pepper.

Carolina Perloo

Perloo is a Southern American dish with a colorful and interesting Sephardic Jewish past. The word "perloo" is a colloquialism for "pilau," a Middle Eastern rice dish. Pilau or, as Sephardic Jews call it, *pilaf* or *pilafi* was popular throughout the Mediterranean. The original pilau was made from long grain white rice that was washed and presoaked to remove excess starch and then simmered gently in a spicy, aromatic stock. When done, the rice was golden-colored, glistening with oil, and every grain was perfectly separated. A Sephardic version of this dish, *Arroz de Sabato,* is found on page 205.

This venerable recipe underwent many permutations over the centuries, traveling first throughout the Islamic world and Europe and then going with the Spanish to the Americas. From the simple saffron rice pilau, the Spanish created *paella,* a saffron rice pilav with chicken, shellfish, vegetables, and herbs. The Spanish Jews prepared *Arroz con Pollo* (page 138), a kosher version of *paella* which leaves out the shellfish. Variations of pilau traveled everywhere the Spanish—Jewish or Catholic—settled. It went to the Spanish colonies in the West Indies and eventually made it to the Southern United States. In Louisiana pilau turned up as jambalaya. In Carolina it became "perloo." By the time the recipe traveled across the Atlantic, tomatoes had been added to the dish. The Caribbean version of *Arroz con Pollo* on page 140, which contains both saffron and tomatoes, reflects this change. Saffron, an expensive spice and difficult to get, was eventually left out of the American recipes altogether.

In Inquisition-dominated Spain and its American colonies, bacon or salt pork was also added to the recipe. Jewish and Muslim converts to Catholicism were forced by the Inquisition to prove that their conversions were sincere by eating pork, which is a forbidden food in both the Jewish and Muslim religions. Pork appeared in many of the new Spanish dishes of the time because the eating of pork was a way to prove to the Inquisition that one was a sincere Christian. Pork and pork products like ham became a common ingredient in the new pilau dishes as well, especially those of the Spanish colonies in Latin America and the Southern United States. Southern cooks are very inventive and have created many kinds of perloos and jambalayas using herbs and spices, green peppers, fruits, seafood, and all kinds of meats.

Here is my recipe for a kosher Carolina perloo. I've tried to stay true to some of the more important Carolina traditions, like using long grain white rice and washing the rice carefully so that the grains will be kept dry and separate during cooking. But pork and shellfish are missing, for obvious reasons. Use this recipe as a guideline and be inventive yourself. You'll never get bored with perloo. It provides endless opportunities for the creative cook.

PREPARATION TIME: $1^1/_2$ hours
SERVINGS: 6–8

One $3^1/_2$–4-pound chicken
  8 cups chicken stock
  2 cups long grain white rice
  4 tablespoons corn oil
  1 large onion, peeled and very finely chopped
  2 large stalks celery, finely diced
  1 large clove garlic, peeled and very finely chopped ($^1/_2$ tablespoon)
  4 very large, meaty tomatoes, peeled, seeded, and finely chopped
  1 large kosher knackwurst, thinly sliced
  1 tablespoon fresh thyme leaves
  1 tablespoon minced fresh tarragon leaves
  1 bay leaf
  4 scallions, very thinly sliced
$^1/_2$ cup finely chopped fresh parsley plus additional for garnish
$^1/_8$ teaspoon cayenne pepper
    Dash Tabasco sauce
    Freshly ground black pepper
  1 teaspoon salt

1. Wash and dry the chicken, setting the giblets aside for another purpose. Bring the stock to a rapid boil over high heat in a stockpot. Add the chicken and boil rapidly for 30 minutes. If necessary, skim off any scum that rises to the top with a slotted skimming spoon and discard. Remove the chicken from the stock and cool both to room temperature. Up to this point, the dish can be made in advance. It is actually preferable to do this a day before you make the perloo, because the stock can be skimmed of fat after it is chilled and the meat from the chicken will be easy to remove from the bones when the meat is cold.

2. Put the rice into a sieve and wash with cold water, rubbing your fingers over the grains, to wash away the extra starch. Set the sieve over a mixing bowl and let the rice rest while you prepare the chicken and the casserole.

3. Remove the skin from the chicken and take the meat off the bones. Discard the skin and bones and cut the meat into bite-sized chunks. Put it into a mixing bowl.

4. In a casserole with a tight-fitting lid, heat the oil over medium-high heat. Sauté the onion until soft and translucent (5–7 minutes).

5. Reduce the heat slightly and add the celery and garlic. Cook, stirring constantly, until the celery begins to soften.

6. Add the tomatoes, knackwurst, thyme, tarragon, bay leaf, scallions, parsley, cayenne, Tabasco, black pepper, and salt. Mix together well and cook 5–10 minutes, stirring constantly.

7. Add the chicken pieces and rice and mix again.

8. Pour in 4 cups of the reserved chicken stock. Do not stir again. Reduce the heat to simmer, cover the pot tightly, and cook for 30–35 minutes. When the perloo is done, the liquid will have been completely absorbed by the rice and each grain will be separate and glistening. Discard the bay leaf and serve immediately, sprinkled with fresh chopped parsley.

SERVING SUGGESTIONS:

Carolina perloo is an entree served all on its own. For a real Southern-style dinner, make biscuits, corn bread, and pureed sweet potatoes to accompany the perloo. Serve a tossed green salad before the main course. Conclude the meal with a seasonal fruit pie and coffee.

Arroz con Fidellos

RICE PILAV WITH ANGEL HAIR PASTA

 Fidellos are a Sephardic pasta that resembles angel hair pasta (which is what the word *fidellos* means) or vermicelli. They are prepared in two different ways—cooked together with rice in a pilav or on their own as *fidellos tostados.*

To prepare *arroz con fidellos*, simply cook $^1/_2$ pound angel hair pasta or vermicelli in rapidly boiling salted water for 10–12 minutes or until it is *al dente*. Then drain it and toss it together with 4 cups of *Arroz Pilafi* (page 204) as soon as the rice comes out of the oven. Then, *voilà! Arroz con fidellos!*

This recipe for *arroz con fidellos* serves, as a side dish, 6–8 or more, if the diners have smaller appetites. Use *arroz con fidellos* in a menu the same way you would use an *arroz pilafi*.

Fidellos Tostados

TOASTED FIDELLOS

 Toasted *fidellos* is a very old Spanish-Jewish dish that survived in the Jewish kitchens of Latin America. The preliminary toasting of the pasta is actually a sautéing in olive oil and it imparts a nutty flavor to the finished dish.

PREPARATION TIME: **25–30 minutes**
SERVINGS: **6–8**

$^1/_3$ cup plus 2 tablespoons olive oil
  1 pound angel hair pasta or vermicelli, broken into 2-inch pieces
  1 medium onion, peeled and finely chopped
  3 very large, meaty tomatoes, peeled, seeded, and chopped or 16 ounces good quality canned tomatoes, chopped
  1 teaspoon salt
  4 cups cold water

1. Heat $^1/_3$ cup oil in a deep, wide sauté pan over medium heat and brown the pasta in the oil until it is golden brown. Remove it with a slotted spoon and set aside.

2. Heat the remaining 2 tablespoons oil in a large deep saucepan over medium-high heat. Sauté the onion until translucent (5–7 minutes).

3. Add the tomatoes and salt, stirring constantly until the tomatoes begin to soften (about 10 minutes).

4. Add the cold water and bring to a boil. Then add the pasta and reduce the heat to low. Simmer, partially covered, about 15–18 minutes, stirring from time to time to prevent the pasta from sticking. When all the liquid is absorbed, the dish is done. Remove from the heat and allow the flavors to meld together and the pasta to solidify into a cake. Turn it onto a flat plate and serve, cut into wedges as a side dish. *Fidellos tostados* can be served warm or at room temperature.

SERVING SUGGESTIONS:

Fidellos tostados is a delicious side dish with just about anything that does not contain a tomato-based sauce. Try it with *Pollo al Forno* (page 125) or with *Kodredo al Forno* (page 151). It can also be eaten as a vegetarian entree with a tossed green salad.

Couscous

Couscous is the national dish of Morocco. The main ingredient, a grain, is semolina (durum wheat), which is cooked by steaming. The steaming is done in a special pot called a *couscousière,* a type of steamer pot fitted with a small tray with holes in it that holds the grain in place and steams it while it sits above simmering liquid. The liquid is usually a stew made of vegetables, meat, and spices but *couscous* can also be steamed over plain water. The *couscousière* is widely available in housewares stores or by mail order. However, this pot is not absolutely necessary for preparing good *couscous*. An ordinary steamer pot, a steamer tray, or a colander set above a stockpot works just as well, provided that it fits tightly into the pot and rests high enough away from the bottom of the pot to prevent any contact between the liquid and the grains of *couscous*. The important thing to keep in mind about cooking *couscous* is that no water vapor can escape during cooking. All of the vapor should be directed upward through the holes of the colander and into the grains.

The method of cooking the *couscous* follows an orderly procedure that must be strictly adhered to. If you do this correctly, you can prepare a large variety of dishes using *couscous* and be very creative as well. To serve *couscous* as a grain side dish, follow the procedure outlined below, using plain water instead of the stew.

Basic Couscous

PREPARATION TIME: **1 hour**
SERVINGS: **6–8**

  2 cups *couscous*
$6^1/_2$ cups cold water
    Olive oil
    Salt (optional)

1. The grains of *couscous* should be soaked and washed. Put the grains in a mixing bowl. Pour a ratio of three parts water to one part grain over the *couscous* grains. Stir the grains quickly after you pour the water over them. Then, pour the excess water out of the bowl; most of the water will be discarded. The grain will absorb a little of the water left in the bowl. After you pour the water off, let the grains rest 10 minutes. They will swell a little.
2. After 10 minutes have passed, wet your hands and work them gently but thoroughly through the grains, breaking up any lumps that have formed.
3. Have the stockpot you are going to use for steaming the grain close at hand. Fill it half full with cold water if you are preparing the *couscous* as a grain side dish and bring the water to a steady boil. If you are preparing the *couscous* with a stew, the stew will already have been

cooking in this pot for a while. If you are using a *couscousière,* this next step is simple. Place the steamer tray on top of the stockpot. Gently dribble the *couscous* grains into the steamer tray. Do not cover the pot. Steam 20 minutes, remove the tray, and pour the *couscous* back into the mixing bowl. If you are using a makeshift *couscousière* made of a colander or steamer tray, place a damp towel around the rim of the stockpot and rest the colander or steamer tray on the towel.

4. Pour the remaining $^1/_2$ cup cold water over the grains. Pour a little olive oil over your hands. Then mix the grains gently with your oiled hands, breaking up any lumps that have formed in the grains. The grains will absorb both the water and the oil. If you wish, you may add a little salt at this point. When you have finished mixing the grains, let them rest for 10 minutes.

5. Repeat step 3, cooking the *couscous* for another 20 minutes. After this final steaming, the *couscous* can be served.

There are many variations on the recipe for *couscous.* Morocco alone has so many that entire books have been written about it. (See *Couscous and Other Good Food from Morocco* by Paula Wolfert [Harper & Row, 1973].) While Moroccan recipes are complex and subtly flavored, Tunisian *couscous* dishes are very spicy and robust. Here are three different *couscous* recipes:

Couscous con Siete Legumbres
(*Couscous* with Seven Vegetables)

Couscous with seven vegetables, also called in French *couscous au sept legumes,* is traditionally served on Rosh Hashono by the Jews of Fez, Morocco. The number seven is considered lucky, and since Rosh Hashono occurs on the first and second days of *Tishri,* the seventh month of the Hebrew calendar, a dish with seven different vegetables is felt to be lucky.

Rabbinic tradition teaches that Rosh Hashono is the date of the first day of Creation of the world. According to Jewish belief, the world was created in six cycles (Days of Creation), beginning on Rosh Hashono, and God rested on the seventh. So there are mystical and metaphysical meanings to the number seven. Eating a dish with seven vegetables in it connects the diner with both the Creator and the act of Creation. The theme of seven is also incorporated into the *Yehi Ratsones* ceremony on Rosh Hashono (page 323) and into the menu for the Rosh Hashono meal for Fez Jews, which traditionally includes seven different courses. *Couscous con siete legumbres* is the main entree of this meal.

The seven vegetables used in the stew are onions, tomatoes, pumpkin, zucchini, turnips, carrots, and cabbage. Chick-peas are also cooked in the stew but they are not counted as a vegetable because the standard *couscous à la mode du Fez* ("*couscous* in the style of Fez") always uses chick-peas as a main ingredient.

Moorish influence is evident in this dish in the beguiling use of sweet and savory spices combined with raisins and herbs. Turmeric is traditional among Jews of Moroccan origin but was not used by the *Moriscos* (Jews of Spanish origin), who disdained it as an inexpensive substitute for saffron. This Moroccan-style recipe uses both turmeric and saffron.

When I prepare the stews for *couscous* dishes, I use a nontraditional approach. I use meat stock instead of water in order to enrich the flavor of the stew. I also brown the meat before starting to cook the stew. Fez cooks never do either of these things. But I personally feel that these two alterations make a better-tasting dish.

SOAKING TIME (CHICK-PEAS): **12 hours or overnight**
PREPARATION TIME (CHICK-PEAS): **1 hour**
PREPARATION TIME (STEW): **2$^1/_2$ hours**
PREPARATION TIME (COUSCOUS): **1 hour**
(included as part of the 2$^1/_2$-hour preparation time for the stew)
SERVINGS: **8–10**

 1 cup dried chick-peas
    Cold water plus 6$^1/_2$ cups cold water for preparing *couscous*
 4 tablespoons olive oil plus additional oil for preparing *couscous*
 2 pounds stewing lamb or beef, cut into 2-inch cubes
 2 medium onions, peeled and very finely chopped, and 4 medium
    onions, peeled and quartered or cut in wedges

$^1/_2$ teaspoon turmeric
$^1/_2$ teaspoon ground ginger
$^1/_4$ teaspoon ground allspice
$^1/_8$ teaspoon ground cloves
$^1/_4$ teaspoon ground coriander seeds
   8 cups meat stock
   5 large tomatoes, peeled, seeded, and finely chopped, or 24 ounces good
      quality canned chopped tomatoes
   1 teaspoon cayenne pepper
$^1/_2$ teaspoon black pepper
$^1/_4$ teaspoon saffron threads dissolved in $^1/_4$ cup boiling water
   2 sticks cinnamon
   1 bouquet garni, consisting of 7 sprigs fresh parsley, 7 sprigs fresh
      cilantro, and 1 bay leaf, tied together with kitchen string
   4 large carrots, peeled and cut into $^1/_2$-inch rounds
   4 medium turnips, peeled and cut into quarters or wedges
$^1/_2$ small head green cabbage, cored and cut into 8 or 10 wedges
$2^1/_2$ cups cubed, peeled pumpkin or Hubbard squash
$^1/_3$ cup dark raisins
   3 cups *couscous*
   4 medium zucchini, sliced into $^1/_2$-inch rounds
      Salt
   2 tablespoons *Harissa* (page 303)

1. Soak the chick-peas 12 hours or overnight in water to cover by 1 inch. Drain and wash. Put the chick-peas into a large stockpot and cover with fresh cold water. Bring to a boil. Reduce the heat and cook gently for 1 hour. Drain and set aside.

2. In a large stockpot or the stockpot that comes with the *couscousière,* heat the 4 tablespoons oil over medium-high heat. Brown the meat a few pieces at a time and set aside in a bowl when they are browned.

3. Sauté the chopped onions in the same oil until they are soft and translucent (5–7 minutes). Reduce the heat to low and add the turmeric, ginger, allspice, cloves, and coriander. Cook an additional 3 minutes, stirring constantly.

4. Deglaze the pot with 1 cup of the meat stock, stirring and scraping up the browned bits with a wooden spoon.

(continued)

5. Add the remaining stock, tomatoes, cayenne and black pepper, saffron, cinnamon sticks, and bouquet garni. Mix together well.

6. Bring to a boil and return the chick-peas and meat, together with any meat juices that have accumulated, to the pot. Cover the pot, reduce the heat to simmer, and cook for 1 hour.

7. Add the quartered onions, carrots, turnips, cabbage, pumpkin, and raisins to the stew. Cover again and keep the pot simmering.

8. Prepare the *couscous,* steps 1 through 4, as described above (pages 216–217).

9. After completing the first steaming of the *couscous,* add the zucchini to the pot.

10. Finish steaming the *couscous,* as described in step 5 (page 217). Remove the *couscous* to a mixing bowl. Add salt to the stew and taste for seasoning. Remove and discard the cinnamon sticks and bouquet garni.

11. Mix the *harissa* with $^1/_2$ cup broth from the stew. Set this aside in a small sauceboat or bowl and serve alongside the *couscous.*

12. To serve the *couscous,* use wide, deep soup bowls. Put a portion of the grain into each bowl. Put a portion of the meat and vegetables on top of the grains. Spoon a little of the broth from the stew over the meat, vegetables, and *couscous.* Put a sauceboat of the broth on the table together with the sauceboat of *harissa* sauce for people to pour over their entree as they like.

SERVING SUGGESTIONS:

Serve *couscous con siete legumbres* all by itself. Precede the *couscous* with a variety of Moroccan hors d'oeuvres. *Pastilla* (page 79) makes an outstanding appetizer course to precede the *couscous.* Conclude the meal with baklava, marzipan-stuffed dried fruits (page 251), and coffee or mint tea.

Couscous à la Mode du Tangier

(Couscous, Tangier Style)

The cooking of Tangier, on the north coast of Morocco, is more influenced by Andalusia than that of other parts of the country. Flavors tend toward the sweet, and the spicing is more subtle. The Sephardic Jews of

Tangier do not use turmeric in their cooking. This recipe is less complex than *couscous con siete legumbres* but just as delicious.

SOAKING TIME (CHICK-PEAS): **12 hours or overnight**
PREPARATION TIME (CHICK-PEAS): **1 hour**
PREPARATION TIME (STEW): **2$^1/_2$ hours,**
including precooking of chick-peas
SERVINGS: **8–10**

  1 cup dried chick-peas
     Cold water plus 6$^1/_2$ cups cold water for steaming *couscous*
  4 tablespoons olive oil plus additional oil for steaming *couscous*
  2 pounds stewing lamb or beef, cut into 2-inch cubes
  2 medium onions, peeled and very finely chopped, and 4 medium
     onions, peeled and quartered or cut in wedges
$^1/_4$ cup sugar
$^1/_2$ teaspoon cayenne pepper
$^1/_4$ teaspoon freshly ground black pepper
  1 teaspoon ground ginger
  7 cups meat stock
$^1/_4$ teaspoon saffron threads dissolved in $^1/_4$ cup boiling water or stock
  1 stick cinnamon
  6 large carrots, peeled and cut into $^1/_2$-inch rounds
  4 medium turnips, peeled and cut into quarters or wedges
  1 pound pumpkin or Hubbard squash, peeled and cut into cubes
$^1/_2$ cup dark raisins
  3 cups *couscous*
     Salt
  2 tablespoons *Harissa* (page 303)

1. Soak the chick-peas 12 hours or overnight in cold water to cover by 1 inch. Drain, wash, and put the chick-peas into a stockpot with fresh cold water to cover. Bring to a boil. Reduce the heat to low and simmer the chick-peas for 1 hour. Drain and set aside.

2. In a stockpot or the stockpot which is part of the *couscousière*, heat the 4 tablespoons oil over medium-high heat. Brown the meat a few pieces at a time. Set the meat aside after it is browned.

3. Sauté the chopped onions in the same oil in which the meat was browned until soft and translucent (5–7 minutes). Reduce the heat and

add the sugar, cayenne and black pepper, and ginger. Cook for 1 minute, stirring constantly.

4. Deglaze the pot with 1 cup meat stock, scraping and stirring with a wooden spoon to incorporate all the browned bits.

5. Add the remaining stock, saffron, and cinnamon stick. Bring to a boil. Reduce the heat to simmer and return the chick-peas, meat, and any meat juices that have accumulated to the pot. Cover the pot and cook 1 hour.

6. Add the quartered onions, carrots, turnips, pumpkin, and raisins and continue to simmer the stew as you prepare the *couscous*.

7. Prepare the *couscous* following steps 1 through 5 as directed above (pages 216–17). Remove the *couscous* from the steamer tray after the final steaming and place it in a bowl. Discard the cinnamon stick and serve the *couscous* immediately, as directed in the recipe for *Couscous con Siete Legumbres* (page 217).

SERVING SUGGESTIONS:

Serve the *couscous* all by itself. Precede the *couscous* with a variety of Moroccan-style appetizers or with a *Salata de Verdura* (page 36). *Buleymas* (page 71) with meat filling (page 63), *Olivada* (page 12) with crisp raw vegetables, and Roasted Pepper Salad (page 46) with Simple Lemon Vinaigrette (page 47) are all good appetizers. Conclude the meal with assorted fresh fruit and baklava or baklava-type pastries. Serve coffee or mint tea at the end of the meal.

Cuscussu
(Tunisian-Style Couscous with Fish)

This is the Tunisian-Jewish version of a well-known Sicilian dish, *cuscussu*, which was brought to Sicily by Spanish-speaking Sephardic Jews. The Tunisian dish is much more spicy than the Sicilian. The original Jewish recipe, which came from Spain, is lost in obscurity. All that remains as a living Jewish culinary tradition is this Tunisian dish, redolent with exotic and robust spices. The *cuscussu* of Trapani, Sicily, an equally exquisite dish, is made with tomatoes, garlic, and Italian parsley.

Because fish cooks quickly and takes less time to prepare than the *couscous*, the grain is steamed over plain water and then served with the fish. I personally love *cuscussu*. It is one of my favorite summer dishes.

PREPARATION TIME (COUSCOUS): **1 hour**
PREPARATION TIME (FISH): **45 minutes**
SERVINGS: **8–10**

3	cups couscous
$6^1/_2$	cups cold water for preparing couscous
	Olive oil for preparing couscous plus 6 tablespoons oil
8–10	fish fillets (red snapper, perch, sea bass, and halibut are good choices; $3^1/_2$–4 pounds)
$^1/_3$	cup fresh parsley leaves
$^3/_4$	cup fresh cliantro leaves
4	large cloves garlic, peeled
3	tablespoons freshly squeezed lemon juice
1	teaspoon salt
1	teaspoon cayenne pepper
$^1/_8$	teaspoon freshly ground black pepper
1	teaspoon ground cumin
1	large onion, peeled and very finely chopped
4	large tomatoes, peeled, seeded, and finely chopped

1. Prepare plain *couscous*, steps 1 through 4 as directed above (page 216–17). Wash and dry the fish fillets and put in an 11 × 14-inch baking dish.

2. In a blender or food processor, puree the parsley, cilantro, garlic, lemon juice, salt, cayenne, black pepper, and cumin. Set aside.

3. In a sauté pan, heat the 6 tablespoons olive oil over medium-high heat and sauté the onion until soft and translucent (5–7 minutes). Add the tomatoes and cook 15 minutes or until the tomatoes begin to disintegrate.

4. Preheat the oven to 350 degrees.

5. Add the herb puree to the tomato mixture and mix together well. Cook an additional 10 minutes, stirring constantly.
6. Pour the sauce over the fish fillets. Cover the baking pan and bake for 25 minutes.
7. While fish is baking, finish cooking the *couscous*, following step 5 (page 217). Uncover the fish after 25 minutes of baking and bake 10 minutes longer, uncovered. Fish is done when it flakes with a fork.
8. Serve the *cuscussu* immediately. Make a bed of the *couscous* and lay a fish fillet across it. Cover the fish with some of the sauce. Put any left-over sauce into a sauceboat and serve alongside the entree.

SERVING SUGGESTIONS:

Serve *cuscussu* all by itself. Precede the entree with a selection of appetizers and salads. Roasted Eggplant Salad, Arabic Style (page 51), *Toureto* (page 31), *Salata de Spinaca* (page 40), and marinated green olives (page 11) are all good choices. Conclude the meal with assorted fresh fruit, Sephardic cookies, and mint or lemon verbena tea.

Pilafi de Trahanas

BULGUR PILAV

 Bulgur pilav is a wonderful alternative to rice. It is very popular in Turkey, Syria, and Lebanon.

PREPARATION TIME: **25 minutes**
SERVINGS: **6–8**

2 tablespoons olive oil
1 medium onion, peeled and finely chopped
$1^1/_2$ cups bulgur
$^1/_4$ teaspoon salt
3 cups Vegetable Stock (page 299)

1. Heat the oil in a saucepan over medium-high heat. Sauté the onion until soft and translucent (5–7 minutes).
2. Add the bulgur and sauté for 2–3 minutes. Add the salt and stock and bring to a boil. Reduce the heat to simmer and cover the pot tightly. Cook 10–15 minutes or until the liquid is all absorbed. Bulgur will swell and become very soft. Serve immediately.

SERVING SUGGESTIONS:
Serve as a side dish exactly as you would rice pilav.

The Magic of Saffron

A SEPHARDIC FOLK TALE

Once a peace treaty was made between the Sultan of Turkey and the King of Greece. The Sultan sent beautiful gifts to the King as part of the treaty. There were all kinds of precious jewels, silks and satins, expensive carpets, gold and silver objects, and other luxurious things. When the messenger of the Sultan brought these gifts to the King, he sent a small box back, which was doubly sealed and wrapped. He commanded that no one but the Sultan open the box.

After the messenger returned to Turkey with the box, the Sultan looked at it with a sour expression on his face. "This gift certainly is small," he said. "But maybe it contains something so precious that there are only a few of them in the world. He opened the box and found that all it contained was a small bag with a handful of saffron threads.

"Look how that pig makes fun of me?" huffed the Sultan. "I send him all kinds of expensive things from my palace—precious jewels and cloth and carpets and gold and silver and look at what he sends me! A handful of flower stamens!"

The Sultan was ready to call out his fleet of ships and sail to Greece to wage war again when an old rabbi, one of his advisers, came up to him and said, "Your Excellency, you are a very wise and lucky man. I heard about the gift that the King of Greece sent you. This gift is very precious. It can protect you from evil."

"How do you know that?" bellowed the Sultan.

"Tomorrow, travel to the north of the kingdom, where the wild bears live, and you will see. When you show them the package, they will run away."

So the Sultan did as the rabbi suggested. He went to a place where many wild bears lived. And as soon as he showed them the saffron, they ran away. So the Sultan proclaimed the wisdom of the rabbi and because of it, he praised and honored all the Jewish people who lived in Turkey. And that is why the Jews consider saffron a magical plant and cook their Shabbat rice with it.

Egg Dishes

Huevos Haminados (EGGS BRAISED IN A HAMIN STYLE)

Huevos con Tomates (EGGS WITH TOMATOES)

    Eggs with Tomatoes, Macedonian Style

    Eggs with Tomatoes, Syrian Style

    Chakchouka (TUNISIAN-STYLE EGGS AND TOMATOES)

    Menemen (A TURKISH VERSION OF CHAKCHOUKA)

Huevos con Spinaca (POACHED EGGS WITH SPINACH)

Bumuelos de Verdura (MACEDONIAN HERB FRITTERS)

Fritadas

    Fritada de Kalabasa, Sautéed (ZUCCHINI FRITTATA, SAUTÉED)

    Fritada de Berenjenna, Baked (EGGPLANT FRITTATA, BAKED)

Bumuelos de Masa and *Masa Tiganitas*

    Bumuelos de Masa (MATZOH MEAL PANCAKES)

    Masa Tiganitas

Huevos Haminados

EGGS BRAISED IN A HAMIN STYLE

Huevos haminados is one of the most ancient dishes in the Mediterranean and it is uniquely Jewish. The eggs are cooked like *Hamin* (page 170) in a slow oven for 12 or more hours and served as a hot dish for the Sabbath. The eggs are braised in water, a large amount of onion skins, and sometimes coffee grounds, both of which impart flavor and a golden brown color to the eggs through the porous egg shells. Eggs made with coffee grounds get a darker color than those prepared only with onion skins. The *Hamin* method of cooking the eggs results in eggs that are beige-colored, soft, and creamy, with none of the rubbery texture of ordinary hard-boiled eggs.

In Ladino-speaking communities, *huevos haminados* were served together with savory pastries and salads as a kind of Sabbath morning brunch called *desayuno* after Saturday morning synagogue services during warm-weather months. In cool weather, Mediterranean Jewish communities put the eggs into a *Hamin* containing meat. Cooking the eggs in the *Hamin* gives them the same creamy texture described above, the difference being that the *huevos haminados* absorb the cooking flavors of all the other ingredients in the stew instead of those imparted by onion skins or coffee grounds.

Leftover *huevos haminados* are eaten like hard-boiled eggs and are used for garnishes or in different kinds of salads, like Sephardic *Salata de Atun y Sardellas* (page 15).

PREPARATION TIME: **12 or more hours**
SERVINGS: **8–10**

8–10 eggs
      Skins of 10–12 medium onions
  2 tablespoons coffee grounds
      Cold water

My favorite way of cooking *huevos haminados* is in an electric crock pot set on the lowest temperature. Just put everything into the pot and let it cook for a minimum of 12 hours. More will not hurt. Lacking this appliance, simply put everything into a 2-quart ovenproof saucepan, cover it tightly, and set it into a preheated 175-degree oven. Leave it alone for at least 12 hours. When ready to serve the eggs, just take them out of the pot with a slotted spoon and let them cool slightly, until they can be handled. Shell the eggs and serve them.

SERVING SUGGESTIONS:
Serve *huevos haminados* as part of a *desayuno* or vegetarian buffet.

Huevos con Tomates

EGGS WITH TOMATOES

There are several variations on this recipe. Some cooks stew the tomatoes into a thick puree and then poach the eggs in the puree. Others scramble the eggs together with the tomatoes and herbs. Here are three different recipes for *huevos con tomates*.

Eggs with Tomatoes, Macedonian Style

PREPARATION TIME: **45 minutes**
SERVINGS: **4–6**

- 4 tablespoons olive oil
- 1 large onion, peeled and very thinly sliced
- 2 large cloves garlic, peeled and finely chopped (1 tablespoon)
- 1 teaspoon Hungarian hot paprika
- 6 very large tomatoes, peeled, seeded, and finely chopped
- 1 teaspoon dried marjoram
- 1 tablespoon finely chopped fresh rosemary leaves
  Salt and freshly ground black pepper
- 6 large eggs
- $1/4$ cup finely chopped fresh parsley

1. Heat the oil in a large, deep sauté pan over medium heat. Sauté the onion until soft and translucent (5–7 minutes).
2. Reduce the heat to low and add the garlic and paprika. Cook, stirring constantly, for 5 minutes.
3. Add the tomatoes, marjoram, and rosemary. Stir well and simmer for 20–25 minutes, or until the tomatoes soften and begin to turn into a very thick stew.
4. Stir in the salt and pepper. Make six depressions in the tomato mixture and break an egg into each depression. Turn the heat down to the lowest simmer and cover the pot. Cook 15 minutes or until the whites are set but yolks are still soft. Serve one or two eggs and some of the tomato puree, sprinkled with fresh parsley, to each diner.

SERVING SUGGESTIONS:
Serve this dish with crusty Mediterranean bread. Precede the eggs with a selection of salads and appetizers. *Salata de Spinaca* (page 40), marinated black and green olives (page 9), and *Toureto* (page 31) are all good choices. Conclude the meal with fresh fruit, Sephardic cookies, and coffee or mint tea

Eggs with Tomatoes, Syrian Style
In this variation, the eggs are scrambled with the tomatoes and herbs.

PREPARATION TIME: **25 minutes**
SERVINGS: **4–6**

  4 tablespoons olive oil
  1 large onion, peeled and finely chopped
  2 large cloves garlic, peeled and finely chopped (1 tablespoon)
  5 large tomatoes, peeled, seeded, and finely chopped
$1/_4$ cup finely chopped fresh parsley
  1 tablespoon finely chopped fresh mint leaves
    Salt and freshly ground black pepper
  6 large eggs, beaten

1. In a large, deep sauté pan, heat the oil over medium-high heat and sauté the onion until soft and translucent (5–7 minutes).

(continued)

2. Reduce the heat and add the garlic and tomatoes. Cook 7–10 minutes or long enough for the tomatoes to begin to disintegrate.

3. Add the herbs and stir in. Add salt and pepper and the beaten eggs. Scramble the egg mixture, stirring from time to time as the eggs cook. Do not cook the eggs too long—just until set. Remove immediately from the heat and serve.

SERVING SUGGESTIONS:

Serve these eggs and tomatoes with pita bread, butter, olives, and a glass of white wine. Precede or accompany the eggs with a variety of salads. *Salata de Spinaca* (page 40), one of the Roasted Pepper Salads (page 46), and *Humus* (page 7) make excellent choices. Conclude the meal with fresh fruit, baklava, and coffee or mint tea.

Chakchouka
(Tunisian-Style Eggs and Tomatoes)

PREPARATION TIME: **40 minutes**
SERVINGS: **4–6**

4	tablespoons olive oil
1	large onion, peeled and finely chopped
1	large clove garlic, peeled and finely chopped ($^1/_2$ tablespoon)
3	medium green bell peppers, cored, seeded, and cut in strips
5	large tomatoes, peeled, seeded, and chopped
$^1/_4$	teaspoon cayenne pepper
$^1/_2$	teaspoon ground cumin
	Salt and freshly ground black pepper
6	large eggs

1. Heat the olive oil in a large, deep sauté pan over medium heat. Sauté the onion until soft and translucent (5–7 minutes). Add the garlic and green peppers and cook an additional 5 minutes, stirring constantly.

2. Lower the heat and add the tomatoes, cayenne pepper, and cumin. Cook 10–12 minutes, stirring constantly.

3. Add salt and black pepper and the eggs. The eggs may be either broken and added in whole by making depressions into the simmering vegetables or they may be beaten and scrambled. If cooking the eggs whole, lower the heat to the lowest simmer, cover the pot, and cook 15 minutes. If scrambling in beaten eggs, cook at a low temperature, stirring once in a while, until eggs are set. Serve immediately.

SERVING SUGGESTIONS:
Serve *chakchouka* with pita bread or crusty Mediterranean bread. *Buleymas* (page 71) filled with cheese (page 63), Roasted Eggplant Salad, Arabic Style (page 51), and marinated black olives (page 10) may be served alongside the *chakchouka*. Conclude the meal with fresh fruit, baklava, and coffee or mint tea.

VARIATION:
Menemen (A Turkish Version of *Chakchouka*)
To make *menemen*, omit the cayenne pepper and cumin from the *chakchouka* recipe and add $1/4$ cup chopped fresh parsley and $1/4$ cup crumbled feta cheese. Prepare as directed above, using the scrambled egg version of *chakchouka*. Add the cheese toward the end of cooking. Serve *menemen* with yogurt, marinated olives, and crusty Mediterranean bread.

Huevos con Spinaca

POACHED EGGS WITH SPINACH

 This Turkish dish is similar to eggs Florentine but the seasonings are different. Sweet butter is used to make *huevos con spinaca* rather than olive oil.

PREPARATION TIME: 35 minutes
SERVINGS: 3–6

- 4 tablespoons sweet butter
- 1 medium onion, peeled and finely chopped
- 2 pounds fresh spinach, washed and dried
- $1/2$ cup crumbled feta or brynza cheese
- $1/4$ cup finely chopped fresh dill leaves
  Salt and freshly ground black pepper
- 6 extra large eggs

1. In a deep, wide sauté pan, melt the butter over medium heat. Sauté the onion until soft and translucent (5–7 minutes).
2. Add the spinach and cook until the leaves wilt and begin to give off liquid. Reduce the heat and cook down until most of the liquid has evaporated.
3. Stir in the cheese, dill, salt, and pepper. Make six depressions in the spinach and break an egg into each depression.
4. Reduce the heat to the lowest simmer and cover the pan tightly. Cook 15 minutes or until the eggs are set. Serve immediately.

SERVING SUGGESTIONS:

This entree is delicious with crusty Mediterranean bread. Precede it with some complementary salads and appetizers like *Borekas* (page 61) filled with eggplant (page 65), marinated black olives (page 10) and sliced tomatoes and cucumbers. Conclude the meal with fresh fruit, baklava, and coffee, mint tea, or lemon verbena tea.

Bumuelos de Verdura

MACEDONIAN HERB FRITTERS

 These fritters, made of fresh herbs, are considered a springtime delicacy in Macedonia and Bulgaria. Any type of fresh herbs can be put into the fritters, depending on what is in season. The only two constants are parsley and scallions.

PREPARATION TIME: **25 minutes**
YIELD: **makes approximately 16–18 fritters**

> 3 large eggs, beaten
> 1 cup finely chopped fresh parsley
> $^1/_2$ cup thinly sliced scallions
> $^1/_2$ cup chopped fresh herbs (dill, chervil, mint, rosemary, thyme, oregano, marjoram), alone or in combination
> $^1/_2$ teaspoon salt
> 3 tablespoons sweet butter or more as needed
> 3 tablespoons olive oil or more as needed

1. Combine everything except the butter and oil in a mixing bowl.
2. Heat the butter and oil together in a 12-inch skillet over medium heat. When the butter melts and the foam subsides, take $^1/_4$ cup of the herb mixture and put it into the fat in the skillet. Repeat until you have three fritters cooking.
3. Fry each fritter approximately 3–4 minutes, turning over once. When ready, fritters will be delicately browned. If necessary, you may add more butter or oil to the skillet. Drain on paper towels. Keep warm in a 250-degree oven until all are fried. Serve immediately.

SERVING SUGGESTIONS:
Serve *bumuelos de verdura* with brynza cheese, sliced tomatoes and cucumbers, thick yogurt, good Mediterranean bread, and marinated black and green olives (page 9). Conclude the meal with fresh fruit, Sephardic cookies, and mint or lemon verbena tea.

Fritadas

 Sephardic *fritadas* are very much like those made in Italy and very different from those made in France and Spain, where bacon or ham is almost invariably one of the ingredients. These are vegetarian *fritadas,* dominated by one vegetable. One type of Sephardic *fritada,* prepared for Passover, uses *matzoh* meal, which thickens the finished dish into a kind of quiche.

There are essentially two different methods of making Sephardic *fritadas.* One kind is sautéed on top of the stove on both sides. In the second method, the *fritada* is baked in the oven. You will need an oven-proof skillet to try out the second method. An oversize spatula is also a great asset when you are cooking *fritadas* as it makes them very easy to turn.

Here are two Sephardic *fritadas:*

Fritada de Kalabasa, Sautéed
(Zucchini Frittata, Sautéed)

PREPARATION TIME: **25–30 minutes**
SERVINGS: **4**

> 6 tablespoons olive oil
> 6 small zucchini, cut into thin rounds
> Salt and freshly ground black pepper
> $1/4$ cup finely chopped fresh parsley
> 6 large eggs, beaten

1. Heat 3 tablespoons oil in a 12-inch skillet over medium-high heat. Sauté the zucchini until they are lightly browned on both sides. Remove the zucchini with a slotted spoon and set them on paper towels to drain as they finish cooking. Add the remaining oil to the skillet.

2. Mix the salt, pepper, parsley, and cooked zucchini into the beaten eggs. Pour this mixture into the skillet. Reduce the heat to the lowest temperature and cover the pot. Cook the *fritada* for 15 minutes, shaking from time to time to keep the *fritada* from sticking to the bottom

of the skillet. This cooks the bottom and most of the center of the *fritada*.

3. When the bottom has cooked and is set, uncover the skillet. Turn the *fritada* over on its other side. If you have a very large spatula, this can be done easily. Another method is to place the *fritada*, cooked side up, onto a plate and then slide it back into the skillet. You will lose a little egg this way, most of which can be poured back carefully around the sides of the skillet as the flip side of the *fritada* cooks. If it gets messy the first time, practice. Eventually, you will be able to do this with no trouble.

4. Slide the cooked *fritada* onto a flat plate, cut into wedges as you would a pizza, and serve immediately.

SERVING SUGGESTIONS:

Serve zucchini *fritada* with brynza or feta cheese, thick yogurt, sliced tomatoes and cucumbers, marinated green and black olives (page 9), and plenty of crusty bread. Conclude the meal with fresh fruit, Sephardic cookies, and mint or lemon verbena tea.

Fritada de Berenjenna, Baked
(Eggplant Frittata, Baked)

SALTING TIME (EGGPLANT): **1$^1/_2$ hours**
PREPARATION TIME: **1 hour**
SERVINGS: **4–6**

   1 small eggplant (6–8 ounces)
      Coarse salt
   6 tablespoons olive oil
   1 medium onion, peeled and finely chopped
   1 large clove garlic, peeled and finely chopped ($^1/_2$ tablespoon)
$^3/_4$ cup feta cheese, crumbled
   3 tablespoons *matzoh* meal
$^1/_4$ cup yogurt
      Salt and freshly ground black pepper
   6 extra large eggs, beaten

1. Cut the unpeeled eggplant into small dice. Place it in a colander in the sink. Sprinkle it with coarse salt. Cover it with plastic wrap and place several plates on top of it to weight it down. Let rest for $1\frac{1}{2}$ hours. Remove the plates and plastic wrap. Rinse, squeeze to remove bitter juices, and dry on paper towels.
2. Preheat the oven to 350 degrees.
3. Heat the oil in a skillet over medium-high heat. Sauté the onion until soft and translucent (5–7 minutes).
4. Add the eggplant and sauté, turning constantly, until nicely browned.
5. Add the garlic and reduce the heat. Cook 1 minute longer and remove from the heat. Pour the contents of the skillet into a mixing bowl.
6. Add the remaining ingredients to the mixing bowl and combine well. Bake 45 minutes or until the *fritada* is golden brown. Cut into wedges and serve hot or at room temperature.

SERVING SUGGESTIONS:
Serve the *fritada* with thick yogurt, sliced tomatoes and cucumbers, or a *Salata Sepharadi* (page 34), marinated black olives (page 10) and crusty Mediterranean bread. Conclude with fresh fruits, baklava, and coffee.

Bumuelos de Masa and *Masa Tiganitas*

Ashkenazic Jews are very well acquainted with two kinds of Passover specialties—*matzoh* meal pancakes called *chremslach* and fried *matzoh* with eggs called *matzoh brei*. Sephardic Jews make similar dishes on Passover. The main difference between the Sephardic and the Ashkenazic dishes is that Sephardim serve their *matzoh* meal pancakes and their fried *matzoh* with *arrope*, a raisin syrup, or with honey and sprinkled with walnuts. Here are the Sephardic variations of these two Yiddish-Jewish favorites.

Bumuelos de Masa
(Matzoh Meal Pancakes)

PREPARATION TIME: **30 minutes**
YIELD: **makes 15–16** *bumuelos*

3 large eggs
$1/4$ teaspoon salt
1 cup cold water
1 cup *matzoh* meal
Sunflower oil for frying
Arrope (page 297) or honey
Finely chopped walnuts

1. In a deep mixing bowl, beat the eggs well. Add the salt and cold water, whisking well and thoroughly.
2. Mix in the *matzoh* meal. The batter should be like a thin pancake batter.
3. Pour $1/4$ inch of oil into a 12-inch skillet. Heat over medium-high heat.
4. Pour $1/4$ cup batter into the skillet. It will spread into a little pancake. Repeat until you have four or five pancakes frying. Regulate the heat, adjusting it to prevent burning as the *bumuelos* cook. Fry 3–4 minutes on each side and drain the *bumuelos* on paper towels. Serve with *arrope* or honey poured over the pancakes and sprinkle with chopped walnuts.

SERVING SUGGESTIONS:

Bumuelos de masa make a delicious breakfast with coffee, fresh fruit, and thick yogurt served on the side.

Masa Tiganitas

This Sephardic variation of *matzoh brei* is much richer and creamier than the Ashkenazic dish. The method is also totally different. *Masa tiganitas* is a little like French toast made out of *matzoh*.

PREPARATION TIME:
SERVINGS: **4–6**

- 6 whole *matzot*
  Whole milk to soak *matzot* (about 4 cups)
- 4 large eggs
- $^1/_4$ cup yogurt
  Sunflower oil for sautéing
  Arrope (page 297) or honey
  Finely chopped walnuts

1. Place the whole *matzot* into a wide, deep mixing bowl or a square baking pan that can accommodate them all without breaking them. Pour the milk over them to cover. Soak the *matzot* in the milk until they soften enough so that they can be cut but are not so soft that they will disintegrate (about 2–$2^1/_2$ minutes).

2. While the *matzot* are soaking, beat the eggs in a mixing bowl together with the $^1/_4$ cup yogurt.

3. When the *matzot* are soft enough, gently remove them, one at a time, and lay them on paper towels. Cut each *matzoh* into four quarters. Stack the squares on top of one another on paper towels or on a plate.

4. Pour enough oil into a 12-inch skillet to come up the sides $^1/_4$ inch. Heat the oil over medium-high heat until it is sizzling but not smoking.

5. Dip one square of *matzoh* from each stack into the beaten egg. Allow the excess to drip back into the mixing bowl. Place the square in the skillet. A 12-inch skillet will hold 2–3 *tiganitas* (squares) while they

are frying. Fry the *tiganitas* until golden brown on both sides. Keep the *tiganitas* warm in a 250-degree oven until all are ready. Apportion the *tiganitas* onto serving plates. Serve with *arrope* or honey poured over the *tiganitas* and sprinkle with chopped walnuts.

SERVING SUGGESTIONS:
Serve *masa tiganitas* with thick yogurt, fresh fruit, and coffee for a very special breakfast.

The Egg Seller and His One Thousand Eggs

A SEPHARDIC FOLK TALE

Once there was a Jewish egg seller who sold eggs for a very small profit in the market. One day he was walking to the market with a basket of a thousand eggs on his head, bemoaning his fate. "How long do I have to go on working so hard and making so little money? It would be much better if I took the eggs home with me and put chickens on top of them to roost. Then, if each egg would hatch, I would have a thousand chickens. Some of the chickens will be roosters and some of them will be hens. If the hens start to lay eggs, I'll soon have hundreds of thousands of chickens. I'll make it into a big chicken business. I'll sell the chickens at one dinar per chicken and that will make me two hundred thousand dinars. Then I'll give up the chicken business and buy silk. I'll sell the silk in France at a 50 percent markup, use the money to buy other goods there, mark those up 50 percent, and sell them here. If I keep buying and selling like that for five years, I'll have hundreds of thousands of gold dinars to my name. Then I'll buy a mansion and surround it with gardens and orchards and some shops that I can rent out for more money. I'll be a very rich man. I'll have more money than any other Jew in Turkey! And I'll be invited to be an adviser to the Sultan's court. I will go every day to the court of the Sultan and I will bow down to him and to all the members of his court. And when they see me bowing down to them, they will have to bow down to me . . ." As the egg seller said this, he lowered his head a little and the basket fell to the ground, breaking all of the thousand eggs.

Desserts and Sweet Pastries

Macedonia and *Composto*

    Summer Fruit Macedonia

    Composto with Fresh Oranges

    Autumn Quince Composto

Marzipan-Stuffed Dried Fruits

Dried Apricot Balls with Almonds

Sutlach

Sweet Couscous Pudding

Assure

Torta de los Reyes (KINGS' CAKE)

Tishpitti

Pan d'Espanya or *Pan de Esponjada*
(BREAD OF SPAIN OR SPANISH SPONGE CAKE)

Bizcochos de Anis (ANISE COOKIES)

Bizcochos de Vino or *Masa de Vino* (WINE BISCUITS)

Mustachudos (SEPHARDIC HAZELNUT COOKIES)

Travados

Los Siete Cielos (BREAD OF THE SEVEN HEAVENS)

Orejas de Haman (HAMAN'S EARS)

Bumuelos de Hanuka (HANUKKAH FRITTERS)

Macedonia and Composto

 Macedonia is a fresh uncooked fruit compote that can be made with virtually any seasonal fruit. The fruits are macerated in a sugar syrup flavored with lemon, orange flower water, or rosewater. Sometimes brandy or anise-flavored liqueur is put into *macedonia* instead of the lemon juice or the flower essences. *Composto* is a compote made with one or more fruits, cooked or uncooked. Here are three recipes for *macedonia* and *composto* for different seasons.

Summer Fruit Macedonia

PREPARATION TIME: **35 minutes**
MACERATION TIME: **2 or more hours**
SERVINGS: **6–8**

> 1 cup sugar
> 2 cups cold water
> 4 large peaches, peeled, pitted, and cut into wedges
> 8 apricots, peeled, pitted, and cut into quarters
> 2 cups cut-up well-ripened Persian or Crenshaw melon, cut into 1-inch chunks (well-ripened honeydew or cantaloupe can be substituted)
> 1 cup cherries, pitted
> $1^1/_2$ teaspoons rosewater
> Shelled green pistachio nuts for sprinkling

1. To make the sugar syrup, dissolve the sugar in the water in a saucepan and bring to a boil. Boil rapidly for 10–12 minutes and remove from the heat. Cool to room temperature.
2. Put all of the fruit into a glass serving bowl. Combine gently.
3. Mix the rosewater into the syrup and pour over the fruit. Stir to combine and cover the bowl tightly. Refrigerate at least 2 hours before serving. Sprinkle pistachio nuts over each serving of *macedonia*.

Composto with Fresh Oranges

PREPARATION TIME: **25 minutes**
MACERATION TIME: **2 or more hours**
SERVINGS: **6–8**

> 2 tablespoons honey (preferably citrus flower honey)
> $1^1/_2$ cups freshly squeezed orange juice
> 6–8 large seedless navel oranges
> Finely grated zest of 1 large orange (1 heaping tablespoon)
> $1^1/_2$ teaspoons orange flower water
> Sliced almonds for sprinkling

1. In a mixing bowl, dissolve the honey in the orange juice by stirring it briskly with a wire whisk.
2. Peel the oranges and cut them crosswise into thin slices. Layer them in a glass bowl, sprinkling finely grated orange zest over each layer.
3. Mix the orange flower water into the orange juice mixture and pour it over the oranges. Cover the bowl tightly and put in the refrigerator. Allow to rest undisturbed for at least 2 hours before serving. Sprinkle thinly sliced almonds over each portion of *composto* before serving.

Autumn Quince Composto

PREPARATION TIME: **$1^1/_4$ hours**
MACERATION TIME: **2 or more hours**
SERVINGS: **6–8**

> 3 pounds fresh quinces
> 4 cups cold water mixed with the juice of 1 lemon
> 2 cups cold water
> 1 cup sugar
> Seeds of 1 pomegranate

1. Peel and core the quinces and slice thickly. Save the peels and the cores. Put the sliced quinces into 4 cups cold water acidulated with the lemon juice to prevent discoloration. Refrigerate the quince slices while you do the next step.

2. Put the quince peels and cores into a saucepan together with the 2 cups cold water and the sugar. Dissolve the sugar by stirring with a spoon and bring to a boil. Reduce the heat to simmer and cook 30 minutes. The fruit cores and peels will release pectin, which will cause the syrup to thicken almost to the point of jelling. Strain this syrup through a sieve into another saucepan.

3. Remove the quince slices from the acidulated water and cook them in the syrup until soft (about 20 minutes).

4. Transfer the *composto* to a glass serving bowl, cover tightly, and chill at least 2 hours before serving. Sprinkle each portion with pomegranate seeds before serving.

Marzipan-Stuffed Dried Fruits

 Prunes, dates, and dried apricots are all made into elegant confections by stuffing them with marzipan. Here is a supremely beautiful and delicately flavored sweet to enjoy with coffee or tea after a meal.

PREPARATION TIME: **30 minutes**
YIELD: **makes approximately 30 sweets**

1 pound pitted prunes, pitted dates, or dried apricots
1 cup marzipan (page 291)

Stuff each dried fruit with $^1/_2$–1 teaspoon marzipan, depending on the size of the fruit. Dates have to be cut in half and then pressed together after they are stuffed. Prunes and apricots only need to be opened at the top in order to be stuffed. Apricots are particularly attractive when stuffed with green pistachio marzipan (page 291). Lemon Marzipan (page 292) is especially nice with prunes.

VARIATION:
A slightly different and very elegant variation can be made with dates by pureeing 1 pound pitted dates in a food processor, then taking 1 heaping

tablespoon of the date puree, rolling it into a ball, making a well in the center, stuffing it with $^1/_2$ teaspoon marzipan, and then closing up the ball. The ball of stuffed date puree can then be rolled in powdered sugar and set into chocolate cups for serving.

Dried Apricot Balls with Almonds

 In this sweet confection, the dried apricots are cooked and then rolled into a paste. It is a very rich sweet and goes particularly well with lemon verbena or mint tea.

PREPARATION TIME: **1 hour**
YIELD: **makes 18–20 apricot balls**

$1^1/_2$	pounds dried apricots
$^2/_3$	cup cold water
$^3/_4$	cup sugar
2	tablespoons rosewater
18–20	whole blanched almonds
$^1/_2$	cup confectioners' sugar

1. In a food processor or blender, grind the apricots into a coarse puree.
2. Place the apricots in a saucepan together with the water. Bring to a boil. Reduce the heat to simmer and cover the pot. Cook 15 minutes or until the liquid is absorbed by the apricots.
3. Uncover the pot and add the sugar and the rosewater. Cook another 12–15 minutes. The apricots will have softened and cooked down to a thick paste. Remove from the heat and cool to room temperature.
4. Have the almonds and the confectioners' sugar at your side while you work. Take 1 tablespoon of the apricot mixture into your hand and roll it into a ball. Flatten the ball into a disk and roll it in confectioners' sugar. Press an almond into the disk and set it on a plate. Repeat until you have used up all the apricot puree and the almonds. Serve arranged attractively on cookie plates.

Sutlach

 Sutlach is one of the great delicacies of Turkish and Greek Sephardic cooking. It is a sweet pudding made of rice flour or semolina. In Salonika, a special oven called a *kanun* and a special copper pan called a *kazandibi* were used to make *sutlach*. The *kanun* was a portable charcoal brazier that stood on a pedestal. The *kazandibi* fit perfectly into the *kanun* and the pudding would simmer very, very slowly, being stirred every once in a while by the cook, until it was ready. *Sutlach* was a traditional Friday night dish for Salonika Jews, who served it following a dairy dinner with fish as the main entree.

In today's kitchen, the *kanun* and the *kazandibi* are as essential to the making of *sutlach* as a *samovar* is to preparing tea. A perfectly delicious *sutlach* can be made on top of the stove and then baked in the oven with much less fuss. The proper kind of rice flour can be purchased at any health food store. If you can find it, I recommend a coarse rather than a fine grind.

The closest equivalent to *sutlach* I have found in other cuisines is that old New England favorite Indian pudding, a Puritan dish made of cornmeal, milk, and molasses that is baked in the oven for hours and turns into a mouthwatering caramel-flavored custard. If you like Indian pudding, you will love *sutlach*.

The main thing to remember about preparing a good *sutlach* lies in the method of mixing the rice flour with the milk. It must be done slowly and thoroughly or the pudding will be lumpy. The microwave comes in handy for the first step as it does an excellent job of cooking the milk with the sugar.

PREPARATION TIME: **2 1/2 hours**
CHILLING TIME: **2 or more hours**
SERVINGS: **6–8**

$1^3/_4$ cups sugar

4 cups whole milk (Do not try to make a "light" version with 2 percent or skim milk. The insipid flavor isn't worth the bother.)

1 cup rice flour

$^1/_4$ cup ground almonds

$^1/_4$ teaspoon ground cinnamon

1. Preheat the oven to 350 degrees.
2. Dissolve 1 cup sugar in the milk in a 2-quart saucepan or microwave casserole. On top of the stove, bring the mixture to a boil and simmer for 7–8 minutes to reduce and thicken it. (In the microwave, 3–4 minutes at full power is enough.) Stir with a wire whisk to prevent a skin from forming. When the mixture is reduced slightly, stop cooking and remove it from the heat. Cool slightly.
3. Put the rice flour into a deep mixing bowl. Add 2 tablespoons of the milk mixture to the rice. Stir in well with your fingers. Continue to do this, 2 tablespoons at a time until the mixture becomes fluid enough to be stirred with a wire whisk. Be very, very thorough as you mix. Eventually you will have a smooth liquid.
4. Spread $^1/_2$ cup sugar over the bottom of a 9 × 12-inch baking dish and place it in the oven. Allow the sugar to caramelize (about 3 minutes); remove immediately from the oven. Reduce the oven temperature to 250 degrees.
5. Pour the rice flour mixture over the caramelized sugar. Bake in the oven for at least 2 hours or until a rich brown crust has formed. Remove the pudding from the oven and cool to room temperature. Then cover with plastic wrap and chill for at least 2 hours.
6. Before serving the *sutlach,* mix together the remaining $^1/_4$ cup sugar, the ground almonds, and the cinnamon. Remove the pudding from the refrigerator. The caramelized sugar will have formed into a caramel syrup, similar to that found in a crème caramel. Cut the *sutlach* into squares or diamond shapes and put in individual bowls. Pour a little caramel syrup over each portion of the pudding and sprinkle with the almond-cinnamon mixture before serving.

Sweet Couscous Pudding

 Moroccan Jews serve this delicious simple dessert following a meal that features a *tajin* or stew. Sweet *couscous* pudding is considered a festive dish made generally only on special occasions.

PREPARATION TIME: **1 hour**
SERVINGS: **6**

> 6 cups *Couscous* (page 216)
> 1 cup blanched almonds
> $^2/_3$ cup sugar plus $^1/_3$ cup mixed with 1 teaspoon ground cinnamon
> 16–18 pitted dates

1. Prepare the *couscous* according to the instructions on pages 216–217.
2. Grind the nuts together with $^2/_3$ cup sugar in a food processor.
3. Have the nut paste, cinnamon/sugar mixture, and the dates ready at your side. After the final steaming of the *couscous,* pile the grain onto a platter or into a deep, wide pasta bowl. Shape it into a round mound.
4. Sprinkle alternating rows of nut paste and cinnamon/sugar over the *couscous.* Surround the *couscous* with a row of dates and use the remaining dates to decorate the top. Present and serve to your guests.

Assure

Assure is a grain and dried fruit pudding that has many variations throughout Turkey, Greece, and Armenia. The name of the dish, *assure,* is the Turkish word for "ten" (phonetically similar to *esser,* the Hebrew word for "ten"). Turkish Muslims prepare the pudding as a gift for relatives, friends, and the poor on the festival of Assure Gunn, which commemorates the deaths of Hassan and Hussein, grandsons of the prophet Muhammad. Greeks call the pudding *kolyvas* and they serve it as a funeral dish. Armenians call the dish "Noah's Pudding" and have their own legend connected with the Great Flood that says *assure* was served by Noah's wife on the last day they spent on the ark as a way of using up the leftover stores of grain and fruits.

Jews embrace none of the folkloric associations of their Muslim and Christian neighbors. Instead, they connect *assure* with an important Jewish festival—Tu B'Shevat (the New Year for the Trees). On Tu B'Shevat, Sephardic Jews have formal ceremonies to mark the end of the winter season and to welcome the season of spring. Special blessings are made over grains and fruits, which are eaten in many different forms as a prayer for abundance during the coming growing season. In this way, Jews acknowledge the role of the Creator in providing the people of the earth with crops in their season.

The number ten (or *esser*), for Jews, refers to the Ten Commandments. The Jewish recipe for *assure* symbolically contains ten different ingredients, an ingredient for each of the Ten Commandments given by God to the Jewish people. *Assure* is eaten at the end of a ritual meal on Tu B'Shevat called the Tu B'Shevat Seder. This custom was developed by Jewish mystics, the Kabbalists, as a way of spiritually connecting with the turning of the season and the beginning of a new planting and growing cycle. A more detailed description of the Tu B'Shevat Seder is found on pages 331–333.

Here is the classic recipe for *assure* made by the Sephardic Jews of

Turkey, Greece, and Armenia. *Assure* is time consuming to make but should definitely be prepared once a year for the special festivity of Tu B'Shevat. The result is worth the time it takes to prepare the pudding.

SOAKING TIME: **overnight**
PREPARATION TIME: **$3^1/_2$–4 hours**
CHILLING TIME: **2 or more hours**
SERVINGS: **12–15 small portions**

$^1/_4$ cup dried chick-peas
1 cup dark raisins
$^1/_2$ cup chopped dried apricots
1 cup brandy
$10^1/_2$ cups cold water for cooking
2 cups whole wheat berries
1 cup long grain brown rice
2 cups sugar
2 cups whole milk (do not substitute 2 percent or skim)
$^1/_4$ cup pine nuts
$^1/_4$ cup slivered almonds
Confectioners' sugar (optional)

1. Soak the chick-peas in water to cover by 1 inch overnight. Soak the raisins and apricots in the brandy overnight.
2. Drain, wash, and put the chick-peas into a pot of boiling, unsalted water. Reduce the heat to simmer, partially cover the pot, and cook the chick-peas for 1 hour or until tender. When done, drain and set aside.
3. While the chick-peas are cooking, bring two saucepans of salted water to a boil, one containing 8 cups and the other containing $2^1/_2$ cups.
4. In the saucepan containing 8 cups water, put the wheat berries. Reduce the heat to medium. Cook the wheat berries for 2 hours. The berries will absorb about half the water in the pan during cooking. The wheat berries are done cooking when they are soft. Drain them and set them aside but do not discard the liquid in which they have cooked.

5. In the saucepan containing $2^1/_2$ cups water, put the rice. Reduce the heat to simmer and cover the pot. The rice will be done after 1 hour of cooking and all of the water should have been absorbed.

6. Take the water in which the wheat berries were cooked and put it into a large saucepan. Dissolve the sugar into this water and bring to a boil. Cook this mixture until it thickens into a thick syrup (about 20 minutes). The syrup will be ready when it is thick enough to coat the back of a spoon.

7. Add the milk to the syrup. Mix together well. Reduce the heat and cook, stirring often, until the milk is absorbed into the syrup and the mixture is thick and creamy. Do not do this at a rapid boil or the milk will curdle. This process will take about 30–45 minutes.

8. Reduce the heat under the syrup to low and add the raisins and apricots and any brandy left from the soaking. Cook over low heat for 20 minutes until tender.

9. Add the wheat berries, rice, and chick-peas to the mixture and cook until all the liquid has been absorbed (about 15–20 minutes).

10. Stir in the nuts. Remove the *assure* from the heat and mound the pudding in a large deep bowl or in individual serving bowls. Chill, covered, in the refrigerator 2 or more hours before serving. If you wish, sprinkle each portion with confectioners' sugar before serving. *Assure* is a very rich dish and a small portion goes a long way.

Torta de los Reyes

KINGS' CAKE

 This almond cake, made with orange rind and orange flower essence, is a typical Sephardic Sabbath cake. The almonds take the place of flour and bind the rest of the ingredients together. This cake does not rise very much. While its appearance may be flat, it is very moist and very rich and a small slice is quite filling. This is an easy sweet to prepare because it is too moist to ever be overbaked or to dry out.

PREPARATION TIME: $1^1/_4$ hours
SERVINGS: 6–8

      Butter, oil, or nonstick spray
5 large eggs
$1^1/_2$ cups sugar
2 cups whole, unblanched almonds
$^1/_3$ cup bread crumbs
1 teaspoon ground cinnamon
1 tablespoon grated orange zest
1 tablespoon orange flower water
      Confectioners' sugar

1. Preheat the oven to 375 degrees. Butter, oil, or spray the sides and bottom of a 9-inch springform cake pan.
2. Beat the eggs well in a large mixing bowl together with the sugar.
3. Add all the remaining ingredients except the confectioners' sugar and mix together thoroughly. Pour into the prepared cake pan and bake on the middle shelf of the oven for 1 hour. Cool the cake in the pan and then unmold. Sprinkle with confectioners' sugar before serving.

VARIATION:

A Passover version of *torta de los reyes* can be made by substituting $^1/_3$ cup *matzoh* meal for the bread crumbs and leaving out the confectioners' sugar. Confectioners' sugar contains cornstarch and therefore is not kosher for Passover.

Tishpitti

Tishpitti is another Sephardic nut cake baked for Sabbaths and holidays. *Tishpitti* is traditionally made with walnuts but it is equally good with almonds, hazelnuts, or pecans.

PREPARATION TIME: **1¼ hours**
CHILLING TIME: **24 hours**
SERVINGS: **8–10**

1½ cups cold water
1½ cups plus ¾ cup sugar
  2 tablespoons Grand Marnier, Cointreau, or triple sec
1½ cups bread crumbs, *matzoh* meal, or a combination
1½ cups ground walnuts
  ½ teaspoon ground cinnamon
  ¼ teaspoon ground cloves
  ¼ teaspoon freshly grated nutmeg
  2 large eggs, beaten
  ⅔ cup freshly squeezed orange juice
  1 tablespoon freshly grated orange zest
  ½ cup peanut, corn, or sunflower oil
8–10 whole walnuts

1. In a saucepan, combine the water and 1½ cups sugar. Dissolve by stirring well with a wire whisk. Bring to a boil over high heat. Cook until the syrup is thick enough to coat the back of a spoon (about 15–18 minutes). When ready, remove from the heat, stir in the liqueur, and set aside to cool.

2. Preheat the oven to 350 degrees. Oil or spray the sides and bottom of an 8-inch-square baking pan.

3. Combine the dry ingredients (including the remaining sugar) in a mixing bowl and mix well.

4. Mix in the eggs, orange juice and zest, and the oil to form a rather stiff dough.

5. Press the dough into the prepared baking pan. Using the tip of a small paring knife, cut the cake into square or diamond shapes. Press a whole walnut into each cut shape.

6. Bake 45–50 minutes or until nicely browned.

7. Remove the cake from the oven and pour the syrup slowly over it. Practically all of the syrup will be absorbed by the cake. Cool to room temperature and allow the flavors to marry for 1 day in the refrigerator before serving.

VARIATION:

Substitute $1^1/_2$ cups ground almonds for the walnuts and 1 teaspoon freshly grated lemon zest for the cinnamon, cloves, and nutmeg. Substitute rosewater or orange flower water for the liqueur in the syrup. Prepare cake as directed above.

Pan d'Espanya or *Pan de Esponjada*

BREAD OF SPAIN OR SPANISH SPONGE CAKE

Sponge cake is a very important element of the cuisines of both Sephardic and Ashkenazic Jews. It is quite possible that European bakers in France, Germany, and Holland learned to make sponge cakes from Jewish bakers. The sponge cake traveled north and east from the countries where Sephardic Jewish tradition dominated into the heartland of Yiddish-speaking Eastern Europe and became so important in the cuisine of Yiddish-speaking Jews that its origin was forgotten. In Russia and Poland, sponge cake became the standard Passover cake because it was helped to rise by the separation of egg whites from the egg yolks. The whites were beaten into a stiff meringue that would help the cake rise without the assistance of yeast or other leavening agents.

Sephardic Jews call the sponge cake *pan d'Espanya* or "Spanish bread" because unlike the other low-rising, syrup-soaked Middle Eastern pastries, this one was light and high rising and reminded them of baking in their former Iberian home. Sponge cakes today are still popular in the Iberian peninsula but in other parts of the Mediterranean, only the Sephardic Jews have retained them as part of their cuisine.

Pan d'Espanya is always made with flour—never with *matzoh* cake meal. So for Sephardic Jews, sponge cake is a non-Passover pastry. *Pan d'Espanya* gets its golden color from the egg yolks and the orange juice. It should be made only with the freshest of eggs.

PREPARATION TIME: **1 hour**
SERVINGS: **8–10**

Slivered almonds for coating
9 large eggs, at room temperature
1$\frac{1}{2}$ cups unbleached white pastry flour
Finely grated zest of 1 orange
Finely grated zest of 1 lemon
1 cup sugar
$\frac{1}{4}$ cup sunflower, corn, or peanut oil
$\frac{1}{4}$ cup freshly squeezed orange juice
Pinch salt (optional)

1. Preheat the oven to 350 degrees. Prepare a round springform pan by oiling it or coating it with nonstick spray. Coat the bottom and sides of the pan with slivered almonds.
2. Carefully separate the egg yolks from the egg whites. Be sure that no egg yolk gets into the whites, or the whites will not foam up and stiffen properly when they are beaten, ruining the sponge effect of the cake.
3. Beat the egg yolks until creamy. While beating, add everything but the egg whites and the salt to the yolks.
4. Using separate beaters or washing and drying the beaters carefully, take the clean beaters and beat the egg whites until very stiff. You may add a pinch of salt to help the egg whites stiffen, if you wish.
5. Carefully fold the egg whites into the egg yolk mixture using a spatula. The mixture should be frothy but the whites should be thoroughly mixed into the yolk batter.

6. Pour the batter into the prepared springform pan and bake 45 minutes. Be careful not to move about in the kitchen while this cake bakes or it will fall. When 45 minutes have passed, test the cake for doneness by inserting a toothpick into the center. If it comes out clean, the cake is ready. Remove it from the oven and cool completely before unmolding.

7. As the cake cools, it may fall slightly and pull away from the sides of the pan. This is to be expected. The almonds will pull away and adhere to the sides of the cake. When the cake is completely cool, turn it over and unmold onto a platter. The cake will have an attractive coating of slivered almonds. For a special treat, serve it with a little brandy poured over it. Sponge cake acts like a sponge and absorbs liqueur or syrup. That is how it got its name!

Bizcochos de Anis

ANISE COOKIES

In 1984, I escorted a group of United Church of Canada ministers to Israel on a mission. I helped organize meetings for this group with Israeli political and religious leaders and was invited by them to join in meetings with Palestinian and Israeli Arab leadership. One of these meetings took place in Nazareth with members of the Nazareth City Council. I, as the only Jew in the group, was given the "seat of honor" next to our host.

The table was set with bottles of arak, Arabic sweets, assorted fresh and dried fruits, and demitasses of Middle Eastern coffee. Our gracious host kept pouring arak into my glass while we engaged in lively and heated discussion. I do not remember how many hours this meeting lasted. I only know that it was one of the most pleasant and memorable of the entire trip.

Arak is a very potent anise-flavored liqueur. That evening it went down so easily and smoothly that I was hardly conscious of how much of it I had imbibed until we were ready to leave. I remember trying to get up out of my seat and having to be supported by one of my colleagues on both my right and left sides. Everybody was laughing, especially me, as I queried, "Is this what it feels like to get drunk?"

Needless to say, I also discovered the salubrious pleasures of the prairie oyster the next morning as I attempted to cure the buzzing headache that I correctly perceived to be a "hangover." As my poor head throbbed away, I not-so-jubilantly exclaimed, "I had to drink arak with a bunch of Protestant ministers from Canada and Christian Arabs in Nazareth, where Jesus established his community, in order to understand for the first and only time in my life what it feels like to get "shikkur" enough to be unable distinguish between 'Cursed be Haman' and 'Blessed be Mordecai'! And it isn't even Purim!"

This delicious Sephardic cookie does not get nearly as drunk as I did that evening. It is a tasty sweet—made with lots of anise-flavored liqueur—and very refreshing after dinner with coffee or mint tea.

PREPARATION TIME: 35–40 minutes
REFRIGERATION TIME: overnight
YIELD: makes 25–30 cookies

- 1 cup anise-flavored liqueur (raki, arak, anisette, Pernod)
- $1/_2$ cup sugar
- $1/_3$ cup peanut or sunflower oil
- 1 tablespoon baking powder
- 3 cups unbleached white pastry flour
- 2 tablespoons anise seeds
- 1 egg beaten with 1 tablespoon cold water (egg wash)

1. In a mixing bowl, combine all the ingredients except the anise seeds and the egg wash. Cover and refrigerate overnight.
2. Preheat the oven to 375 degrees. Prepare well-oiled cookie sheets.
3. Knead the anise seeds into the dough. Cut it into twenty-five or thirty pieces.

4. Roll each piece of dough into a ball and then shape the ball into a miniature bagel by gently poking a hole in the center and twirling the cookie gently around your finger. Lay the cookies on the prepared cookie sheets.

5. Brush each cookie with egg wash. Bake the cookies in the oven for 15 minutes or until they are golden in color. Cool on wire racks. The cookies will keep fresh for weeks stored in tightly sealed tins.

Bizcochos de Vino or Masa de Vino
WINE BISCUITS

Wine biscuits are a Sephardic Passover specialty, particularly popular in Rhodes and Salonika. They were originally made out of *matzoh* ground to a fine texture to resemble flour. *Matzoh* cake meal, which is the commercial version, works perfectly. These cookies are just as tasty made with unbleached white pastry flour for use year round. The version made with flour is called *bizcochos de vino* and the version made with *matzoh* cake meal is called *masa de vino* (wine *matzot*). The potato starch makes the cookie crumbly.

PREPARATION TIME: **35–40 minutes**
YIELD: **makes 25–30 cookies**

1 cup peanut oil
$^3/_4$ cup sweet red wine
$^3/_4$ cup sugar
1 large egg
2 cups *matzoh* cake meal or unbleached white pastry flour
$^1/_2$ cup potato starch
$^1/_2$ cup chopped walnuts
1 tablespoon finely grated fresh orange zest
25–30 walnut halves

1. Preheat the oven to 350 degrees. Oil cookie sheets.

2. Beat the oil, wine, sugar, and egg together with a wire whisk until frothy. Add the remaining ingredients except for the walnut halves. If the mixture seems too soft, add a little more cake meal or flour to achieve the correct consistency. The mixture should hold tightly together, like a sugar cookie dough.

3. On a well-floured board (on Passover, use *matzoh* cake meal), roll the dough to a thickness of $^1/_2$ inch. Cut into 1-inch rounds with a cookie cutter.

4. Place each cookie on the prepared cookie sheets. Set a walnut half into each cookie.

5. Bake for 20–25 minutes or until the cookies are golden in color. They will be very crisp. Cool on wire racks. The cookies keep well for weeks stored in tightly sealed tins.

Mustachudos

SEPHARDIC HAZELNUT COOKIES

 These cookies are a specialty of the Jewish community of Rhodes. *Mustachudos* are similar to macaroons but they contain egg yolks as well as egg whites. Unlike macaroons, they do not harden after they have cooled but remain quite soft. They are delicate in flavor and a little tricky to get right the first time but with a little practice, you, too, can make delicious *mustachudos*.

PREPARATION TIME: **40–50 minutes**
YIELD: **makes 25–30 cookies**

- 3 cups whole, shelled hazelnuts
- 1 cup sugar
- 1 tablespoon finely grated fresh orange zest
- 1 teaspoon ground cinnamon
- $^1/_2$ teaspoon ground cloves
- 2 large eggs, well beaten
- 1 tablespoon honey (preferably citrus flower honey)
    Confectioners' sugar

1. Preheat the oven to 350 degrees. Cover two cookie sheets with wax paper.

2. Place the hazelnuts and the sugar in a food processor or blender. Pulse/chop until the mixture is ground into a paste. Pour it into a mixing bowl.

3. Add the remaining ingredients except the confectioners' sugar and mix together well. The mixture should form a stiff paste.

4. Drop teaspoonsful of the nut batter onto the wax paper, leaving a 2-inch space between each cookie.

5. Bake 25–30 minutes or until golden brown. Remove the cookies from the oven and cool completely before attempting to remove them from the paper. Separate slowly and carefully. Sprinkle the cookies with confectioners' sugar before serving. Stored in tightly closed tins, the cookies keep well for weeks.

Travados

 Travados are a favorite Sephardic pastry prepared for many Jewish holidays. Despite their triangular shape, they are unrelated to *hamantaschen,* the Yiddish Purim cake. There is no Sephardic Purim lore associated with *travados.*

PREPARATION TIME: **1 hour**
YIELD: **makes 25–30 *travados***

> 2 cups unbleached white pastry flour
> 3 cups confectioners' sugar plus additional for dusting
> 8 tablespoons (1 stick) unsalted butter, melted
> $^3/_4$ cup sweet red wine (I like to use port or Madeira instead of the sweet American kosher wines. Hungarian Tokay is also a good choice.)
> $^3/_4$ pound blanched almonds
> $1^1/_2$ tablespoons rosewater, orange flower water, brandy, or liqueur
> 1 medium egg beaten with 1 tablespoon cold water (egg wash)

1. In a deep mixing bowl, mix the flour with 1 cup confectioners' sugar. Add the melted butter and the wine and mix well into a soft dough. Roll the dough into a ball and place on a floured board while you prepare the filling.

2. Preheat the oven to 350 degrees. Oil two cookie sheets.

3. Grind the almonds in the food processor using the pulse/chop motion until they become a paste. Place in a mixing bowl. Add the remaining 2 cups confectioners' sugar and flower water, brandy, or liqueur. Mix together well. This will be the filling.

4. Roll the dough to a thickness of $^1/_4$ inch. Using a cookie cutter, cut the dough into 2-inch rounds.

5. Place 1 teaspoon filling onto the center of each round. Shape each pastry round into a triangle. Place on the cookie sheets.

6. Repeat the rolling and shaping of the dough until the dough and filling are all used up.

7. Brush the pastries with the egg wash and bake for 20–25 minutes or until they are golden in color. Remove from the oven and cool on wire racks. Dust with confectioners' sugar before serving.

Los Siete Cielos

BREAD OF THE SEVEN HEAVENS

This exquisitely crafted bread for the holiday of Shevuot is the most elaborate bread recipe found in any Jewish cuisine. It is heavily laden with religious symbols.

In order to appreciate how this bread came to be created, it is necessary to understand a fundamental Jewish belief about the meaning of life and death. Jews have a strong belief in life after death. They also believe that there is a strong connection between life on earth and life after death. According to Jewish tradition, every human being is a union of body and soul. Human beings are born to live short lifetimes on earth and, while there, do things that will make the world a better and more spiritual place. When a person dies, the body and soul separate. The body returns to earth but the soul does not die. It begins a journey toward eternal life, which can last over several lifetimes. A soul can also return to earth again if God requires it.

Los siete cielos is a symbolic representation, through bread, of the connection between this world and the world-to-come for Jewish people. The centerpiece of the bread is a round, braided loaf called *el monte* ("the mountain"), said to represent Mount Sinai. Seven rings of dough, the *siete cielos* ("seven heavens"), surround *el monte*. The rings of dough around the mountain are decorated with various folkloric and religious symbols shaped out of dough.

The "seven heavens" refers to the "seven holy living spaces through which the soul ascends to heaven." There are seven "living spaces" between heaven and earth through which the soul passes on its journey back to the Creator. Each "living space" is endowed with special characteristics. The soul, as it passes through each of these spaces, gains spiritual knowledge that helps it move closer and closer to its final resting place with God.

The holiday of Shevuot is one of the most spiritual occasions of the Jewish calendar year. On this holiday, Jews celebrate the birth of the Jewish religion. Judaism was a gift given by God to the Jewish people to help them live their lives on earth in a moral and godly way. The way life is to be lived on earth is recorded in the *Torah*. The *Torah* contains Judaism's most important religious teachings. By living their lives according to the *Torah,* Jews prepare their souls for their journey back through the seven heavenly spheres to eternal life with God.

The *Torah* was given to Moses, and through him to the Jewish people, on Mount Sinai, hence the symbol of *el monte* on the Shevuot bread. The *Torah* consists of three parts: a "written tradition," represented by the Hebrew Scriptures, an "oral tradition," represented by the *Talmud* and the codes of Jewish law, and the mystical tradition, represented by the *Kabbalah*. All of the symbols created on the *los siete cielos* bread come from these three traditions. So, by celebrating the giving of the *Torah* on Mount Sinai, the Jews thank God for giving them the gift that will help them live good lives on earth and connect them with the passage of the soul into eternal life. And by eating *los siete cielos* on Shevuot, they take in the spiritual lessons of the holiday and give their lives extra meaning.

PREPARATION TIME (SPONGE): **1 hour**
PREPARATION TIME (BREAD): **$2^1/_2$–$2^3/_4$ hours**
SHAPING TIME: **45 minutes**
YIELD: **makes 1 *siete cielos* bread**

1 teaspoon plus $1^{1}/_{2}$ cups sugar
$^{1}/_{2}$ cup lukewarm water
1 tablespoon active dry yeast
7–8 cups unbleached white bread flour
5 tablespoons sesame oil
$^{1}/_{2}$ cup whole milk
4 large eggs, beaten
1 teaspoon salt
1 tablespoon anise-flavored liqueur (ouzo, arak, raki, Pernod, anisette)
$^{1}/_{4}$ cup dark raisins
1 egg yolk mixed with 1 tablespoon cold water (egg wash)

1. Dissolve the teaspoon sugar in the lukewarm water. Stir in the yeast and set aside in a draft-free place to proof (about 10 minutes). The yeast will be ready when it is bubbly.

2. While waiting for the yeast to proof, put 3 cups flour into a mixing bowl. Make a well in the center of the flour.

3. Add the yeast mixture to the flour and stir in well. The mixture will be somewhat liquid, thicker than pancake batter, but not stiff enough to shape into a dough by hand. Cover the mixing bowl with plastic wrap and set aside for 45 minutes in a draft-free place. The flour mixture will bubble up and begin to rise. This is called the sponge.

4. After 45 minutes have passed, add 4 tablespoons oil, milk, beaten eggs, $1^{1}/_{2}$ cups sugar, salt, and anise liqueur to the sponge. Begin to knead in the remaining flour. Mix and knead steadily until the dough has achieved a soft, moist, but not sticky consistency. You will use more or less flour depending on the quality of the flour and the humidity of the day. Practice will give you a feel for the correct consistency.

5. After the dough has the right consistency, knead in the raisins. Knead the dough and roll it into a ball.

6. Place the remaining tablespoon oil in a mixing bowl and put the ball of dough into this. Roll it over and over to make sure the dough is covered with oil. Cover with a damp cloth and let rise until doubled in bulk (about $1^{1}/_{2}$–2 hours). Dough prepared by the sponge method takes less time to rise than dough prepared by regular mixing and kneading.

7. Take one fourth of the dough and set it aside. Divide the remaining dough into two parts. Set one of the halves aside. Cover this and the other quarter of the dough with a damp towel.

8. Divide the piece of dough you are working with into three pieces. Roll each into a 24-inch-long rope.

9. Pinch the ends of the ropes together and braid them into a three-braid loaf (see figure 1).

Figure 1

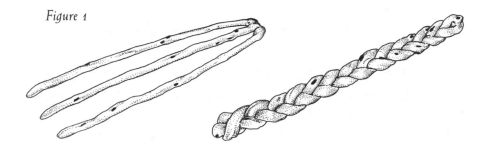

10. Coil the loaf into an ascending spiral (see figure 2). Lay it on the center of a well-oiled baking sheet. This is your *el monte,* representing Mount Sinai. Cover *el monte* with a damp cloth after you finish.

Figure 2

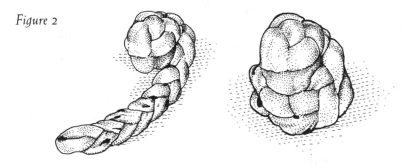

11. Take the second large piece of dough and separate it into seven pieces of varying sizes. These are going to be the "seven heavens" and they will be coiled around the *el monte.* As they coil, they will need to be larger in size. Roll the smallest piece of dough into a rope that will fit snugly around the *el monte* (see figure 3). Repeat with the remaining pieces (see figures 4–6). Cover this with a damp cloth after you finish.

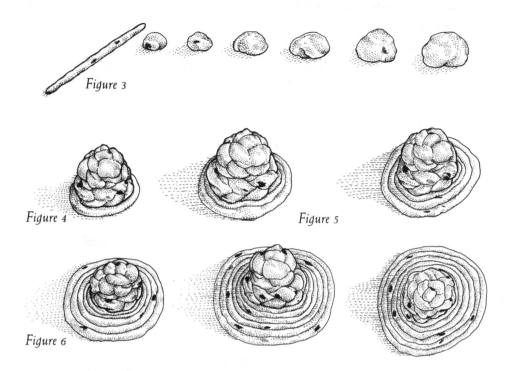

Figure 3

Figure 4

Figure 5

Figure 6

12. The remaining piece of dough will be used to make the various Shevuot symbols that will be placed on the "seven heavens." Divide this piece of dough into five equal pieces. Take one piece and set the other pieces aside, covered with the damp cloth, while you work on the first piece.

13. The first piece of dough will be used to make the *luchot habrit* (the two tablets of stone on which the Ten Commandments were written). Divide it in half and shape each half into an oblong tablet. Set it on top of the "seven heavens" as shown in figure 7.

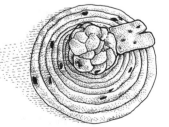

Figure 7

14. Take the second piece of dough. This piece will be shaped into a hand, called a *yad*. The hand in Sephardic folkloric tradition is a symbol of good luck. It contains the number five, symbolizing the five books of Moses (the first five books of the Hebrew Bible). Shape it into a hand and set it down on the "seven heavens" as shown in figure 8.

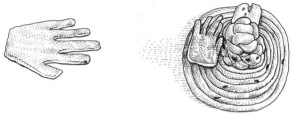

Figure 8

15. Take the third piece of dough and shape it into a fish. The fish is another symbol of good luck to Sephardic Jews, because, unlike other animals, fish were not destroyed by God during the great flood of Noah's time. Fish also symbolize the Messiah and the Messianic era of peace on earth. Lay the fish down on the "seven heavens," as shown in figure 9.

Figure 9

16. Take the fourth piece of dough and shape it into a bird. Birds are a symbol of peace for Sephardic Jews because the dove brought back an olive branch to Noah, which told him that the great flood was

over and that a great peace would now be coming to the earth. Birds are also a symbol of ascendance—the ascendance of the soul into the "seven heavens." Lay the bird onto the "seven heavens," as shown in figure 10.

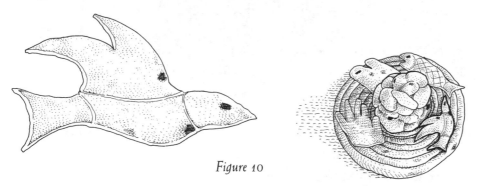

Figure 10

17. The last piece of dough will be used to make Jacob's ladder. Jacob's ladder symbolizes the connection between earth and the "seven heavens" and, ultimately, God's world. This represents the story told in the book of Genesis about the dream Jacob had of angels moving up and down a ladder between heaven and earth. To make Jacob's ladder, divide the piece of dough into three parts. Roll two parts into thin pencils and lay them down on the "seven heavens," as shown in figure 11.

Figure 11

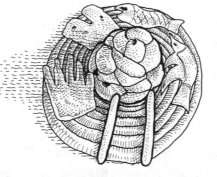

18. Divide the remaining piece of dough into five pieces and roll them into short pencils. These will serve as the steps of the ladder. Lay them in between the "poles" of the ladder as shown in figure 12.

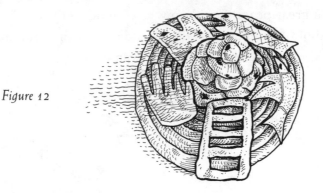

Figure 12

19. Cover the bread with the damp towel and let it rise until doubled in bulk (about 1 hour).
20. Preheat the oven to 350 degrees.
21. Brush the bread with egg wash and bake 40–45 minutes. The bread will be golden brown in color when it is done baking. To test for doneness, gently lift the bread from the baking sheet and tap the bottom. If it sounds hollow, it is done. Set on a rack to cool.

Some versions of the recipe for *los siete cielos* also call for a shape of an oil lamp, called *lampara,* which symbolizes eternity—the eternal flame that burns in the synagogue and that also burned in the ancient Hebrew Temple. Some recipes include a book shape, called *livro,* which symbolizes the various Rabbinic writings including the *Talmud,* the *Kabbalah,* and the codes of Jewish law.

It is always easier to make *los siete cielos* working with a partner in the kitchen so that there will be less waiting time and, more importantly, less time for the already shaped pieces of dough to rise while you are working on the later pieces. It is a good idea to minimize this amount of time so that the dough will not rise too high before you finish shaping it. If you need to work alone, I recommend putting the shaped pieces, beginning with the *el monte,* in the refrigerator, covered by a damp cloth. The dough will not rise while you are working on shaping the last pieces. Then you can take it out of the refrigerator for its final rising before baking.

SERVING SUGGESTIONS:

Los siete cielos is not an ordinary bread and it is not served as part of an ordinary meal. In Sephardic homes, it is placed in the center of the table during the Shevuot dinner for decoration and left there throughout the meal. Following dinner on the night of Shevuot there is a tradition among Jews to return to the synagogue for a *mishmar,* an all-night study session in which holy books (Bible, *Talmud,* and other Rabbinic texts) are read and studied throughout the night. A special collection of readings called *Tikkun Layl Shevuot* (anthology for the evening of Shevuot) is very popular in some Jewish communities and forms the basis for the all-night study session. Midway through the evening, shortly after midnight, people take a break from studying and go home to have something to eat. It is then that *los siete cielos* is eaten, with coffee or tea, as a midnight snack. After this, people return to the synagogue to complete the all-night *Torah* study session. At sunrise the morning services are recited. Then people go home to sleep, their minds filled with the holy words of the *Torah* and their spirits strengthened and uplifted by spending an entire evening immersed in the study of religious texts. In this way, the Jewish community thanks God for the gift of the *Torah* and for the spiritually enriching way of life contained in observance of the Jewish religion.

Orejas de Haman

HAMAN'S EARS

 These are a well-known Sephardic Purim confection. They are made to resemble the shape of a human ear, in this case the ear of Haman, who was defeated in his attempt to murder the Jews of Persia by wise Queen Esther and her uncle Mordecai. It is good that *orejas de haman* are made only once a year because, being deep fried and then soaked in a rich sugar syrup, they are not fare for the girth-conscious!

PREPARATION TIME: $1^1/_2$ hours
YIELD: makes about 25–30 *orejas de haman*

$1^1/_2$ cups sugar
$1^1/_3$ cups cold water
  2 tablespoons orange flower water
  3 large eggs
  Pinch salt
$^1/_2$ cup freshly squeezed orange juice
  Finely grated zest of 1 orange
$^1/_2$ cup confectioners' sugar
  2 cups unbleached white pastry flour
$^1/_4$ cup slivered almonds
  Peanut oil for deep frying

1. Prepare the syrup by dissolving $1^1/_2$ cups sugar in $1^1/_3$ cups cold water in a saucepan. Bring to a boil and cook until the syrup is thick enough to coat the back of a spoon. Remove it from the heat, stir in the orange flower water, and set it aside to cool.
2. Beat the eggs well until frothy in a large mixing bowl. Add the salt, orange juice and zest, and confectioners' sugar.
3. Mix in the flour and slivered almonds. Knead the dough on a floured board or use the dough hook of a standing mixer for 10 minutes.
4. Roll the dough to a $^1/_2$-inch thickness and cut into 4-inch rounds with a wide glass or cookie cutter.

5. Cut each circle in half. Draw the two pointed ends of each half circle together and pinch them to form a small hump in the center which buckles up a little. This piece of dough is now shaped to roughly resemble an ear.

6. Heat peanut oil in a wok to a depth of 2 inches or in a deep fryer to a depth of 3 inches. Fry the pastries a few at a time until they are golden brown in color. Drain on paper towels. Do not crowd the pastries. They will puff out a little as they fry.

7. When you have finished frying and draining all the pastries, arrange them on a long platter and drizzle the syrup over them. Let cool and then serve. Fattening and delicious!

Bumuelos de Hanuka

HANUKKAH FRITTERS

Fritters fried in oil are the Hanukkah specialty of Sephardic Jewry. This is how the Sephardic and other Jews of the Mediterranean celebrate the miracle of the burning oil lamp connected with the Hanukkah story. The lamp in the ancient Hebrew Temple, which burned pure olive oil continuously, was rekindled after being captured by Jewish guerrillas from the Syrian Greek army in 166 B.C.E. but there was only enough oil to last for one day. The miracle is that the oil lasted for eight days, allowing the priests enough time to press and bless fresh oil.

In earlier centuries, olive oil was the only acceptable frying oil for this dish because it was the oil used in the Temple. However, today, any oil is acceptable. I use sunflower, peanut, or safflower oil.

The *bumuelos* are made with yeast dough and various aromatic seasonings. The most traditional is anise or licorice. In Spain and Portugal, anise or fennel seeds were kneaded into the dough to provide this flavor but as Sephardic Jews settled in the Ottoman Empire, raki, arak, and ouzo replaced the seeds. Romanian Jews use fennel seeds. You may vary the seasoning in the dish to create new flavors if you wish. Here is the traditional recipe.

PREPARATION TIME: 1 hour plus $1^1/_2$ hours rising time
YIELD: makes 25–30 *bumuelos*

> 1 tablespoon active dry yeast
> 2 cups lukewarm water
> 1 teaspoon plus 1 cup sugar
> 3 cups unbleached all-purpose white flour
> Pinch salt
> $1^1/_2$ tablespoons anise or fennel seeds or 2 tablespoons ouzo, raki, arak, anisette, or Pernod
> 1 large egg, beaten
> $^1/_2$ cup honey
> 1 cup cold water
> Peanut, sunflower, or safflower oil for deep frying
> Sesame seeds for sprinkling

1. Dissolve the yeast in the lukewarm water mixed with 1 teaspoon sugar. Set aside to proof (about 10 minutes). The yeast is ready when it is bubbly.
2. Mix the flour, $^1/_2$ cup sugar, salt, and anise or fennel seeds (if using) in a mixing bowl. Add the egg, yeast mixture, and liqueur (if using) and knead into a dough. Knead the dough for about 10 minutes. Roll into a ball, place in an oiled mixing bowl, and cover with a damp cloth. Set aside in a draft-free place like an unlit oven to rise until double in bulk (about $1^1/_2$ hours).
3. While the dough is rising, prepare the syrup. Dissolve the honey and remaining sugar in 1 cup cold water in a saucepan. Bring to a boil and cook until thick enough to coat the back of a spoon. Keep the syrup warm over very low heat while you make the fritters.
4. After the dough has sufficiently risen, punch it down and knead it again. Pour oil into a wok to a depth of 2 inches or into a deep fryer to a depth of 3 inches and heat it to just before smoking. Take 1 heap-

ing teaspoonful of the dough and roll it into a ball. Place it in the sizzling oil. Repeat, frying a few of the fritters at a time. Do not crowd the fritters as they cook. Fritters will puff up until they are about double in size. Turn once during frying. They are done when golden in color. Drain on paper towels.

5. To serve *bumuelos,* place two or three on a plate, ladle a little of the warm syrup over them, and sprinkle with sesame seeds. Delicious with coffee!

VARIATIONS:

Substitute any of the following liqueurs for the anise-flavored liqueurs: brandy, Galliano, Sambuca Romana, Strega, amaretto, Frangelico, kirsch, triple sec. Substitute any of the following seasonings for the anise or fennel seeds: ground cinnamon, ground cloves, freshly grated nutmeg, ground mace, ground cardamom seeds.

The Baklava Story
A SEPHARDIC FOLK TALE

Baklava is a popular sweet throughout the Middle East. There are many different recipes for baklava and none is uniquely Jewish. Instead of a recipe for baklava, which can be found in any Greek or Middle Eastern cookbook, I offer this delightful Sephardic folk tale about baklava.

A Christian, a Jew, and a Muslim went to Istanbul together to see if they could make a living. As they walked along the street, they found a coin and decided, after a lengthy discussion, to spend it on baklava. The coin was only enough to buy one pastry. After the men bought the baklava, they decided to save it until morning and the one who dreamed the most beautiful dream would be given the baklava to eat.

In the middle of the night, the Jew got very hungry. He tossed and he turned, unable to fall asleep. He tried to wake up his comrades but they were deep in dreamland. He stretched and he turned over. He scratched his back and then his neck. He rubbed his nose and finally he got up and took a small bite out of the baklava. Then he went back to bed, hoping to fall asleep. But sleep was not to come to him that night. He tossed and turned some more, and every time he tossed and turned, he got up to take another bite out of the baklava until finally the pastry was all gone. No more baklava. When the baklava was gone, the Jew finally fell asleep.

When morning came, the men woke up to find that the baklava was missing. Where had it gone to? The Muslim and the Christian searched here and there, all through the room. The Jew made as if he was searching too. Finally, the three hungry men decided to go to a café. There they had coffee and breakfast and a crowd gathered around to talk. The men started to tell the "café society" the story of how they had found the coin and bought one baklava, planning to give it to the one who would dream the most beautiful dream.

"Let us be the judges," said the people in the café. "Let us decide who had the most beautiful dream. And we will buy that person a baklava as a replacement."

First the Christian spoke. "I dreamed that Jesus came to me and carried me away with him to Nazareth. When we arrived there, all the saints were there to greet us. I bowed to all the saints and then Jesus showed me where the Gates to Paradise stood. What could be more beautiful than that?"

Then it was the Muslim's turn. "I dreamed that the Prophet Muhammad himself appeared before me and whisked me away on a magic carpet to the Holy City of Mecca. We looked at all the *Hajji* marching around the *Ka'aba* and got a glimpse of Eternal Life. What could be more beautiful than that?"

Finally it was the turn of the Jew to speak. "Well, my friends, my dream was different from both of yours. I was not lucky enough, like you, to see the Garden of Eden. But Moses, our teacher, came to me and said, 'Christos is with his Master Jesus in Nazareth. Suleiman is with his Master Muhammad in Mecca. Who knows if either of them is going to come back?' Then he told me to eat the baklava."

"Did you eat it?" asked both of his comrades.

"Who am I to disobey Moses, our teacher?" answered the Jew.

Odds and
Ends

Salt-Preserved Lemons

Sephardic Haroset

Susam (SESAME NUT BRITTLE)

Mazapan or *Almendrada* (MARZIPAN)

    Lemon Marzipan

Dulces

    Dulce de Bimbrio (JELLIED QUINCE CONFECTION)

    Dulce de Mansana (JELLIED APPLE CONFECTION)

    Dulce de Guyaba (JELLIED GUAVA CONFECTION)

    Dulce de Sharope (SWEET LEMON CONFECTION)

Arrope (RAISIN SYRUP)

Soumada and *Pepitada*

    Soumada (ALMOND SYRUP)

    Pepitada (PUMPKIN SEED SYRUP)

Vegetable Stock

Fresh Tomato Sauce

P'kaila

Harissa

Agristada (EGG/LEMON SAUCE)

Caldo de Vinagre (SWEET AND SOUR TOMATO SAUCE)

Salsa con Ajo (GARLIC SAUCE)

Turkish, Greek, or Arabic Coffee

Salt-Preserved Lemons

 Salt-preserved lemons are a Moroccan specialty. They are used as a pickle or condiment and also in cooking special recipes like *Pollo con Olivos y Limon* (page 135). This is a long-lasting condiment and can be replenished just by adding new lemons to the old brine.

PREPARATION TIME: **15 minutes**
MARINATING TIME: **30 days or more**
YIELD: **makes 1 quart preserved lemons**

    2 tablespoons coarse salt
  6–7 small lemons
    1 cup freshly squeezed lemon juice

1. Put the salt into a 4-cup sterilized glass jar with a tight-fitting lid. A French pickling jar with a clamp lid works well. To sterilize the jar, just run it through one cycle in the dishwasher or, lacking this, wash it and dry it carefully and then pour boiling water over it before drying it again.

2. Wash and dry the lemons and cut lengthwise into quarters but do not cut all the way through.

3. Press the lemons down into the jar. Cover with the freshly squeezed lemon juice. Cover the jar tightly and turn it over and over to dissolve the salt and disperse it throughout the jar.

4. Set aside in a cool, dark place for 30 days, turning the jar over once a day. The preserved lemons are now ready. They can be used immediately in recipes. Store on the pantry shelf rather than in the refrigerator. They will keep well indefinitely.

Sephardic Haroset

 Haroset, prepared for the Passover *seder,* is enjoyed throughout the holiday with *matzot.* There are many Sephardic variations—this particular recipe is a favorite. A composite of the Egyptian and Turkish traditions, it includes dates, which are an important ingredient for Egyptian Jews. Walnuts, pine nuts, and almonds are important in Turkey. Orange is ubiquitous throughout the Sephardic world.

SOAKING TIME (FRUIT): **overnight**
PREPARATION TIME: **15 minutes**
YIELD: **makes 3 cups** *haroset*

  1 cup pitted dates
$^1/_2$ cup dark raisins
$^1/_3$ cup (or more) sweet red wine
  1 large seedless navel orange, washed and dried
$^1/_2$ cup citrus flower honey
$^1/_2$ teaspoon ground cinnamon
$^1/_4$ teaspoon ground cloves
$^1/_3$ cup whole almonds
$^1/_3$ cup walnuts
$^1/_3$ cup pine nuts

1. Soak the dates and raisins in the wine overnight. Make sure there is enough wine to cover the fruit.
2. Cut the orange into chunks. Put everything into the food processor and pulse/chop until the mixture is ground to a paste. If necessary, add sweet red wine to achieve the correct consistency. Turn out into a container and use for the *seder* and all through Passover.

Susam

SESAME NUT BRITTLE

 Susam is a favorite Sephardic candy served any time of the year. The combination of sesame seeds and nuts is uniquely Sephardic.

PREPARATION TIME: **20–25 minutes**
YIELD: **makes 3 cups**

- 1 cup sugar
- 2 cups toasted almonds or walnut halves
- 2 tablespoons sesame seeds

1. Cover the kitchen counter or a large wooden board with a piece of heavy-duty foil. This will be used to pour the candy mixture on.
2. Put the sugar into a large, heavy sauté pan and caramelize it over very low heat, stirring constantly.
3. When the sugar begins to caramelize, pour in the nuts and sesame seeds and mix together well. Work very quickly so the caramel does not burn.
4. Pour the mixture immediately onto the foil surface. Use a large rolling pin or a wooden spoon to spread it into a thick layer.
5. Allow the candy to cool and harden and then break it into chunks. Like any brittle, *susam* breaks up into uneven pieces.

Mazapan or Almendrada

MARZIPAN

Marzipan began as a Passover sweet, one of dozens which could be prepared without flour. The marzipan could be eaten on its own or used as a stuffing for dried fruits. Almonds are the most common nut to use in making marzipan, hence the Ladino name *almendrada,* but pistachios, walnuts, and hazelnuts can also be used to make the confection. A combination of almonds and pistachios gives the dish a beautiful pale green color.

PREPARATION TIME: **30 minutes**
YIELD: **makes approximately thirty to forty $^1/_2$-inch-round marzipan balls**

    2 cups sugar
    1 cup cold water
    3 cups blanched almonds, shelled pistachios, or a combination
 $1^1/_2$ tablespoons rosewater
       Confectioners' sugar

1. Dissolve the sugar into the 1 cup cold water in a saucepan. Bring it to a boil and boil 15 minutes or until the syrup is thick enough to coat the back of a spoon.
2. While the syrup is boiling, grind the nuts in a food processor or blender using a pulse/chop motion until they are finely ground.
3. When the syrup is ready, remove it from the heat, stir in the ground nuts and rosewater; set aside to cool. The mixture will absorb the syrup completely and become a sticky, pasty dough.
4. Pour the marzipan out of the saucepan onto a board or cold marble slab and knead it for a few minutes. The marzipan can then be rolled into a half-inch cylinder and cut into small rounds or shaped into balls. Roll each of the rounds or balls in confectioners' sugar. Marzipan can also be used to stuff dried fruits (see page 251). Allow the flavors of the confection to mellow for 24 hours before serving.

VARIATION:

Lemon Marzipan

Lemon marzipan is a specialty of the Jews of Greece. To make it, take the large hole of a citrus zester and strip off the zest of ten lemons. Put the zests into a bowl and cover completely with cold water. Allow the lemon zests to soak for 2 days, changing the water a few times. On the third day, rinse off the zests and put them into a saucepan with water to cover. Simmer over low heat until the zests are very soft. Drain them and mash the zests into a fine pulp by hand or in the food processor together with the 3 cups almonds. Do not use pistachios or any other nuts for making lemon marzipan. Follow the instructions in the recipe above. Lemon marzipan is delicious on its own or stuffed into dried fruits, especially prunes.

Dulces

Dulces are mouthwatering sugary confections that are popular today in Turkey, Greece, and all over Latin America. In Mexico and other Latin American countries, the sweet is cut into thin strips and served together with bread and sliced yellow or white cheese. Sweets similar to *dulce de bimbrio* can be found in Mexican and Latin American markets all over the United States made of tropical fruits. *Dulce de bimbrio* originated as a Sephardic specialty; it traces its origin back to Spain. It was most likely brought by *conversos* (Jewish converts to Catholicism) to the Spanish colonies in the Americas. Many *conversos* settled in these colonies, particularly in Mexico and the Caribbean islands, to escape the Inquisition, which was less oppressive there than it was in Spain itself. Some of these *conversos* practiced Judaism in secret.

The *dulces* (sweets) can be made with many different kinds of fruits. Quinces (*bimbrios*) were particularly popular in Spain because the large amount of pectin in the fruit aided in its jelling. But bitter oranges, apricots, and apples were also used to prepare this sweet. In the tropical climates of the Caribbean islands and Latin America, fruits like guavas and mangoes grew in abundance and were readily used to prepare *dulces* by Jewish cooks. Today, jellied pastes made of these fruits (*dulce de membrillo* and *dulce de guyaba*) are commonly found throughout Mexico, Puerto Rico, Cuba, and other Latin American countries. The guava is especially loved because it resembles quince but is much sweeter and has a heady, "roselike" aroma.

This sweet was also brought to the countries of the Ottoman Empire by Sephardic Jews and today is popular in many Middle Eastern countries.

Here are three recipes for jellied *dulces* from three of my favorite fruits. Try this with any fruit you enjoy.

Dulce de Bimbrio
(Jellied Quince Confection)

> PREPARATION TIME: $1^1/_2$ hours
> DRYING TIME: 3–4 days
> YIELD: makes 2 sheets of *dulce*

> 2 pounds quinces
> 1 pound sugar
> $^1/_2$ cup freshly squeezed lemon juice
> $^1/_2$ cup cold water

1. Wash the quinces and cut them in chunks but do not peel or remove the cores. Put them in a *couscousière* or a steamer and steam for 30 minutes over boiling water.
2. When the fruit has cooked through, rub it through a fine sieve into a mixing bowl. The seeds and extra cellulose will remain in the sieve.
3. Dissolve the sugar in the lemon juice and water in a heavy saucepan (enameled cast-iron is best) by whisking it with a wire whisk. Bring to a boil and reduce the heat to simmer. Simmer until the mixture turns into a syrup (10–15 minutes). Reduce the heat to its lowest possible temperature.

4. Add the quince puree and cook for 20–25 minutes, stirring once in a while. When the paste is thick enough, it will begin to pull away from the sides of the saucepan.

5. Put the thick paste into a wide, shallow mold or tray like a large baking pan. Spread it out evenly. It should be no more than $^3/_4$ inch thick.

6. Allow it to dry in a cool, dry place for 3 or 4 days. When it is ready, it will have the texture of a jellied candy. Cut into squares, diamond shapes, or triangles and wrap in greaseproof paper or foil. This confection will keep well for months. Eat very small pieces as it is a very rich, very sweet confection.

Dulce de Mansana
(Jellied Apple Confection)

> My master put this lovely delicacy into your hand
>   Note its smell. Forget what else you yearn for.
> On all sides it is blushing, like a young maiden
>   at the first touch of my hand on her breast.
> It is an orphan, it has no father or mother
>   and it is far away from its leafy home.
> When it was picked, the other apples on the tree were jealous.
>   They envied its journey and they called out to it,
> "Give greetings to our master Isaac.
>   You are so lucky to be kissed by his lips."
>   SOLOMON IBN GABIROL (1021–58)

Apples are not commonly thought of as a Mediterranean fruit. Yet Mediterranean writers of many centuries, including Jewish writers, composed odes to the apple. This *dulce* is a favorite of apple lovers around the world.

PREPARATION TIME: $1^1/_2$–2 hours
DRYING TIME: 3–4 days
YIELD: makes 2 sheets of *dulce*

  12 medium Jonathan or McIntosh apples
    4 cups sugar
$^1/_2$ cup freshly squeezed lemon juice
    1 cup cold water

Follow the same procedure, steps 1 through 6, outlined above for *Dulce de Bimbrio* (pages 293–294). Apples are moister than quinces so the final cooking and thickening will take a little longer. Like apple butter, the *dulce de mansana* will turn a dark, rich brown as it cooks.

Dulce de Guyaba
(Jellied Guava Confection)

Substitute 2 pounds guavas for the quinces and proceed as directed for *Dulce de Bimbrio,* steps 1 through 6 (pages 293–294).

Dulce de Sharope
(Sweet Lemon Confection)

This unusual confection comes out of a body of recipes prepared in Turkish and Greek homes that was adopted by Sephardic Jews when they settled in the Ottoman Empire. There is an art to the preparation and presentation of this type of *dulce*. Made from every kind of fruit that grows in the Mediterranean, the *dulces* are used to extend hospitality to special guests. Mireille Varol, formerly of Izmir, Turkey, describes the ritual of preparing and serving *dulce de sharope* in her grandmother's home.

"My grandmother, Matilda Navarro, would come from Istanbul every year to stay about a month with us. That was the time for cooking [the best part] and for sharing my room with her [not always the best part]. My memory of my grandmother's visits is filled with the smells of freshly made pastas [*filas*], pickles, *salados* [cured fish]. But the best part was the homemade jams [*dulces*].

"*Dulce* was very important and every family had several kinds made with the freshest of seasonal fruits. The *dulce* was arranged in a specially designed tray [*tavia*] to serve for the holidays. Since most men were self-employed, they would close their shops and, after synagogue services, pay visits to friends and relatives. This was the occasion to see people that we would not see on an everyday basis. Women would prepare their homes weeks ahead for the purpose of receiving the male guests.

"The *dulce* tray was made of silver and it had silver spoons to match. In the center of the tray was a beautiful glass or crystal bowl which held the *dulce*. It sat on a high pedestal and the spoons were arranged around it, each spoon in its special holder. Small glasses of water were arranged around the bowl. The tray and spoons were highly polished for the occasion.

"The serving of the *dulce* was the duty of the daughter whose turn it was to find a *novyo* or "husband." The men would dip their spoons into the *dulce,* take a spoonful of it, savor it slowly, and then put their spoons into the glasses filled with water. They would then proclaim the virtues of the *dulce* and of the woman who made it. The making of *dulce,* in the old days, was considered one of the very desirable marriage traits a man would look for in a woman."

Here is Mireille Varol's recipe for *dulce de sharope,* which she received from her mother, Sara Abuaf, who in turn got it from Grandmother Matilda Navarro.

PREPARATION TIME: $1^1/_4$ hours
YIELD: **makes 1 cup of very rich *dulce de sharope***

  1 **cup plus 2 tablespoons sugar**
$1^1/_2$ **cups cold water**
  1 **teaspoon freshly squeezed lemon juice**

1. Mix the sugar and water together in a saucepan and bring it to a boil. With a slotted spoon, skim off any foam that rises.
2. Lower the heat and add the lemon juice. Keep cooking the syrup until it begins to form ribbons when taken between the fingers. The syrup will turn clear.
3. Remove the syrup from the heat and let it cool for 1 hour.
4. After the syrup is cool, beat it with a 1-inch-thick wooden dowel. Beat well in the same clockwise direction until the syrup thickens and turns white. Keep beating in the same direction. This is important to give the correct texture and color to the *dulce*. Transfer the *dulce* to a glass container with a tight-fitting lid, where it will keep for months. Serve in the manner described above or as a jam on sweet breads or muffins.

Arrope

RAISIN SYRUP

 Arrope was traditionally prepared by Turkish Jews as a syrup to pour over *Bumuelos de Masa* (page 241) or *Masa Tiganitas* (page 242) as an alternative to honey. It is a delicious alternative to maple or other syrups to pour over any kind of pancake or crepe.

PREPARATION TIME: $2^1/_2$–3 hours
YIELD: makes $2^1/_2$–3 cups *arrope*

$^1/_2$ cup sugar or more to taste
 5 cups cold water
 1 pound sweet dark raisins
 1 tablespoon freshly squeezed lemon juice

1. Dissolve the $^1/_2$ cup sugar in the water in a saucepan and bring to a boil. Reduce the heat and add the raisins. Simmer uncovered for 2 hours. The liquid will cook down to half the original amount and the raisins will render sugar and flavor. When done *arrope* will have the consistency of very thin maple syrup.

2. Strain the syrup through a sieve, pushing as much pulp through as possible. To do this you might have to pour the strained juice back through the sieve two or three times. After you have completed this, discard what is left of the raisins.

3. Put the syrup back into the saucepan and add the lemon juice. Taste for sweetness and, if necessary, add more sugar.

4. Return the syrup to a boil and cook until it is thick enough to coat a spoon. Cool and use as a syrup, poured over *bumuelos* or any other kind of pancake.

Soumada and Pepitada

 These syrups are popular all over the Middle East and North Africa and as far west and north as Sicily. Mixed with ice cold water, they make a much loved and refreshing beverage.

Soumada
(Almond Syrup)

PREPARATION TIME: **30 minutes**
RESTING TIME: **24 hours**
YIELD: **makes 1 quart** *soumada*

3 cups cold water
2 cups ground blanched almonds
4$\frac{1}{2}$ cups sugar
1 teaspoon almond extract

1. Bring the water to a boil in a saucepan. Add the ground almond paste and remove from the heat. Cover and allow to rest for 24 hours.
2. Strain the contents of the saucepan through a sieve lined with a double layer of cheesecloth into another saucepan. The liquid will be white.
3. Add the sugar to the saucepan and dissolve it with a wire whisk. Bring to a boil and reduce the heat to simmer. Cook until the syrup is thick enough to coat the back of a spoon (about 20 minutes).
4. Stir in the almond extract and bottle the syrup in a vinegar bottle with a clamped top. Store in a cool, dark place.
5. To use the *soumada,* put 3 tablespoons of the syrup into a glass and dissolve it in ice cold water. Delicious!

Pepitada
(Pumpkin Seed Syrup)

> PREPARATION TIME: **30 minutes**
> RESTING TIME: **24 hours**
> YIELD: **makes 1 quart *pepitada***

    4 cups cold water
    2 cups *pepitas* (ground toasted pumpkin seeds)
    1 cup sugar
    1 teaspoon almond extract

Follow steps 1 through 5 for *soumada,* substituting the above ingredients. Serve as you would *soumada. Pepitada* is the traditional drink to break the fast on Yom Kippur in many Sephardic Jewish homes, especially those of Rhodes, Greece, and Turkey.

Vegetable Stock

This is a useful and flavorful stock, easy to make, and flexible within limits. Broccoli, cauliflower, cabbage, and brussels sprouts are strongly flavored and will dominate rather than blend into the dish. Green peppers should not be used to make stock.

> PREPARATION TIME: **1 1/2 hours**
> YIELD: **makes 1 1/2–2 gallons**

    4 tablespoons peanut or sunflower oil
    3 large onions, peeled and chopped
    3 cloves garlic, peeled
    2 large carrots, peeled and chopped
    4 large stalks celery, chopped
    2 leeks, white part and 2 inches greens, washed and halved
    4 cups additional vegetables (green beans, spinach, turnips, parsnips,
       zucchini, kohlrabi, celery root, etc.)
    1 bouquet garni, consisting of 6 sprigs fresh parsley, 3 sprigs fresh
       thyme, and 1 bay leaf, tied together with kitchen string
    4 black peppercorns
    1 tablespoon coarse salt

1. Heat the oil in a stockpot over medium-high heat. Sauté the onions until soft and translucent (5–7 minutes).
2. Reduce the heat to medium and add the garlic, carrots, and celery. Cook another 5 minutes, stirring constantly. Add the remaining vegetables and cook 5–7 minutes more. Cover with cold water by 2 inches.
3. Bring to a boil. Add the remaining ingredients, reduce the heat to simmer, partially cover the pot, and cook for 45 minutes to 1 hour. The vegetables will be very soft.
4. Pour the contents of the pot through a sieve into another pot, pressing down hard on the vegetables to extract all the flavor. Stock will keep well for 2 or 3 days in the refrigerator and frozen for 2 or 3 months.

Fresh Tomato Sauce

Fresh tomato sauce is as essential to good Mediterranean Jewish cooking as it is to Italian or other Mediterranean cuisines. While the preparation of this sauce is lengthy, the result is well worth the time and effort. Quantities can be increased proportionally. An acceptable variation can be prepared with good quality canned tomatoes.

PREPARATION TIME (WITH FRESH TOMATOES): **5–6 hours**
PREPARATION TIME (WITH CANNED TOMATOES): **$2^1/_2$–3 hours**
YIELD: **makes 4 quarts**

    8 pounds best quality fresh garden tomatoes
    1 cup olive oil
    2 large onions, peeled and chopped
    2 large carrots, peeled and chopped
    4 large stalks celery, chopped
    1 teaspoon sugar
    1 or more tablespoons salt

1. Cut the tomatoes into chunks and put them into a large stockpot. The tomatoes are full of juice and will provide all the liquid needed to make the sauce. Cover the pot and bring it to a boil. Reduce the heat to simmer, partially cover the pot, and cook the tomatoes for $1\frac{1}{2}$ hours. Remove from the heat and cool slightly.

2. Pour the contents of the stockpot through a sieve into another pot. Press down hard on the vegetables to put the pulp through the sieve. Discard the seeds and skin that remain in the sieve.

3. Wash and dry the stockpot. Heat the oil over medium-high heat and sauté the onions until soft and translucent (5–7 minutes).

4. Add the carrots and celery and cook another 7–10 minutes, stirring constantly, until the vegetables begin to soften.

5. Add the tomato puree and the sugar to the vegetable mixture. Cover the pot and bring to a boil. Reduce the heat to simmer and cook another 2–$2\frac{1}{2}$ hours. This sauce will be thick.

6. Puree the sauce in a food processor or blender and put it through a sieve. Almost all the solids will pass through the sieve; discard what remains. Season the sauce with salt. The sauce can be kept in the refrigerator for a week. If you do not plan to use the sauce within 1 week, you must process it.

7. To process the sauce, sterilize four quart-size glass canning jars and their lids by running them through one cycle in the dishwasher. Alternately, wash the jars and lids with warm, soapy water, dry them, and pour boiling water over them. Dry again.

8. Fill each jar with tomato sauce, cover with the cap, and twist it until it is as tight as possible.

9. Bring a large stockpot of water to a boil. Place a rack into the stock-pot. The jars will rest on this rack while they are being processed. If you own a canning pot, the rack that comes with the pot does this job well, if the jars are the correct size for the pot. You should be able to process all four jars at one time. Place all the jars onto the rack, making sure that they are completely submerged in boiling water.

10. Cook the jars at a slow, steady simmer for 15–18 minutes, covered. Remove from the pot and cool. Store on a cool, dark shelf. The processed tomato sauce will keep for months.

VARIATION:

Substitute six 28-ounce cans of best quality tomatoes. Puree them in a food processor or blender and pass the puree through a sieve. Proceed with the recipe as described above, beginning with step 3.

P'kaila

 P'kaila is a savory herb essence prepared by Tunisian Jews from a variety of fresh herbs. It is used as both a condiment and a seasoning ingredient in sauces. Moroccan cooks make a similar dish called *charmoula,* which does not contain spinach. *P'kaila* can be used with plain boiled or roasted meats, fish, and vegetables as a dipping sauce. It is equally delicious with just bread. For an unconventional dish, serve *p'kaila* instead of pesto with freshly cooked pasta. It makes a wonderful pasta sauce.

PREPARATION TIME: **35–40 minutes**
YIELD: **makes $2^1/_2$ cups**

- 4 pounds fresh spinach
- 2 tablespoons plus $^1/_3$ cup olive oil
- 1 large onion, peeled and finely chopped
- 5 large cloves garlic, peeled and finely chopped
- $^1/_4$ cup chopped celery leaves
- $^1/_3$ cup chopped fresh cilantro leaves
- $^1/_3$ cup chopped fresh parsley leaves
- $^1/_4$ cup chopped fresh mint leaves
- 4 scallions, finely chopped
- $1^1/_4$ teaspoons or more salt

1. Carefully wash the spinach leaves to remove all the sand and put them into a pot of cold water. Cover and bring to a boil over medium heat. Reduce the heat and cook until the spinach leaves wilt. Drain and pour cold water over them to stop the cooking. When cool, squeeze dry and chop.
2. Heat 2 tablespoons oil in a deep, wide sauté pan over medium-high heat and sauté the onion until soft and translucent (5–7 minutes). Reduce the heat and add the garlic. Cook an additional 5 minutes.
3. Add the remaining ingredients, except for the salt and the remaining oil, and cook over low heat, stirring constantly, until everything is cooked through.
4. Puree the mixture in a food processor or blender a little at a time. When the mixture is pureed, put it into a mixing bowl, stir in the salt, and taste for seasoning. Add more salt, if necessary.
5. Heat the remaining oil in a large, deep sauté pan; add the puree. Cook for 5–10 minutes, or until the mixture turns into a paste with a pesto-like consistency. Remove from the heat and cool to room temperature. Store *p'kaila* in the refrigerator in a sealed glass container. *P'kaila* will keep fresh for about 2–2$^1/_2$ weeks.

Harissa

Harissa is a hot-flavored Tunisian and Moroccan condiment. In Tunisia it is eaten with practically everything. When Tunisians prepare *couscous,* they mix a tablespoon or two of *harissa* into $^1/_2$ cup of the stock in which the stew was cooking and serve it as a hot sauce to pour over the *couscous* and meat.

Harissa is easy to make and it keeps well for a long time in the refrigerator. It can be made with either fresh or dried red hot chili peppers. There are many kinds of chili peppers on the market but the only two that are traditional in Moroccan and Tunisian cooking are cayenne peppers and hot paprika peppers. Therefore, I specify only these varieties.

PREPARATION TIME: 15 minutes if using fresh peppers,
1 hour 15 minutes if using dried
YIELD: makes about $1/_2$ cup *harissa*

$1/_2$ cup fresh cayenne or hot paprika peppers or 1 ounce dried cayenne or hot paprika peppers
  1 large clove garlic
  1 tablespoon cumin seeds
  2 teaspoons salt
$1/_3$ cup olive oil

1. If using fresh peppers, cut them in half and remove the seeds and cores. If using dried chili peppers, they need to first be soaked in boiling water for 1 hour in order to be reconstituted. After doing this, remove the seeds and cores of the reconstituted dried peppers.
2. Put the peppers into a food processor together with the garlic and cumin seeds. Process until smooth.
3. Put the puree into a small mixing bowl and mix in the salt and the olive oil.
4. Put the *harissa* into a glass jar and store in the refrigerator. Use as directed in recipes or serve alongside plain boiled or roasted meats, fish, and *couscous* dishes. It will keep up to 3 months if refrigerated.

Agristada

EGG/LEMON SAUCE

Agristada is the Sephardic egg/lemon sauce. It is made specially to serve alongside fried or grilled fish, *Keftedes* or *Albondigas de Pescado* (page 120), or stuffed vegetables. Vegetable stock is traditional but fish stock or fish fumet makes a wonderful base for *agristada* if you are poaching fresh fish. Poaching was not a cooking technique employed by Sephardic cooks for any kind of fish except *albondigas,* hence the use of vegetable stock.

PREPARATION TIME: **15–20 minutes**
YIELD: **makes 1$^1/_2$ cups *agristada***

- 2 **large eggs, beaten**
- $^1/_3$ **cup freshly squeezed lemon juice**
- 2 **tablespoons olive oil**
- 1 **teaspoon salt**
- 2 **cups Vegetable Stock (page 299)**
- $^1/_4$ **cup snipped fresh chives**
- $^1/_4$ **cup finely chopped fresh parsley**

1. Beat the eggs together with the lemon juice, oil, and salt in a mixing bowl.
2. Heat the vegetable stock in a saucepan over medium-high heat.
3. Ladle a small amount of the stock into the egg/lemon mixture and dissolve it by whisking with a wire whisk. Beat well.
4. Slowly pour the egg/lemon mixture into the simmering stock, whisking all the time until it thickens.
5. Remove the sauce from the heat, mix in the fresh herbs, and pour into a sauceboat.

Caldo de Vinagre

SWEET AND SOUR TOMATO SAUCE

 This is another traditional Sephardic sauce to serve with fried or grilled fish. The sugar and vinegar are balanced by the tomato sauce, which fuses with both the sweet and the sour flavors. Celery leaves add a savory touch.

PREPARATION TIME: **35–40 minutes**
YIELD: **makes $1^1/_2$ cups**

- 3 tablespoons olive oil
- 1 small onion, peeled and finely chopped
- 1 clove garlic, peeled and finely chopped
- 3 tablespoons red wine vinegar
- $3^1/_2$ teaspoons sugar
- $1^1/_4$ cups Fresh Tomato Sauce (page 300)
- 2 tablespoons finely chopped fresh celery leaves
- 1 teaspoon salt
- 2 tablespoons finely chopped fresh parsley

1. Heat the oil over medium-high heat in a saucepan. Sauté the onion until soft and translucent (5–7 minutes). Reduce the heat to low and add the garlic. Cook 3 minutes longer, stirring constantly to prevent burning.
2. Add the vinegar, sugar, tomato sauce, and celery leaves to the saucepan. Cook, stirring constantly, for 15–20 minutes or until the sauce thickens.
3. Remove from the heat, stir in the salt and parsley, and serve immediately in a sauceboat.

Salsa con Ajo

GARLIC SAUCE

 This is the simplest sauce of all to serve with fried or grilled fish. It is basically a warm, lemon-scented vinaigrette with lots of *ajo,* or "garlic."

PREPARATION TIME: **15 minutes**
YIELD: **makes $^3/_4$ cup salsa**

2 tablespoons olive oil
2 very large cloves garlic, peeled and finely chopped
1 tablespoon cold water
$^1/_2$ cup freshly squeezed lemon juice
$^1/_2$ teaspoon salt
1 tablespoon snipped fresh chives
1 tablespoon finely chopped fresh dill leaves
1 tablespoon finely chopped fresh parsley

1. Heat the oil over medium heat. Add the garlic, water, lemon juice, and salt; cook 5 minutes.
2. Remove from the heat and stir in the fresh herbs. Pour into a sauceboat and serve with fried or grilled fish.

Turkish, Greek, or Arabic Coffee

 It was difficult enough for a student in an Orthodox Yeshiva (Rabbinic school) in Israel to get to know nonobservant Israeli Jews, much less to get to know Arabs. I succeeded, despite the odds, at both of these undertakings. Mahmoud, a Muslim, worked at a kiosk in the Old City of Jerusalem that had an excellent selection of dried fruits and nuts. Because I came so often to buy his merchandise,

Mahmoud and I struck up a warm and friendly acquaintanceship. I taught him some Hebrew and English words and he taught me some Arabic.

One day he invited me into a room behind the kiosk to join him for coffee. He took down off a shelf what appeared to me to be a grime-encrusted *ibrik* (coffeepot) that seemed to never have been washed since the day it was first used. I knew that the most heinous insult I could commit in this situation was to refrain from drinking Mahmoud's coffee. So I gritted my teeth and mentally prepared myself for an eventual attack of *shilshul* (Hebrew for diarrhea) later that day. After the coffee was made and poured, I sipped tentatively and was immediately overcome by a feeling that can only be described in one word—rapture. I have always loved strong, black coffee. But this was truly one of the best cups of coffee I had ever tasted. Mahmoud had put a small amount of mixed spices into the coffee grounds together with the sugar and water before he made the coffee. "What am I tasting, Mahmoud?" I asked. "Is it the spices you put in here? What makes this coffee taste so good?"

"No, it was not only the spices." He beamed with pleasure. "It was the oil from the coffee."

"Oil from the coffee? What is oil from the coffee? I didn't know there was any oil in coffee beans."

Mahmoud went over to a sink and carefully washed out the *ibrik* with cold water and dried it. "I wash this only with cold water. Never anything else." He pointed to a residue that coated the bottom and sides of the *ibrik*. "This is oil from the coffee." This was the same residue I had mistaken for grime. "Wash the coffeepot only with cold water. The oil from the coffee sticks to the pot and every time you make fresh coffee, it gives it extra flavor. You cannot buy anything like this anywhere. The best coffee is made in an old, used pot."

This tasty strong coffee, served Middle Eastern style in tiny cups, is a mark of hospitality throughout the Mediterranean in Jewish as well as in Muslim and Christian homes. In Israel it is nicknamed *kaffe botz* or "mud coffee" because of the sediment that settles at the bottom. Among Sephardic Jews, this coffee is popular as far north as Serbia.

There is a real art to preparing this coffee and to do it correctly, you need the special coffeemaker called an *ibrik*. The *ibrik* is a thin, tall saucepan with a long pouring handle and a notch for a spout on one end of the top of the pot. *Ibriks* are available in just about any Middle Eastern or Greek grocery, most gourmet shops, or through a number of the mail-order catalogs that sell cookware. The proportions of coffee grounds, sugar, and water need to be measured exactly. The boiling procedure follows a ritual. Most important, the coffee has to be ground to a fine powder. This is best done by hand.

I first grind my beans in an electric coffee grinder set to the finest grind. Then I put these grounds into a special hand grinder I bought in Greece. The hand grinder is made of brass and is somewhat difficult to turn, which is why I begin the process in the electric grinder. I find that hand grinding the grounds is essential if the coffee is to taste just right.

Here is my recipe for *kaffe botz,* without any "oil from the coffee."

PREPARATION TIME: **15–18 minutes**
YIELD: **makes 6 Turkish coffee cups or 3 demitasses of coffee**

> 2 tablespoons coffee beans
> 2 tablespoons sugar
> 1¹/₂ cups water
> Pinch ground cloves, cardamom, or cinnamon (optional)

1. Grind the coffee to a very, very fine powder.
2. Dissolve the sugar in the water in the *ibrik* by whisking it with a small wire whisk. Bring it to a boil over high heat.
3. Remove the *ibrik* from the heat and add the coffee grounds and ground spices, if using. Stir well.
4. Return the *ibrik* to the burner and bring to a boil again. When the coffee begins to froth upward, remove the *ibrik* from the burner. The froth will disappear back into the *ibrik*.
5. Rap the bottom of the *ibrik* on a flat surface to settle the grounds and put the *ibrik* back on the burner. Bring to a boil again.
6. When the coffee froths upward, remove from the heat and rap the *ibrik* on the flat surface again.

7. Repeat steps 5 and 6. You will be bringing the coffee just to a boil three times during the preparation and rapping the *ibrik* on a flat surface three times.
8. After the third time, serve the coffee as soon as the grounds have settled. Pour it out into the Turkish coffee cups or the demitasses. The *botz* ("mud") will settle to the bottom of each cup. Drink the coffee black and enjoy!

VARIATIONS:

The amount of sugar can be varied to suit the taste. The recipe above is called "medium sweet." Another delicious variation, from Turkey, is orange-flavored Turkish coffee. To make this, prepare one recipe Turkish coffee using cinnamon. Serve a strip of orange zest on the side of the coffee, which can be put into the coffee to flavor it. This is similar to the way Italians serve espresso with a strip of lemon zest.

Recipe for a Tormented Soul

A LADINO FOLK TALE

A man once went to visit a *m'kubbal* (a rabbi who is learned in *Kabbalah*, the Jewish mystical teachings) who was also a physician to ask his advice on a matter of great importance. "I am very sick in my soul," said the visitor. "I have committed so many sins. Give me a medicine that will cure my spiritual sickness and help me stop committing sins."

The *m'kubbal* looked soulfully at the man and said, "For a person like you whose spirit is so tormented, take a root of humbleness and two leaves, one of patience and one of hope. Mix them with branches of *Torah* and with the rose petals of wisdom. Place all of this in a mortar of repentance, and crush it together well with lots of love and affection. Add some waters of fear of God and blend well. Place this mixture in the oven and light a fire of thanksgiving underneath it. After it is properly cooked, preserve it in a bottle of understanding and drink it out of a cup of goodwill. If you do this, you will never again commit a sin and your spirit will be completely at peace."

Traditions,
Customs,
and Menus

SHABBAT: THE SABBATH

Twilight is such a sweet time to me!
   Because I can see the face of Shabbat as if it were a new face
   Come and bring apples and many sweet raisin cakes,
   Because this is my beloved day of rest.
   I sing to you, Shabbat, songs of love.
   Songs that suit you well.
Because you are a day filled with joy!
   A day of pleasures and banquets,
   Of three sumptuous feasts.
A day of the pleasures of the table and of the couch.

From "Peace Be Unto You, Oh Shabbat"
YEHUDA HALEVI (1075–1148 c.e.)

*t*he Sabbath is the most important day of the week in the Jewish community. The seventh day, which represents God's rest from the activity of Creation, is a day dedicated by Jews to rest, relaxation, and spiritual nourishment. The tastiest and most beautiful meals are prepared in honor of the Sabbath. Food is cooked for the Sabbath on Thursday and Friday before sundown. Hot dishes are eaten Friday night or kept warm in an extremely low oven or on very low heat on top of an oven burner covered with a metal sheet to diffuse the heat and serve as a barrier between the heat source and the food.

Many of the Shabbat dishes also have folkloric and symbolic meanings. Best known among the Mediterranean Jewish Sabbath foods are fish dishes, *Huevos Haminados* (page 231), Hamin (page 170), savory pastries, *Sutlach* (page 253), and various kinds of sweets. The savory pastries, for example, symbolize plentitude and richness. They also symbolize the food placed between double portions of manna given by God to the Hebrews when they wandered in the desert. The savory pastries are modern forms of an ancient Jewish dish called *pashtida,* mentioned in the *Talmud* and many other Rabbinic writings. Bread is blessed at two or three different meals on the Sabbath according to Jewish tradition. Wine is blessed twice for meals and once at the conclusion of the Sabbath.

Preparing for the Sabbath is likened by Mediterranean Jews to the preparations for a wedding. Sephardic poets have compared the Sabbath to a queen or a bride to which the people of Israel get married and renew their wedding vows every week. Jewish women engage in elaborate bathing and grooming of their bodies and cleaning of their clothes in order to become Sabbath queens or brides.

Sabbath preparation usually begins on Thursday with the cleaning of the house, clothes, and tableware. Some foods, like appetizers and fillings for savory pastries are made on Thursday. One of the curious peculiarities mentioned by writers about the Sabbath preparation of the Jews of southern Greece and Turkey is the whitewashing of the courtyards of their houses every Friday before the Sabbath. Most homes in this part of the world are built around courtyards festooned with potted flowers, herbs, and colorful rose gardens. Whitewashing the courtyards is a way of making the home clean and festive for the coming of the Sabbath bride.

SHABBAT MENUS
Friday Night Dinners

Friday Night Dinner
    Sabbath Bread
    Ajada (Roasted Garlic Spread)
    Anjinara (Herb-Marinated Artichokes)
    Roasted Pepper Salad with Simple Lemon Vinaigrette

Black Olives in Savory Herb Marinade
Pescado Ahilado con Tomate (Baked Fish Fillets with Tomato Sauce)
Arroz de Sabato (Sabbath Rice Pilav with Saffron)
Assorted Fresh Fruits
Torta de los Reyes (Kings' Cake)
Coffee or Tea

West Indian Sephardic-Style Friday Night Dinner
Sabbath Bread
Marinated Fried Fish, Dutch Style
Salata de Verdura (Romaine Lettuce and Arugula Salad,
    Andalusian Style)
Arroz con Pollo (Savory Chicken with Saffron Rice)
Summer Fruit *Macedonia*
Bizcochos de Anis (Anise Cookies)
Coffee

Spring Dinner for Friday Night
Sabbath Bread
Toureto (Herbed Cucumber Puree)
Roasted Pepper Salad with Simple Lemon Vinaigrette
Salata de Haminados (Turkish Egg and Potato Salad)
Salata de Spinaca (Sephardic-Style Spinach and Yogurt Salad)
Olivada with Black Olives and Raw Fresh Vegetables
Pescado Ahilado (Baked Fish with Fresh Herbs)
Sutlach
Assorted Seasonal Fresh Fruits
Coffee

Friday Night Meat Dinner
> Sabbath Bread
> *Impanadas*
> *Salata Sepharadi* (Sephardic Summer Salad)
> *Sopado con Sedano* (Braised Beef with Celery)
> *Arroz de Sabato* (Sabbath Rice Pilav with Saffron)
> Assorted Seasonal Fresh Fruits
> *Bizcochos de Vino* (Wine Biscuits)
> Coffee

Moroccan-Style Friday Night Dinner
> Sabbath Bread
> Roasted Eggplant Salad, Arabic Style
> *Buleymas* with Spinach and Herb Filling
> *Toureto* (Herbed Cucumber Puree) with Assorted Fresh Vegetables
> Black Olives in Savory Herb Marinade
> Braised Chicken with Tomatoes and Honey
> *Couscous*
> *Composto* with Fresh Oranges
> Almond Macaroons
> Mint Tea

Shabbat Hamin *Dinner*
> Sabbath Bread
> Hot and Savory Carrot Salad
> *Toureto* (Herbed Cucumber Puree)
> *Olivados Marinados* (Green and Black Olives in Herb Marinade)
> *Salata de Panjar y Carnabeet* (Beet and Cauliflower Salad)
> *Hamin,* Salonika Style
> Pickled Mixed Vegetables
> Assorted Seasonal Fresh Fruits
> *Bizcochos de Vino* (Wine Biscuits)
> Tea Spiced with Cloves and Cinnamon

Moroccan-Style Hamin *Dinner*

    Sabbath Bread
    Roasted Pepper Salad with Simple Lemon Vinaigrette
    Buleymas with Spinach and Herb Filling
    Hot and Savory Carrot Salad
    Moroccan *S'kheena*
    Assorted Fresh Fruits
    Dates Stuffed with Almond Marzipan
    Moroccan *Cigares* (Cigar-Shaped Baklava Pastries)
    Mint Tea

MAJOR JEWISH FESTIVALS

The major Jewish festivals are the High Holy Days (Rosh Hashono and Yom Kippur), Sukkot, Pesach (Passover), and Shevuot. The two days of Rosh Hashono, Yom Kippur, the first and last two days of Sukkot and Pesach, and the two days of Shevuot are all treated by Rabbinic law just like Sabbaths. Creative work is strictly forbidden on these days and Jews spend them in prayer, study, and spiritual pursuits. Passover and Sukkot also have intermediate days on which work is permitted but during which special things are done to make the days more festive than ordinary weekdays. Special culinary traditions are a part of each of the major Jewish holidays. The Jewish communities of the Mediterranean region have some customs and traditions uniquely their own.

Rosh Hashono, Yom Kippur, and Sukkot

When the shofar pours out its notes
    and you hear its plaintive sound
You shall offer up praises to the Almighty.
    You shall praise God's great works
According to their measure of greatness.
    Oh praise God with the sound of the shofar.

            From "An Introductory Poem to the Shofrot Service"
            SOLOMON IBN GABIROL (1021–58 C.E.)

The High Holy Days of Rosh Hashono and Yom Kippur occur during the autumn harvest season. Mediterranean gardens are at their most abundant. Great quantities of fresh fruits and vegetables fill the markets. The most luscious eggplants and tomatoes; brilliant-hued bell peppers; tart pomegranates; sweet, juicy quinces; crisp apples; sweet grapes, fragrant rose petals; vivid autumn greens; and golden winter squash with saffron-colored flesh are all at their prime at this time of year. Sweet-tasting dishes to usher in a sweet new year are part of the Sephardic Jewish tradition.

Baked apples soaked in honey, jellied rose petals, and slices of *Dulce de Bimbrio* (page 293) are eaten at the beginning of the Rosh Hashono feast. A special ceremony called the *Yehi Ratsones* (the "May It Be Your Will" ceremony) uses these and other symbolic foods. Each food is blessed with a special blessing beginning with the words *Yehi Ratson* ("May It Be Your Will"). This ceremony is based on a passage in the *Talmud* that says there is a custom of eating "the head of a sheep, pumpkin, black-eyed peas, leeks, beets, and dates for a 'good siman,' a sign to the Almighty that we recognize God's sovereignty and hope that God will, in turn, recognize our pleas for a good and prosperous year." Later Rabbinic writings mention other foods that provide a "good siman"—apple dipped in honey, pomegranates, and the head of a fish. The *Yehi Ratsones* foods eaten traditionally by modern Sephardic Jews include:

1. Apples: Slices of apple, baked and dipped in honey or made into a compote with a honey syrup called *mansanada*. Alternatives to this are a spoonful of jellied rose petals or slices of *Dulce de Bimbrio* (page 293). On eating a portion of this food, we recite: "May it be Your Will, O Creator, that we be sent a sweet and fruitful year from beginning to end."
2. Dates: Dates are listed first among the seven species of plants found in the Land of Israel by the Hebrews on their return from slavery in Egypt. The Hebrew word for date is *tamar,* which is close in spelling to the word *tamah,* meaning "causing wonder or amazement." Before eating a date, we recite: "May it be Your Will, O Creator, to create a sense of wonder and amazement in the eyes of our enemies, make them acknowledge Your Greatness, and respect You as Sovereign of the World."

3. Pomegranates: On eating a piece of pomegranate, we recite: "May it be Your Will, O Creator, that our year be rich and replete with blessings as the pomegranate is rich and replete with seeds." An alternative to pomegranate is black-eyed peas, which are called *rubiah* in Aramaic. *Rubiah* is similar in spelling and pronunciation to the Hebrew word *rabah,* meaning "many." If using *rubiah* for a *Yehi Ratson,* recite "May it be Your will, O Creator, that You multiply that which is worthy of blessing in us."

4. Pumpkin: The Hebrew word for pumpkin or gourd is *karah,* which is close in spelling and in pronunciation to the word for "to be torn or ripped away." Pumpkin is eaten in the form of *Rodanchas* (page 74) (savory pumpkin-filled pastries). On eating a *rodancha,* we recite: "May it be Your Will, O Creator, that the stern decree be torn up and that we be remembered for the good deeds we did this past year."

5. Leeks: Leeks are eaten in the form of *Keftedes de Prasa* (page 193) (leek fritters). The Hebrew word for leek, *karti,* is a pun on the word *koret,* which is a biblical form of punishment meaning "to be cut off." When eating a leek fritter, we recite: "May it be Your Will, O Creator, that our enemies be cut off."

6. Beets: Beets are eaten after being baked and peeled. The Hebrew word for beet is *selek,* which is a pun on the word *saluk,* meaning "to remove" or "to take away." On eating a piece of baked beet, we recite: "May it be Your Will, O Creator, that our enemies be removed."

7. Head of a Fish: The evening meal consists of both a fish course and a meat course. The fish course always features a whole fish with the head left intact. The head symbolizes the hope that our fortunes will place us at the head and not at the tail of things during the coming year. On eating a piece of the head of the fish, we recite: "May it be Your Will, O Creator, that we be at the head and not at the tail in the coming year."

8. The meat course for Rosh Hashono is sometimes an assortment of *Legumbres Yaprakes* (page 177) (stuffed vegetables). The stuffing symbolizes the hope for a rich and full year filled with blessings and prosperity. A stuffed, roasted bird is another popular way to serve meat on Rosh Hashono.

The theme of sweet and stuffed foods continues through the ten days between Rosh Hashono and Yom Kippur and into Sukkot, where stuffed vegetables and fruits, savory stuffed pastries, and honeyed sweets are always main attractions. When served on Sukkot, stuffed vegetables symbolize a plentiful harvest and are eaten as a symbolic way of thanking God for providing a good and plentiful crop. There is also a spiritual linkage between Rosh Hashono and Sukkot because Rabbinic tradition teaches that, while the "final judgment" is sealed on Yom Kippur, the gates of repentance do not close completely until after Sukkot. Eating stuffed vegetables on both Rosh Hashono and Sukkot establishes a symbolic linkage between these two holidays and the blessings that go hand-in-hand with them.

Bizcochos, fresh fruits, and myrtle leaves are used by Mediterranean Jews to decorate the *Sukkah*. The leaves give off a sweet herbal scent.

On the day before Rosh Hashono, the last day of the old year, a beautiful custom used to be practiced by the Jews of Salonika. Fresh water was drawn from the wells, mixed with honey, and poured into clay jars. The jars were then set outdoors in the courtyards at twilight just before the rising of the new moon in order to receive the first rays of *la serena,* the first moon of the spiritual new year. Some of this moon water was blessed and drunk with the evening meal as a way of internalizing the light of the new moon.

Roast chicken is eaten at the meal before the fast of Yom Kippur. In some Sephardic communities, the *shochet* (ritual slaughterer) slaughters a hen for each female and a cock for each male of the household and drains the blood over a bed of ashes. A dab of the ashes is placed on the forehead of the man or woman who brought the chicken to the *shochet* to be slaughtered as a sign of forgiveness. The slaughtered birds are then roasted and eaten.

Rosewater is the traditional aromatic essence used for Yom Kippur. It is sniffed by worshipers during *Ne'ilah,* the last service of the day. Worshipers dab a little on their handkerchiefs before the service begins and sniff it in order to fill their being with its sweet fragrance as the prayers of atonement are concluded. The rosewater is an aromatic symbol of God's mercy and forgiveness.

The fast is broken on Yom Kippur with a drink of *Pepitada* (page 299) and a spoonful of *dulce* made with rose petals.

Salonika-Style Rosh Hashono Dinner

Yehi Ratsones Platter: Baked Apple and Honey
                           Dates Stuffed with Marzipan
                           Pomegranate Pieces
                           Rodanchas (Pumpkin-Filled Pastries)
                           Keftedes de Prasa (Leek Fritters)
                           Baked Beets, Slices or Quarters
                           Head of a Baked or Poached Fish

Holiday Bread
Pescado Ahilado con Abramela (Baked Fish in Sour Plum Sauce)
Sautéed Eggplant with Walnut Sauce
Pollo Relleno con Trahanas (Roast Stuffed Chicken, Sephardic Style)
Fennel Braised in Tomato Sauce
Sautéed Green Beans
Assorted Seasonal Fresh Fruits
Tishpitti
Coffee or Herbal Tea

Moroccan Rosh Hashono Dinner

Yehi Ratsones Platter: Baked Apple and Honey
                           Dates Stuffed with Marzipan
                           Pomegranate Pieces
                           Rodanchas (Pumpkin-filled Pastries)
                           Keftedes de Prasa (Leek Fritters)
                           Baked Beet Slices or Quarters
                           Head of a Baked or Poached Fish

Holiday Bread
Cold *Pescado Ahilado con Abramela* (Baked Fish in Sour Plum Sauce)
Sweet Carrot Salad
Humus (Arabic-Style Chick-Pea Dip)
Toureto (Herbed Cucumber Puree)
Pastilla
Couscous *con Siete Legumbres* (*Couscous* with Seven Vegetables)

Baklava with Almond Filling
Coffee

Dinner Before Yom Kippur Fast
Holiday Bread
Pollo al Forno (Sephardic-Style Roast Chicken)
Arroz Pilafi (Plain Rice Pilav)
Apio (Braised Celery Root and Carrots)
Keftedes de Prasa (Leek Fritters)
Sautéed Green Beans
Assorted Seasonal Fresh Fruits
Pan d'Espanya (Bread of Spain or Spanish Sponge Cake)
Tea, Mint Tea, or Lemon Verbena Tea

Sukkot Dinner
Holiday Bread
Buleymas with Savory Meat Filling
Yaprakes de Oja (Stuffed Vine Leaves)
Ajada de Aves (Turkish-Style Bean Dip) with Fresh Vegetables
Assorted Meat-Stuffed Vegetables
Autumn Quince *Composto*
Travados, Dulce de Mansana (Jellied Apple Confection), and
Mustachudos (Sephardic Hazelnut Cookies)
Coffee

Pesach (Passover)

Your beloved children are singing a new song:
   Just now the Egyptians have drowned in the sea.
   And the righteous people heaped praises on God
When the wheels of their chariots were stuck in the waves.
   Your beloved children were tired and weeping
     When the roaring waves crashed down on their enemies
And Your Outstretched Hand led them safely to freedom.

From "Passover Psalm"
SOLOMON IBN GABIROL (1021–58 C.E.)

One of the greatest feasts of the year for Jews is the Passover *seder*. A special *seder* plate used in the Passover *seder* displays ritual foods which symbolize different aspects of the Passover holiday, including the things that happened during the Exodus from Egypt and the sacrifices performed by the Hebrews in the ancient Temple in Jerusalem. The ritual foods include vinegar, sweet- and bitter-flavored greens, lamb, eggs, and a sweet fruit and nut paste called *haroset,* which is said to look like the color of the mortar used by the Hebrew slaves. The vinegar symbolizes the tears cried by the Hebrews when they were in captivity (Ashkenazic Jews use salt water instead of vinegar). The sweet greens are usually herbs— the first of the new growing season, symbolizing the arrival of spring. These herbs are dipped in the vinegar before they are eaten. The bitter herbs are to remind us of the bitterness of slavery. They are eaten during the *seder* together with the *haroset*. The lamb and eggs symbolize the Temple sacrifices. They are kept on display and not eaten during the meal.

The foods of the *seder* meal parallel the ritual foods of the *seder* plate. The first course is always one of fish, a symbol of peace and Messianic hope. It is served with a walnut sauce in Turkey and Greece or with an almond paste in Morocco and other parts of North Africa. The sauce is similar in color to the *haroset*. There is a salad, called *Salata de Maror* (page 37), made of sweet herbs and bitter lettuces, symbolizing spring and the *maror* (bitter herbs) used in the *seder* ritual. The main course is always roasted lamb, which was the sacrifice roasted and eaten by the people of Israel in the days of the Temple.

Several different vegetables and herbs make their first appearance on the Mediterranean Jewish table at the Passover *seder* because they are just coming into season. These are artichokes, fava beans, and dill, served as a vegetable course to accompany the lamb. *Apio* (page 186), a mixture of celery root and carrots, is also traditional, as the supply in the winter root cellar dwindles. Some Sephardic Jews also serve rice pilav or a chicken soup with rice in it at the *seder*.

These Mediterranean Jewish customs may seem strange to Ashkenazic Jews, who refrain from eating lamb, roasted meats, legumes, and rice during Passover. The reasons are nothing more than difference in custom (see page xxxii).

One unusual Sephardic Passover *seder* custom is a special blessing called *Santak Khadra*. The head of the household holds a small sheaf of new wheat in his hand and taps each member of the family and each guest on the head with it while he recites a blessing for a good, fruitful, and productive year.

Sephardic-Style Passover Seder Meal
Matzoh
Pescado con Tarator (Turkish-Style Fish with Walnut Sauce)
Chicken Soup with *Agristada* (Egg/Lemon Sauce)
Salata de Maror (Passover Bitter Herb Salad)
Kodredo Relleno al Forno (Roast Stuffed Lamb with Egg/Lemon Crust)
Anjinara con Aves (Braised Artichokes and Fava Beans)
Apio (Braised Celery Root and Carrots)
Assorted Seasonal Fresh Fruits
Torta de los Reyes (Kings' Cake, Passover Version)
Coffee

Passover Meat Dinner
Matzoh
Anjinara (Herb-Marinated Artichokes)
Mina de Cordero (Lamb and Spring Herb Filling)
Mina de Pollo (Chicken and Spring Herb Filling)
Patata y Sedano (Braised Potatoes with Celery)
Assorted Seasonal Fresh Fruits
Masa de Vino (Passover Wine Biscuits)
Coffee or Herbal Tea

Shevuot

Shevuot, which occurs seven weeks after Passover, is the celebration of the giving of the *Torah* on Mount Sinai to the Jewish people. The most famous Shevuot dish in Mediterranean Jewish cuisines is the special sweet bread called *los siete cielos*. The folkloric symbols and method of preparing *los siete cielos* is explained in detail on pages 269–277.

Shevuot is also a festival of thanksgiving for the harvest of the first fruits of the new year. It occurs during the season when the sheep and goats are nursing their young and dairy products are abundant. Vegetarian and dairy dishes are the main culinary focus of menus for this holiday.

Shevuot Dinner
Holiday Bread
Ajada de Aves (Turkish-Style Bean Dip)
Salata de Haminados (Turkish Egg and Potato Salad)
Cucumber Salad with Kasseri Cheese
Roasted Pepper Salad with Paprika Vinaigrette
Pitta with Spinach and Cheese Filling
Pitta with Eggplant and Cheese Filling
Pitta de Pescado (Fish Pie)
Assorted Seasonal Fresh Fruits
Sutlach
Coffee

Late Evening Snack for Shevuot
Los Siete Cielos (Bread of the Seven Heavens)
Coffee or Tea

MINOR JEWISH HOLIDAYS

The minor Jewish holidays, which include Hanukkah, Purim, Tu B'Shevat, and Tisha B'Av are not holy days and do not have any Rabbinic restrictions against work. Nonetheless, there are special culinary traditions associated with all of them except Tisha B'Av, which is a fast day in memory of the destruction of both the First and Second Temples. Sephardic Jews also accept Tisha B'Av as the date of the exile from Spain in 1492 and mourn on Tisha B'Av for this as well as for the destruction of the Temples. There are no special culinary traditions for Tisha B'Av that differ from those of Ashkenazim. Hanukkah, Purim, and Tu B'Shevat, however, all have unique Sephardic culinary traditions.

Hanukkah

The special miracle associated with Hanukkah occurred around the subject of oil. Specially prepared and blessed olive oil was used in the ancient Hebrew Temple to light the *ner tamid* (the eternal flame), and for various other rituals, including the anointing of priests. The events of Hanukkah date back to the years 169–166 B.C.E. when the Hebrews of Judea, under Syrian-Greek rule, had their Temple confiscated by the government to be used for pagan worship. The Syrian-Greek ruler of Judea, Antiochus II, had decreed that all "local religions," including Judaism, be banned. The Hebrews revolted against the government and recaptured Jerusalem in 166 B.C.E. They immediately set about rededicating the Temple to the worship of the Hebrew God. Part of the rededication of the Temple was rekindling the *ner tamid*. They found only enough oil to light it for one day. It took eight days to press and prepare a new supply of oil for the lamp. Then a miracle occurred in which the one-day supply of oil lasted a full eight days. To celebrate that miracle, Jews all over the world eat foods fried in oil during the eight days of Hanukkah, preferably olive oil if they can get it.

Hanukkah is a minor holiday with very few religious rituals other than the lighting of oil-burning lamps for eight consecutive days. Presents are generally not exchanged either. But all kinds of foods fried in oil are enjoyed during the eight-day celebration.

On the last day of Hanukkah it was traditional in some Turkish-Jewish communities like Izmir and Istanbul for Jews to get together and have a pot-luck dinner called *merenda,* in which various deep-fried dishes dominated the menu.

Sephardic Hanukkah Dinner
Bread or Rolls
Keftedes de Prasa (Leek Fritters)
Salata de Panjar y Carnabeet (Beet and Cauliflower Salad)
Cucumber Salad with Kasseri Cheese
Pescado Sofrito à la Judia (Sephardic-Style Fried Fish) with *Agristada*
and *Caldo de Vinagre*
Assorted Citrus Fruits and Prunes with Lemon Marzipan
Bumuelos de Hanuka (Hanukkah Fritters)
Coffee

Purim

Purim is the last holiday of the Jewish calendar year, occurring on the fourteenth day of the month of *Adar,* exactly one month before Passover. Purim is a joyous feast day, held in order to celebrate the saving of Persia's Jewish community from a genocide plotted by the evil Haman, prime minister to Persia's King Ahasuerus (Artaxerxes II). Purim also marks the imminent arrival of spring and the beginning of "spring cleaning" for Passover. All of the flour stored for winter use needs to be used up between Purim and Passover, so Purim is a kind of festival of pastries.

Purim is a celebratory carnival of eating, drinking, costume parties, singing, dancing, and the putting on of Purim plays that are parodies on the story recorded in the Book of Esther, which records the events of the plot by Haman to murder Persia's Jews and how it was foiled. Esther, the niece of the Jew Mordecai, was chosen by the King as his queen. He did not know she was Jewish until she revealed the treacherous Haman's plan and saved her people from being murdered. Jews today celebrate the holiday of Purim as a symbolic triumph of good over evil. The Book of Esther, called *Megillat Esther* in Hebrew, is read in the synagogue with great rejoicing and levity.

There is a Rabbinic injunction to drink enough wine or liquor on Purim to cloud your ability to "perceive the difference between 'cursed be Haman' and 'blessed be Mordecai.'" This is not considered by religious Jews to be a license to get drunk. Its intent is to enable a person to remove all personal inhibitions and rejoice without restraint in the victory of the Jewish people over their enemies and in the ascendance of God's goodness over the forces of Darkness. In some Middle Eastern Jewish communities, children burn a rag doll effigy of Haman as part of the Purim celebration.

Purim is also the holiday of massive gift giving in Jewish communities. *Matanat L'Evyonim* ("Presents for the Poor") and *Mishloach Manot* ("the Distribution of Portions") are two kinds of ritual gift giving required by tradition as part of the Purim celebration. *Matanat L'Evyonim* is a gift of money, whereas *Mishloach Manot* is a gift of food. Among Mediterranean Jews, the food is always baked goods (sweet and savory), *dulces,* and marzipan-stuffed dried fruits. The Ladino name for *Mishloach Manot* is *platicos,* meaning "platters."

In addition to *Matanat L'Evyonim* and *Mishloach Manot,* children are given money and costly presents. Purim is also a time for visiting relatives and friends and exchanging gifts. In many Sephardic communities, people make visits to various homes and the hosts set out a *mesa allegre,* a specially prepared sweet table laden with all kinds of delicious baked goods.

Besides massive baking and the giving away of home-baked goods, Purim is celebrated with a big dinner. At the end of the day, before the sun sets, Jews sit down to a Purim *seudah* (Purim meal) where savory pastries filled with meat, vegetable pies, and *Fidellos Tostados* (page 214) are among the featured dishes. Lots of wine is drunk at the *seudah* and the sumptuous meal is concluded with a frolicksome and sometimes bawdy Purim play.

Purim Seudah
Bread or Rolls
Borekas with Savory Meat Filling
Olivada with Assorted Fresh Vegetables
Kodredo al Forno (Roast Lamb)
Fidellos Tostados
Sautéed Green Beans or Spinach
Assorted Fresh and Dried Fruits
Orejas de Haman (Haman's Ears)
Coffee

Mesa Allegre *for Purim*
Pan d'Espanya (Bread of Spain or Spanish Sponge Cake)
Tishpitti
Travados
Bizcochos de Anis (Anise Cookies)
Bizcochos de Vino (Wine Biscuits)
Dried Apricots Stuffed with Pistachio Marzipan
Prunes Stuffed with Lemon Marzipan
Susam (Sesame Nut Brittle) Candies
Coffee, Tea, Dessert Wines, Liqueurs

Tu B'Shevat or *Las Frutas*

Tu B'Shevat, the Jewish New Year for the Trees, is celebrated by Sephardic Jews as a major holiday. There are rituals connected with Tu B'Shevat unknown in other Jewish communities. According to the *Talmud*, there are four different "new years" in the Jewish calendar—the spiritual new year celebrated in the autumn at Rosh Hashono, the calendar new year celebrated in the spring at Passover, a new year for livestock celebrated in the early summer, and Tu B'Shevat, the new year for the trees. Tu B'Shevat occurs in the very late winter, when the heavy Mediterranean rains are beginning to slacken and the sun is visibly brighter in the sky. At that time of year, the sap begins to run in the trees, indicating that the winter season is at an end. Natural life is just beginning to renew itself in preparation for the spring.

There is a custom on Tu B'Shevat to read Psalm 104, which speaks about the wonders of the natural world and the magnificence of Creation. Tu B'Shevat is considered a feast of hope for a fruitful and bountiful year. The Jewish mystics link the renewal of life on earth with the eating of fruit and the drinking of wine. A special ritual meal, called the Tu B'Shevat *Seder* or *Las Frutas* (the Fruits) was created by Sephardic Jewish mystics in the sixteenth century to celebrate this important season.

The fruits are served in a succession of courses, together with four glasses of wine. There are four categories of fruits:

Fruits with no shell or hard pits (i.e., apples, grapes, figs, pears)
Fruits with a hard inedible pit (i.e., dates, apricots, plums, peaches)
Fruits with a hard outer shell (i.e., pomegranates, citrus)
Grains, legumes, and nuts represent a fourth category of fruit

Each course of fruits is accompanied by a glass of wine, representing the different seasons. The first course of fruits is eaten with white wine, representing the paleness of winter. The second course is eaten with a glass of white wine made pink by adding a little red, representing the awakening of spring. A glass of red wine lightened by a little white wine is drunk with the third course. This represents the earliest crops and foliage of spring. The fourth and final course, a rich *Assure* (page 256) pudding made with wheat berries, chick-peas, nuts, and more fruits, is eaten with a glass of rich sweet red wine, symbolizing the fullness and fruitfulness of the summer season.

In between each course, appropriate psalms and passages from

Rabbinic texts are read and discussed. Singing, dancing, and general gaiety accompany the celebration of *Las Frutas*. The fruits may be eaten just as they are or prepared into special sweet dishes. Out-of-season fruits, like figs, plums, peaches, and apricots, are always served in their dried form.

In some Mediterranean Jewish communities, the seeds to be used during spring planting are blessed and set aside just before *Las Frutas* is concluded. In Greece and Turkey, seeds for grains, dried fruits of the tree like figs and dates, and *pepitas,* representing fruits of the earth, are put out in separate bowls or trays as part of the blessing of the crops ceremony. Sweet pastries, dried fruits, and *halva* are given to friends and neighbors as gifts in order to share in the blessings for abundance.

Vegetarian Dinner for Las Frutas
Bread or Rolls
Olivada with Assorted Fresh Vegetables
Salata de Haminados (Turkish Egg and Potato Salad)
Salata de Panjar y Carnabeet (Beet and Cauliflower Salad)
Sopa de Spinaca y Lentijas (Spinach and Lentil Soup)
Boyos with Potato and Cheese Filling
Dulces (Jellied Apple and Quince Confections)
Dried Figs
    White Sauterne
Marzipan-Stuffed Apricots
Prunes Stuffed with Lemon Marzipan
    White Sauterne Mixed with Hungarian Tokay
Composto with Fresh Oranges
    Hungarian Tokay Mixed with White Sauterne
Assure
    Hungarian Tokay

Life Cycle Events

Life cycle events are of great importance to the Jewish communities of the Mediterranean. Circumcisions, baby namings, weddings, and funerals are all occasions when people get together, share food, and engage in formal rituals that mark the rites of passage. Each event has unique customs and ceremonies, some of them very elaborate. Special foods are also traditionally served on these occasions.

Brit Milah (Circumcision and the Naming of a Baby)

Circumcision is a covenant (Genesis 17:10–14) and an occasion for great celebration. In earlier centuries, the baby boy was paraded down the street on a cushion by his godmother from his home to the synagogue, accompanied by musicians playing guitars, dancing, and singing. At the synagogue, they were greeted by the godfather and the ritual was performed. Traditional foods served at a *brit milah* party are *Borekas* (page 61), *Buleymas* (page 71), and various kinds of stuffed vegetables. The stuffing symbolizes a life that is full and rich with good experiences.

When a baby girl is born, there is a special naming ceremony called *Las Fadas* (which means "destiny" or "luck"). The word *fadas* is a play on the Spanish word *ladas,* which means "fairies." *Las Fadas* is celebrated so that the "good fairies" will bless the newborn girl with luck and happiness. Guests at a *Las Fadas* celebration will be served *Borekas* (page 61), *Boyos* (page 66), stuffed vegetables, and sweets. Lots of wine and arak are drunk and many toasts are offered to the newborn.

Bar and Bat Mitzvot

Bar Mitzvot are celebrated by Sephardic Jews but without much fanfare or ceremony. The boy is called up to the *Torah* and is pelted with a deluge of candies thrown by the congregation after the ceremony is over. The family gives a modest reception after the services are over, usually a *mesa allegre* (sweet table). Orthodox Judaism is the only form of Judaism in the Sephardic world. Outside the United States, Sephardic Jews generally do not have a formal religious ceremony to celebrate a bat mitvzah.

Funerals and Death Anniversaries

After funerals during the week of mourning, people eat hard-boiled eggs, chick-peas, olives, and round biscuits. The round shape symbolizes the cyclical nature of life. They recite blessings on various foods as a way of sending the soul of the departed off to paradise with a multitude of blessings. For one year, those who are in mourning refrain from eating *dulce* with their coffee. After the year of mourning is over, friends bring *dulce* over to the family as gifts, symbolizing that there is a sweet end to the period of mourning.

On the occasion of a death anniversary, people gather in the home of the family of the departed and observe a *meldado,* a reading of psalms or passages out of the *mishnah* (the early *Talmudic* writings). The first letters of each psalm or *mishna* read spell out the Hebrew name of the departed. In some parts of the Mediterranean, *bizcochos* and sesame candies like *Susam* (page 290) are served at a *meldado.* In other parts of the Mediterranean, the foods of mourning—hard-boiled eggs, chick-peas, olives, and round biscuits are offered to guests.

Weddings

Weddings are occasions for lavish feasting and celebration. The night before a wedding, the groom sends his bride a tray of henna surrounded by candles. The women give the bride a party and enjoy many different kinds of baked sweets. The bride's trousseau is displayed for everyone to see and wedding songs are sung in honor of the bride. This ceremony is called *La Canta de la Novia* ("The Chants of the New Bride").

Rabbi Susan Talve, of Turkish-Jewish ancestry, shared a humorous memory with me about her *Canta de la Novia.* Her husband-to-be, Rabbi James Stone Goodman, who comes from an Ashkenazi family, brought his family to her home for the ceremony. Sephardic food was served. Among the dishes on the table were *Huevos Haminados* (page 231), which none of Jim's family had ever seen before. They thought the *haminados* were old, spoiled eggs, and tried to make themselves as inconspicuous as possible so as to avoid eating them and, at the same time, not offend their hosts. This, of course, was difficult to do, since in a Sephardic home, guests are always the center of attention. When the in-laws noticed them timidly nibbling at the eggs, they asked what the problem was and then explained what *huevos haminados* were. A few of the guests were still unable to eat the eggs but others gleefully devoured several, to the delight of their hosts.

The day before the wedding is called *El Dio de Banio* ("the Day of the Bath"). The bride is taken to the *mikveh* ("ritual bath") for the first time. After an elaborate grooming and bathing procedure, the women who accompany the bride to the *mikveh* eat dainty almond sweets and offer special blessings to the bride to be *bien casada* ("happily married").

On the Saturday after the wedding, the groom is called up to the reading of the *Torah* in the synagogue. Baklava, marzipan candies, and Jordan almonds are among the sweets offered to the congregation. Wedding meals always conclude with a huge and lavish *mesa allegre* (sweet table). Marzipan confections dominate.

A Sephardic Song for Havdallah

The Havdallah prayer is recited at the conclusion of the Sabbath. Wine, aromatic spices, and a braided candle are blessed in this special ceremony to bid farewell to the Sabbath and usher in the new week. This lullaby in Ladino is sung by the Sephardic Jewish mother at the very end of the ceremony.

Buena Semana nos de el Dio
    Alegres y sanos.
A mis ijos bien decir
    Que me los deje el Dio vivir.
Buena Semana.
    Para fadar y cercucir,
    Para poner tefillin,
      Buena Semana.

A Good Week, God will grant.
    A week filled with happiness and good health.
For my children, let them be blessed by God,
    So that they may live a Good Week.
A Good Week to name girls and circumcise boys,
    A Good Week to put on *tefillin*.
      A Good Week.

Index

marinated fried, 16–18

marinated fried, British style, 17

marinated fried, Dutch style, 18

patties, poached, 120

patties, sautéed, 119–120

patties, Turkish style, 120

pie, 78

Sephardic-style fried, 105–107

Tunisian-style couscous with, 222–224

Turkish-style with walnut sauce, 117–118

in *Yehi Ratsones* ceremony, 321

fresh tomato sauce, 300–302

Friday night dinners, 316–319

fried fish, marinated, 16–18

fritadas, 238–240

    de berenjenna, baked, 239–240

    de kalabasa, sautéed, 238–239

fritters:

    Hanukkah, 279–281

    leek, 193–195

    Macedonian herb, 237

fruit:

    assure, 256–258

    autumn quince *composto*, 250–251

    in braised lamb, Moorish style, 168–169

    composto with fresh oranges, 250

    dried apricot balls with almonds, 252

    marzipan-stuffed dried, 251–252

    summer, *macedonia*, 249

    in Tu B'Shevat, 331–333

Frutas, Las, see Tu B'Shevat

funerals, 335

garlic:

    sauce, 307

    spread, roasted, 3–4

    and yogurt soup, 92–93

Greek coffee, 307–310

Greek Romaniot-style herb-marinated artichokes, 30–31

Greek-style marinade for beef, 158

green olives:

    olivada with, 12–13

    in sweet fennel marinade, 11

grilled eggplant salad, Balkan style, 49–51

ground beef or lamb kebabs, 160–162

guava confection, jellied, 295

Haman's ears, 278–279

hamin, xix, xxv, 170–177

    dinner, Moroccan-style, 319

    dinner, *Shabbat*, 318

    Moroccan *s'kheena*, 174–175

    Salonika-style, 173–174

    -style braised eggs, 231–232

Hanukkah, 328–329

    dinner, Sephardic, 329

    fritters, 279–281

harissa, 303–304

haroset, Sephardic, 289

Havdallah prayer, 336–337

hazelnut cookies, Sephardic, 267

herb and spice mixtures:

    Balkan-style, 161

    North African-style, 161

herbed cucumber puree, 31–32

herb-marinated artichokes, 28–31

    Greek Romaniot style, 30–31

    Italian style, 31

hot and savory carrot salad, 45

hot paprika oil, 31–32

huevos:

    con spinaca, 236

    con tomates, 232–236

    haminados, 231–232

humus, 7–8

ibrik, 308–310

impanadas, 72–74

Italian-style herb-marinated artichokes, 31

jellied confections, 292–296

    apple, 294–295

    guava, 295

    quince, 292, 293–294

    sweet lemon, 295–296

spinach and lentil, 96–97

sour plum sauce, baked fish in, viii, 111–113

Southern-style savory chicken with saffron rice, 139–140

Spanish sponge cake, 261–263

spinach:
    braised chick-peas with, 196–198
    and cheese *borekas,* 64
    and cheese *boyos,* 69
    and herb *borekas,* 64
    and lentil soup, 96–97
    pie, 77–78
    p'kaila, 302–303
    rice pilav, 208
    and yogurt salad, Sephardic style, 40–41

sponge cake, Spanish, 261–263

spring dinner for Friday night, 317

stews, xix, xxv
    braised beef with celery, 164–166
    braised lamb, Moorish style, 168–169
    Egyptian-style braised beef with okra, 166–167
    loubia, 176–177
    Moroccan *s'kheena,* 174–175
    Sephardic-style beef, 162–164
    see also hamin

stock, vegetable, 299–300

stuffed vegetables, Sephardic style, 177–181

stuffed vine leaves, 19–21

Sukkot, Sukkot dishes:
    dinner, 324
    menus for, 319–324
    rodanchas, 74–76
    Sephardic-style stuffed vegetables, 177–181

summer fruit macedonia, 249

summer salad, Sephardic, 34–35

susam, 290

sutlach, 253–254

sweet and sour tomato sauce, 306

sweet carrot salad, 44

sweet *couscous* pudding, 255

sweet fennel marinade, green olives in, 11

Syrian-style eggs with tomatoes, 233–234

syrup(s):
    almond, 298
    pumpkin seed, 299
    raisin, 297

taleya, 166–167

Tangier-style couscous, 220–222

tehina sauce, 51–52

Tisha B'Av, xxxii

tishpitti, 260–261

tomato(es):
    eggs and, Tunisian style, 234–235
    eggs with, 232–236
    eggs with, Macedonian style, 232–233
    eggs with, Syrian style, 233–234
    and honey, braised chicken and, 130–132
    rice pilav, 207–208
    in Sephardic-style stuffed vegetables, 177–181

tomato sauce:
    baked fish fillets with, 108–110
    eggplant cooked in, 186
    fresh, 300–302
    sweet and sour, 306
    vegetables in, 185–186

torta de los reyes, 259

toureto, 31–32

travados, 268–269

Tu B'Shevat, Tu B'Shevat dishes, xx, 331–333
    assure, 256–258
    vegetarian dinner for, 333

Tunisian-style:
    couscous with fish, 222–224
    eggs and tomatoes, 234–235
    roast chicken with *p'kaila* and saffron, 128–130

Turkish coffee, 307–310

Turkish-style:
    bean dip, 5–6
    fish patties, 120
    fish with walnut sauce, 117–118